This book seeks to understand the evolution of Soviet policy towards the countries of South Asia, the regional constraints and policy opportunities which influenced the policy process in Moscow, and the relationship between Soviet perceptions and policy objectives. The author divides Soviet foreign policy into three aspects: a perceptual aspect in which assessment of the regional and international environment occurs; a formulative aspect in which aims and strategies are developed; and an implementation aspect. The book analyses Soviet policy objectives and instruments in distinct historical phases: 1970–1978, which covers the Indo-Pakistani War and bilateral relations; 1979–1985, which covers the Soviet invasion of Afghanistan and its impact on regional politics; and 1985–1991, which examines the Gorbachev era and the withdrawal from Afghanistan.

T0382540

SOVIET POLICY TOWARDS SOUTH ASIA SINCE 1970

Soviet and East European Studies

Series list continues on page 000

SOVIET POLICY TOWARDS SOUTH ASIA SINCE 1970

LINDA RACIOPPI
Michigan State University

CAMBRIDGE
UNIVERSITY PRESS

CAMBRIDGE UNIVERSITY PRESS
Cambridge, New York, Melbourne, Madrid, Cape Town, Singapore, São Paulo

Cambridge University Press
The Edinburgh Building, Cambridge CB2 8RU, UK

Published in the United States of America by Cambridge University Press, New York

www.cambridge.org
Information on this title: www.cambridge.org/9780521414579

First published 1994
This digitally printed version 2008

A catalogue record for this publication is available from the British Library

Library of Congress Cataloguing in Publication data
Racioppi, Linda.
  Soviet policy towards South Asia since 1970 / Linda Racioppi.
    p. cm. – (Soviet and East European studies; 91)
  ISBN 0 521 41457 1 (hc.)
  1. South Asia – Foreign relations – Soviet Union. 2. Soviet Union –
Foreign relations – South Asia. 3. Soviet Union – Foreign
relations – 1953–1975. 4. Soviet Union – Foreign
relations – 1975–1985. I. Title. II. Series.
DS341.3.S65R33 1994
327.47054 – dc20 93–19033 CIP

ISBN 978-0-521-41457-9 hardback
ISBN 978-0-521-05502-4 paperback

For Pasquale and Edith

Contents

Tables

Acknowledgments

The topic of this book has been a central focus of my life for many years, and as such, there have been many friends, colleagues, students, and teachers at the University of Maryland and Michigan State University who have sustained me through its conception, research, and writing. I would like to acknowledge the support of James Madison College, Michigan State University, in releasing me from some of my teaching responsibilities so that I could complete this book. At the University of Maryland, the faculty, research associates, visiting scholars, and graduate students of the East–South Project freely gave their time and intellectual energies to discussing Soviet–South Asian relations with me and created an environment where the study of Soviet–Third World relations was taken seriously. I am particularly indebted to Karen Dawisha who generously shared her extensive knowledge of the Soviet Union and offered penetrating criticisms and kind advice throughout this project. Without her encouragement and support, this book would not have been possible. Along with Dawisha, Clifford Foust, Bartlomiej Kaminski, Warren Phillips, Ilya Prizel, and George Quester read and commented on substantial portions of the manuscript. Jonathan Valdez is owed a special debt of gratitude for reading parts of this work and sharing his many insights into the theoretical literature. At Cambridge University Press, I would like to thank Michael Holdsworth for his support and encouragement of this project; thanks also to John Haslam for ushering the manuscript through a long and arduous process, and Sheila McEnery for copyediting. I am grateful to Cambridge University Press' anonymous reviewers for their very incisive comments. Finally, my husband and daughters have my deepest appreciation for their endless patience and good humor.

1 Introduction: South Asia in the USSR's Third World policy

When Nikita Khrushchev plunged the Soviet Union into the Third World, two of the countries he chose to visit on his well publicized 1955 trip to the Third World were Afghanistan and India. Since that time, South Asia (which for the purposes of this study includes Afghanistan, Bangladesh, India, Nepal, Pakistan, and Sri Lanka) remained a critical area for the USSR's security interests and objectives in the Third World. The region was the site of political, military, and economic competition between the Soviet Union, the United States, and China; two countries of the region (Afghanistan and India again) were among the USSR's top ten non-communist Third World trade partners; the region was second only to the Middle East in Soviet arms transfers and received large amounts of Soviet development assistance. Even with the end of the Cold War, geography still made South Asia, an economically underdeveloped, politically unstable region, a concern to an economically weary and politically unstable Soviet Union. Relations between the regional hegemon India, and Pakistan stabilized after the 1971 war, but the competition between the two remained; secessionist movements in many countries threatened the precarious regional stability; success in economic development was uneven at best; and most critical for the USSR and its successor states, the crisis in Afghanistan continued despite the pull-out of Soviet troops and the US–Soviet agreement to end military aid to the contending sides.

The purpose of this study is to examine the development of Soviet policies towards and views of South Asia since 1970. Like many other areas of the Third World, South Asia changed rapidly in its post-colonial period; in the 1970s important transformations continued but the regional military balance of power was established. The 1971 war positioned India as the dominant power on the subcontinent, cemented the close ties between the Soviet Union and that country,

1

and effectively ended prospects for a warm Soviet–Pakistani relationship. By the end of the 1970s, the USSR had consolidated its position in South Asia, having invaded Afghanistan, become India's number one arms supplier, established a joint economic planning commission with India, and extended economic aid to virtually every country of the region. The regional correlation of forces in the early 1970s seemed propitious for the Soviet Union.

And yet, by the mid-1980s, the war in Afghanistan still was not won and as a result of it, Pakistan had received vast quantities of military aid from the United States; India had started diversifying arms suppliers and had lost faith in the ability of the state sector to spur economic development, as had virtually every other country of the region. The Soviet Union seemed bankrupt of ideas to address the critical issues facing South Asia; nonetheless, relations with countries of the region remained relatively stable until the late 1980s. The consistency and the changes in Soviet policy in the region can be explained in part by evolving Soviet views of the international and regional environment, in part by the USSR's assessment of the political and economic potential of the countries of the region (an assessment which supported India's dominant position) and of its own capabilities in the region, and in part by the policies and interests of the South Asian countries. Explaining the relative consistency in Soviet policy in South Asia over the 1970s and 1980s and the remarkable shifts that occurred in the Gorbachev era is the goal of this study. It seeks to understand the evolution of Soviet policy from 1970, the regional constraints and opportunities which influenced the policy process in Moscow, and the development of Soviet perceptions of the international and regional environments and policy objectives. Finally, based on the history of Soviet views and policy in South Asia, it makes some observations about the future of relations with South Asia in the face of the dissolution of the Soviet empire.

South Asia and the Third World prior to 1970

In one sense, patterns of Soviet involvement in South Asia began to evolve long before the break-up of the British colonial empire on the subcontinent. Through the international communist movement, the USSR had relations with communists in several of the countries of the region. The debates between Vladimir Il'ich Lenin and the Indian communist, Manabendra Nath Roy, concerning the proper role of the communist party in the Third World national liberation movement were understandably followed closely by communist parties in South Asia. The Leninist position which advocated pursuit of a United Front in the independence struggle was not automatically accepted in all countries. In India, for example, the Communist Party rejected a national front during the Second World War in order to support the allies (including Britain) against the Nazis.[1] The Sri Lankan communists waged a bitter campaign against the bourgeois United National Party in 1947 and managed to maintain a vibrant, hostile opposition in parliament until 1955. (In 1956, however, they agreed to collaborate with the newly elected and more left-leaning Sri Lanka Freedom Party.)

The decade following independence witnessed no clear move towards socialism and brought repeated questioning of whether the Leninist solution was correct for South Asia. These tactical questions combined with the Maoist alternative offered to the Third World by China led some parties to break with Moscow.[2] Nonetheless, the USSR managed to consolidate ties with some important local communist parties (e.g. the Communist Party of India (CPI), The Sri Lankan Communist Party, the Parcham in Afghanistan). These parties often accepted Moscow's lead, especially on issues of foreign affairs, but also on questions of domestic strategy: where the bourgeois democratic option existed, they opted for a position of collaboration with principled opposition. Sometimes local communists were reluctant to accept the USSR's preferences, as in the case of India where the Communist Party continued into the 1950s to criticize Nehru and bourgeois democracy.

Party-to-party relations, of course, are only a small part of the story. With the dissolution of the British empire in the post-Second World War period the USSR moved to open diplomatic relations with the new states of South Asia. (Diplomatic relations with Afghanistan had been established by the RSFSR in 1919.) Despite its preoccupation with Eastern Europe, the Soviet Union exchanged ambassadors with India in 1947 and with Pakistan in 1948. Diplomatic relations with Sri Lanka were not established until 1956, mainly due to a strong anti-communist independence leadership in Sri Lanka. Formal relations with Nepal were not opened until 1956 because the monarchy pursued a largely isolationist foreign policy; thereafter, Moscow conducted its ties with Nepal through its ambassador in Delhi until 1959 when Nepal and the Soviet Union exchanged ambassadors and established embassies.[3]

Although diplomatic relations, in the cases of Afghanistan, India, and Pakistan, were established by the late 1940s, it was not until the

1950s and particularly under Khrushchev, that any real economic or military assistance was offered by the Soviet Union. Although Pakistan did received some economic aid from the USSR, its close ties to the imperialist United States and later, to China, precluded the development of a close relationship with the USSR. The vast majority of Soviet assistance, including military assistance, therefore, went to Afghanistan and India. From the Soviet perspective then, balance of power (or correlation of forces) considerations were critical in the development of relations and decisions to extend aid.

Personalities were also important in the early years of relations, in part due to the fact that embassies and diplomatic channels were new and not well developed, but more importantly to the high degree of personal control of foreign policy in the leaders of both the USSR (i.e., Khrushchev), and the South Asian countries (e.g., Nehru and Krishna Menon in India; Senanayake in Ceylon; Zafrullah, Mirza, and Ikramullah in Pakistan). In the debate with the Chinese over the nature of the new Indian regime, Khrushchev observed in his memoirs that

> [Nehru] may be a bourgeois politician, but he's the most progressive leader in India outside the Communist Party. His politics have been steadfastly neutralist and anti-imperialist ... If Nehru should be overthrown, you can be sure more reactionary forces would take power. Therefore, what's the point of alienating Nehru or in weakening his position in his own country.[4]

Khrushchev's appraisal of Nehru, which was quite different from Stalin's essentially suspicious assessment of the Indian leader, reflected not only the Soviet estimation of India's prospects for progress towards socialism but also Khrushchev's personal opinion of Nehru as a man of conscience, as a great leader of the independence movement in the Third World. This evaluation was helped by the fact that Jawaharlal Nehru had a rather positive view of the USSR and socialism.

Nehru had visited the Soviet Union in 1927, commenting on the accomplishments of socialism there and its potential worldwide. Despite the initially chilly reception given Nehru's doctrine of neutralism, the USSR began to rely on Nehru for his nationalistic and often anti-Western outlook. Like his Soviet counterparts, Nehru was very much interested in limiting Western influence in South Asia. With the Avadi Resolution of 1955, Nehru urged Indian state planners to develop a "socialist pattern of society." Moscow, and Khrushchev in particular, reacted favorably, yet cautiously, to Nehru's proclamation, recognizing that while the Indian leadership probably did not have in mind a Soviet-style workers' state, it was moving away from the capitalist West. In Soviet eyes, the Indian leadership, and particularly Nehru himself, had demonstrated "progressive" tendencies, allowing for a more rapid evolution of the relationship than might have been possible had Nehru been less favorably disposed towards "socialism."

Substantial Soviet economic aid was awarded to India, the leader of the non-aligned movement, primarily for development of its industrial and state sectors. Afghanistan, too, was the recipient of economic assistance, mainly in the northern part of the country, where assistance was used for road construction and industrial development, among other things. Although economic relations with Pakistan continued to develop, Pakistan's links to the West limited Soviet contacts. By 1961, the USSR had extended to India a licensing agreement for the MiG-21, a license that had been denied to fellow socialists in China (with whom they had been having difficulties), and the following year, they failed to support China in its border war with India. Competition with the capitalist West, and later on, with China, then, was a key component in the Soviet foreign policy calculus in the 1950s and early 1960s, but there could be no doubt of the significance of South Asia, and particularly India, to the USSR's Third World policy.

In many ways then, the successful Soviet mediation of the 1966 Tashkent Conference, which resulted from the 1965 India–Pakistan War, was a clear indication of the USSR's interest and stature in the region. The United States and Britain were considered suspect by India and Pakistan because of their own interests in the region; the USSR's prior neutrality in Indo-Pakistani border disputes had given them the necessary standing to act as intermediary between the two countries. The USSR then was the only superpower capable of intervening in the conflict and bringing about a peaceful settlement which would have been all but impossible if left to the devices of the Indians and Pakistanis themselves. The UN Security Council had worked out a ceasefire to the bitter border war, which had really begun with fighting in the Rann of Kutch in April of 1965. Through Soviet good offices and at the invitation of Premier Alexei Kosygin, India and Pakistan were brought together in the capital of the Republic of Uzbekistan to negotiate a settlement and end of hostilities.[5] Tashkent was a personal triumph for Kosygin; the "spirit of Tashkent" temporarily served to warm Soviet–Pakistani relations; and it signaled the Soviet Union as a major player in South Asia. The USSR's expanding political, military, and particularly economic ties and growing influence in South Asia presaged the promotion of progressive political tendencies and an accelerated transition to socialism by the countries of the region; however by the 1970s, no country in the region was any closer to making that transition to socialism.

These failed revolutionary capabilities and stalled national liberation movements in South Asia and the rest of the Third World coincided with a realization that the Soviet economy could not afford to finance the Third World's transition to socialism.[6] In the case of South Asia, aid to build the state sector and encourage central planning had not led to a diminution of the private sector (nor, by Soviet accounts, of feudal and semi-feudal elements in the economy); moreover, the state sector was recognized by many Soviet analysts as being inefficient. Even if the Soviet Union had been successful in geopolitical terms in South Asia and elsewhere in the Third World, it was forced to recognize that its capabilities might not allow its economic objectives to be implemented in the region. And where issues of economic underdevelopment in South Asia were considered to be crucial to population survivability, let alone regime stability, this inadequacy cost the Soviet Union.

The 1970s, therefore, of necessity witnessed a retraction of the indiscriminate use of economic aid as a policy tool. At the same time, however, many Western analysts saw a new trend towards Soviet activism in the Third World.[7] Although the USSR had suffered setbacks in Egypt and Somalia, it continued a selectively aggressive policy in countries like Angola, South Yemen, Ethiopia, and of course, Afghanistan. In addition, military advisors were sent to many countries; military training of Third World officers in the USSR became widespread; and the direct projection of Soviet military power in the support of local clients was not an infrequent part of many regional conflicts, and was especially notable in South Asia with Soviet military assistance to India. Moreover, arms transfers (particularly to oil rich states) were used widely not only to gain influence in the developing countries but also as a source of hard currency earnings for a beleagured Soviet economy.

With few exceptions (e.g., Egypt, Somalia), there were no major realignments in relations with the Third World countries generally or with countries of South Asia in particular, until the Gorbachev era. Rapidly changing circumstances in the Third World in the 1970s, however, forced Soviet scholars and policymakers alike to reevaluate their images of the developing countries, as well as the place of these countries in international relations. Although the policy effects of that reevaluation would not be evidenced until the Gorbachev era, these years are nonetheless important for understanding the evolution of Soviet foreign policy in South Asia as elements of Gorbachev's new approach to foreign policy can be traced to this period.

New Thinking, Old Thinking, and Soviet policy

After Mikhail Sergeevich Gorbachev ascended to power in 1985, he introduced the concept of New Thinking (*novoe myshlenie*) into Soviet foreign policy. Its significance for domestic and foreign policy cannot be overstated, for New Thinking was an essential part of the reform of the Soviet Union: if perestroika allowed for a reform of Soviet foreign policy, then too, New Thinking helped advance domestic reform in the USSR. The relationship between glasnost, perestroika, and New Thinking may be thought of as the "symbiotic link in Gorbachev's vision between Soviet foreign policy and domestic politics."[8]

The New Thinking represented a shift away from traditional Soviet foreign policy analyses which had relied on *realpolitik* and correlation of forces to one emphasizing interdependence, complexity, and diversity in the international community. Obviously, the potential consequences of such a reformulation for domestic restructuring were startling: more intertwining with the world economy, greater toleration for variations among and within social systems, a recognition of the complex relations and problems connecting people.

Gorbachev argued for international collaboration to promote negotiated ends to regional conflict in the Third World, advocated reducing arms supplies to the Third World, and talked about finding new bases for North–South cooperation. As a result of the New Thinking, the USSR began to reorient its foreign policy, and although Gorbachev's regime put East–West relations at center stage, the changes in Soviet policy in the Third World, and particularly in South Asia, were equally dramatic. In effect, Soviet reliance on the military as an instrument of foreign policy would be abrogated and replaced by a new emphasis on political and economic means under Gorbachev. Thus, the USSR withdrew all its troops from Afghanistan and admitted that their decade-long intervention to protect the fledgling communist government in Kabul had been a mistake, and announced it would require its longtime ally, India, to pay for arms shipments in hard currency. It appeared that objectives and instruments of Soviet foreign policy were undergoing dramatic changes. While the withdrawal from Afghanistan may be seen as an implicit recognition of the ill-fated correlation of forces in Afghanistan, taken in the regional context of the loosening of military ties with India, it also signaled an end to a foreign policy based solely on considerations of correlation of forces and regional balance of power, and it signaled a more sophisticated and complex view of the domestic and foreign policy circumstances of the Soviet Union itself and of the countries of South Asia and the Third World.

Those views, as articulated on a general level in the New Thinking, were not suddenly formulated in 1985. Indeed, the precursors of this less dogmatic, more nuanced view of the Third World can be seen in the debates in the Soviet literature in the 1970s and particularly in the early 1980s. Those debates reflected the delicate position of the USSR in South Asia and the Third World even under Brezhnev.[9] For although they are often portrayed as decades of Soviet activism in the Third World, in many ways, the 1970s and early 1980s were difficult decades for the USSR. Against a backdrop of domestic political and economic stagnation and on and off detente with the West, the Soviet Union pursued a Third World policy that was alternately cautious and aggressive. On the one hand, the Brezhnev regime targeted military and economic assistance at countries ruled by Marxist–Leninist vanguard parties (e.g., Angola, Ethiopia, post-1978 Afghanistan) and at selected countries of geostrategic significance (e.g., India). On the other hand, Brezhnev had rationalized a diminution of Soviet economic assistance to the Third World, declaring that the USSR's first duty was the building of socialism at home. Soviet views of international relations reflected their belief that the international correlation of forces was moving in favor of the socialist system, but at the same time there was a growing realization of the limitations of Soviet capabilities and of the complexities of development in the Third World.

That policy and those views were in marked contrast to Soviet policy in the 1950s and early 1960s, when the USSR had tried to compete with the West in the Third World on all fronts – political, military, and even economic. Soviet views of the Third World were remarkably simplistic and consistent: the Third World was a potential bastion of anti-imperialism, class analysis of these newly independent countries indicated the success of the national liberation movements in the Third World and the coming transition to socialism. The policy position mandated by such views was both extensive and expensive. Beginning under Khrushchev, there was an explicit policy to encourage national liberation movements to struggle for political and economic independence. The newly free countries became key to realignment of the correlation of forces globally, and the USSR under-took to assist these countries in pursuing a non-capitalist path of development. Afghanistan and India were among the first countries targeted by Khrushchev, and they received considerable attention from Soviet policymakers and academics and financial assistance to aid economic development. As Pakistan became more involved with the United States, the stakes for the regional and global competition between capitalism and socialism grew. South Asia early on became central to the USSR's Third World policy. Under Khrushchev, there was an expectation that an active policy in South Asia specifically and the Third World more generally would result in increased political and economic ties with the newly free countries, and correspondingly, more of these countries would opt for a socialist development path.

Khrushchev's simplistic, expensive, and incorrect assessment of the situation in the Third World necessitated a rethinking of Soviet policy under Brezhnev. Brezhnev's corrective was to rely on Soviet military power to achieve Soviet foreign policy goals; however, there was evidence of a more fundamental reassessment of the Third World and the prospects for socialist transformations in the literature of the late 1970s and early 1980s. The policy consequences of that reassessment, however, would not come to fruition until the Gorbachev era. Gorba-chev's New Thinking built on many of the themes introduced in that earlier literature and directly confronted the implications of the most radical of the literature for Soviet policy in the Third World, and as the process of restructuring and democratizing evolved in the Soviet Union, Soviet perceptions about the world and international relations also advanced. The failure of the August 1991 coup seemed to have consolidated the new approach to international relations and foreign policy behavior.

Organization of the study

This study tries to evaluate the development of Soviet policy towards South Asia since 1970 in two ways: first, through an analysis of evolving Soviet views of international relations, the Third World and Soviet, and continuity and changes in Soviet policy objectives and instruments in the region; and second, through investigation of the actual implementation of the policy in the countries of the region.

The most extensive dimension of the study is the examination of Soviet behavior in South Asia, and to some extent, the consequences of Soviet actions in the region since 1970. The study endeavors to show

how Soviet reliance on India (and by the late 1970s, Afghanistan) advanced and constrained Soviet policy in the region at large, to explore how policy objectives, instruments, and capabilities changed or remained the same, and to evaluate to what extent rethinking about the international and regional environments affected Soviet policy, particularly in the Gorbachev era. It argues that in order to appreciate fully the origins and evolution of the transformation in Soviet attitude and policy that occurred under Gorbachev, it is necessary to overview Soviet thinking about the international environment, especially the Third World and South Asia, and to understand the continuity and changes in policy objectives over time.

The study then is organized according to the following format: chapter 2 will focus on Soviet assessments of the external environment, the Third World, and South Asia. Chapter 3 will assess Soviet policymaking for South Asia by examining the development of Soviet objectives and instruments of policy. Chapters 4 and 5, covering the periods 1970–78 and 1978–85 respectively, attempt to ascertain how that policy was implemented in South Asia: what were the regional constraints and opportunities the USSR faced? Chapter 6 examines Soviet policy in the Gorbachev era and attempts to ascertain how the New Thinking affected changes in Soviet policy in the region. Chapter 7 concludes the study and makes some projections about the future of relations with the countries of South Asia.

2 Soviet perceptions of the Third World and South Asia

Introduction

What was the evolution of Soviet thinking about international affairs and the Third World that led the USSR away from a view that the correlation of forces in the Third World was fortuitous for the development of socialism to a view that stressed not only the unreadiness of the Third World for a transition to socialism but also the commonality of interests regardless of path of development? How was it that under Gorbachev the USSR in part turned away from a Third World that figured so prominently in Brezhnev's foreign policy? This chapter attempts to trace the evolution of Soviet perceptions of the international environment, the Third World, and South Asia from the 1970s to the advent of the New Thinking in an effort to ascertain the commonalities and fundamentals in Soviet images of the Third World while pointing up changes in views over time.

It is beyond the scope of this work, of course, to provide a complete review of Soviet analyses of international relations and the Third World, and indeed, there have been already many fine scholarly works which have examined the Soviet scholarly literature and writings by policymakers.[1] What this chapter hopes to accomplish in its limited way is an overview of the main currents in the Soviet literature since the 1970s which indicate the range of debate about international relations and the Third World and which then become an important component of the New Thinking and policies of the Gorbachev regime.

This chapter examines a range of literature on international relations, the Third World, and South Asia; however, it concentrates mainly on the work of academics, CPSU commentators and specialists (particularly from the International Department), and to a lesser extent, journalists. Some of these writers had direct access to the

11

policymaking process under Brezhnev, but many did not. Their works are important for understanding the roots of the New Thinking about foreign policy in part because they are *not* official statements whose primary purpose is political rhetoric or justification (although they may function in these ways as well), nor are they constrained by space, the need for oversimplification, or other considerations as newspaper articles often are. Their writing helped lay the groundwork for the New Thinking on the Third World later.

The constraints of censorship were still evident in much of their writings, often making them less detailed than one might expect.[2] Unlike similar literature in the West, and especially in the United States, which almost routinely makes foreign policy recommendations, policy proposals in the Soviet literature of the 1970s and early 1980s are virtually non-existent. Thus, it is unusual to find discussion of specific policy objectives for Third World regions, although as the following chapters try to indicate it is possible to ascertain general policy objectives. Even more exasperating for the student of Soviet writings, is the lack of specificity on the countries of the region which in part results from limitations posed by censorship and in part from the desire on the part of academics to contribute to general theoretical debates. The volume of writing on India, and to a lesser degree, Afghanistan and Pakistan helps the analyst overcome some of the shortcomings in the literature. However, these problems are compounded for the smaller countries of the region (Bangladesh, Nepal, and Sri Lanka) where there is simply very little written at all. The reader should not be surprised, therefore, by the general nature of the discussion in this chapter. On the other hand, the writings are sufficiently theoretical to allow for generalization about Soviet thinking and policy.

This chapter then endeavors to assess central images, which emerge and reemerge in the theoretical and regional literature, without blurring lines of debate in an effort to find consensus of view. It is worth quoting Galia Golan at some length:

> The problem is that the theoretical works, be they of party or academic origin, tend to concentrate on what they see as facts, with their policy recommendations remaining either secret or merely implied. Certain code words or phrases do appear, in leadership speeches as well, which ostensibly indicate policy preferences. The proper interpretation on the outside analyst's part presumably could be derived only from an empirical study of Soviet behavior itself. Yet, while the study of Soviet behavior is certainly instructive as to which policy option or interpretation has actually been chosen, a continued or apparent dissonance with the theoretical discussions is

not without significance, especially when those discussions are conducted by the very body formulating foreign policy recommendations for the party – the International Department. That controversy or variety of views persist – and are permitted to be expressed – suggests that the policy itself has not been wholeheartedly embraced and may well be subject to change. Indeed ... theoretical debates have preceded changes in leadership pronouncements, and possibly even policies.[3]

What is clear from an examination of Soviet writings on the Third World from 1970 to the early 1980s is the paradoxical nature of developments there. Because of the post-World War II successes of developing countries in establishing their political independence from the colonial West, Third World states were seen as potential allies for the USSR and the socialist countries, but the fact that these countries were also integrally linked into the international political economy, and particularly to the developed capitalist states, made them vulnerable to its exigencies. The Third World then was seen as both a force for progress and a continuing victim of the colonial past. However, as early as the late 1970s, some branches of the literature on South Asia and the Third World began to down-play the role of imperialism in Third World underdevelopment and develop a more complex and nuanced approach, one that emphasized the diversity of conditions in the less developed countries and the role of domestic factors in underdevelopment. With the establishment of the New Thinking as a cornerstone of Soviet foreign policy in the mid to late 1980s, these more complex views of the Third World and South Asia took precedence.

In order to trace the roots of the New Thinking in Third World policy, considerable attention will be paid to pre-Gorbachev writings. The chapter will emphasize two dimensions of the Third World (and South Asian) environment in the 1970–85 period: the international environment, that is, the developing countries as a critical part of the Soviet view of relations between the USSR and the US (and to a lesser extent, China), between socialism and capitalism; and the regional environment, that is, local (Third World) factors and their role in Third World development and foreign policy. The first dimension will concentrate on Soviet perceptions of the global correlation of forces (*sootnoshenie sil'*) in an effort to explain Soviet assessments of the impact of superpower politics on the developing countries and vice versa and on Soviet views of interdependency in the global economy. As subsequent chapters will suggest, it is these views that had the most obvious policy relevance, particularly in the 1970s and early 1980s.

The second dimension will examine Soviet views of social, political, and economic development in South Asia by describing some common issues with which Soviet scholars were concerned. Although the literature on development broadly defined (and particularly on India), raises a number of interesting and important theoretical issues for Soviet social science (e.g., the relevance of the Soviet development model), this study concentrates on analyzing several of the major themes in Soviet writings on general Third World and South Asian development and the possible policy implications of these analyses: (a) the role of the national liberation movement in international politics; (b) a general overview of Soviet perceptions of development, including discussion of the concept of multistructuralism (*mnogoukladnost'*) and the detailed typologies of developing countries; (c) the role of the state in South Asia, which was critical to Soviet writings on development in India in particular; (d) the Soviet view of dependency and interdependency, including discussion of foreign capital as a promoter or inhibitor of development, which played an important part in the literature particularly with regard to Pakistan and its ties to the US; and (e) agricultural and industrial development, which underlay much Soviet debate on development throughout the Third World. Each of these themes not only reflects the breadth of Soviet images of political, military, and economic developments in the Third World and South Asia, their "progressive" or "reactionary" quality, and their relationship to broader trends in international politics and the global correlation of forces, but also, because of their relative specificity, demonstrates the diversity and development of Soviet views over the 1970s and early 1980s. Attention is paid to these debates in the pre-Gorbachev period, because even though their impact on Soviet policy in that period appears negligible, they are important for understanding the underpinnings of the New Thinking on the Third World.

The global environment from 1970 to 1985

During the 1970s, the USSR was faced with a changed international environment. In 1972, the USSR and United States signed the basic principles agreement and the Strategic Arms Limitation Treaty, ushering in the era of detente. But it would come to pass that the two countries had very different ideas of how detente would function with regard to the Third World: the US expected the USSR to refrain from activism in developing countries while the USSR believed that competition between the USSR, the US, and the two social systems they represented would continue in the Third World. To the USSR, American policy in the early 1970s was not entirely clear-cut: on the one hand, the US was seen to be forced to withdraw from Vietnam while pursuing *rapprochement* with China, on the other.

For the USSR's own Third World policy, after recovering from the initial shock of Egypt's realignment, Moscow was presented with opportunities in Angola, the Horn of Africa, Yemen, and most significantly for the purposes of this study, Afghanistan. The recognition of the USSR's military parity with the United States through the basic principles and SALT agreements, coming at a time when the US appeared weakened and internationally ostracized by Vietnam, offered interesting possibilities to developing countries in terms of military and economic support. What most Western scholars have focused on is the USSR's increased willingness in the 1970s to use the military instrument in their Third World foreign policy arsenal.[4] But, for the USSR, while the military balance of power was certainly important, its shifts and changes were seen as part and parcel of a larger phenomenon, the correlation of forces, which was seen as boding well for the forces of socialism worldwide in the 1970s.

Correlation of forces. Sootnoshenie sil' is a multidimensional concept which was used by Soviet analysts to measure the relative strength of the socialist and capitalist blocs.[5] Because of the rough military parity between the United States and the Soviet Union achieved by the 1970s, the military dimension was of course an important component of the correlation of forces. Indeed, this dimension's importance sometimes led Western scholars to interpret *sootnoshenie sil'* to mean "balance of power." This had to do both with US–Soviet nuclear equality and the significance the Soviets placed on protection of socialism in the USSR, a goal which took precedence over the expansion of socialism elsewhere. It was argued that the building of socialism, and ultimately communism, in the USSR would actually help the development of socialist internationalism and the cause of national liberation movements.[6] These doctrinal considerations, of course, placed particular emphasis on the protection of Soviet borders, and by extension, on the reduction of threats from countries adjacent to the USSR. This meant that while USSR military strategy was fundamentally centered on the European theater and on strategic nuclear questions,[7] Soviet leaders also expressed a great concern with the USSR's southern and eastern borders and correspondingly, with US and Chinese intrigues in countries bordering the USSR. Correlation of forces, as will be shown below, extended beyond balance of power, but because of the security dimensions of the concept, was nonetheless compatible with balance of power.

One of the recurrent themes in the Soviet literature was foreign intervention in local crises and wars. As Rajan Menon wrote, "The emphasis on local war as an instrument of Western policy typifies the analyses of Soviet military writers."[8] The United States and other imperialist powers were seen as using local wars in the Third World to try to halt the advance of socialism in the developing countries.[9] This certainly held for Soviet perceptions of the global environment which they confronted in South Asia. As chapter 5 will show, for example, US and Chinese involvement in Afghanistan was seen as a principal cause for the civil war there which led to Soviet intervention. Soviet coverage of all the crises in South Asia had as recurrent themes the underlying convictions, first that without Western and Chinese interference there would be no conflict, and second, that imperialism was desperate to stop the progress of socialism in the Third World. Although the general line in Marxist–Leninist ideology especially during this period considered the advancement of socialism to be inevitable, nevertheless the immediate dangers of imperialist intrigues were recognized as direct and serious.[10]

However, it was possible for these threats to be overcome by Third World revolutionaries. Indeed, Soviet writings stressed that local wars were won not simply by technological superiority alone (witness the American defeat in Vietnam), but by a combination of military and political-moral factors.[11] The winning side triumphs not only through the use of weaponry but because of the support and suffering of the entire society. In the Third World, this approach to war and armed conflict not only meant that a less-well-equipped force could triumph over imperialism and its lackeys, but also required on the part of any Soviet policymaker who would assist potential revolutionaries careful assessment of the degree of support they enjoyed among the citizenry at large. Nonetheless, these considerations did not appear paramount in the case of Afghanistan where the failure of the Kabul regime to gain legitimacy and the effectiveness of the less-well-armed mujaheddin in fighting Soviet and Afghan forces were not openly confronted by policymakers or scholars until after Mikhail Gorbachev came to power.

While the USSR never explicitly linked its conduct of foreign policy in the Third World to East–West relations, during the 1970–85 period the role of American and other imperialist interests in the developing countries was, of course, part of the calculus of the correlation of forces in the Third World. Therefore, under Brezhnev, the Soviet leadership announced that it would not support the export of revolution (after all, revolution would arise as a result of a particular correlation of internal class forces) to the Third World, it would continue to provide "fraternal assistance" to a troubled socialist regime and support to progressive forces in non-socialist countries. The military aspect of Soviet assistance to the Third World seemed to increase in the 1970s, and the military dimension of the correlation of forces was correspondingly strengthened as regimes of socialist orientation were established.

Soviet scholars, however, cautiously avoided equating the correlation of forces with military might alone.[12] Instead they stressed other dimensions to the concept of the correlation of forces.[13] It included an ideological/political element which was concerned with the role and strength of the socialist countries and the international socialist movement; this naturally spilled over into consideration of the economic growth and development of the socialist world *vis-à-vis* capitalism.

There was a final, social dimension which had to do with the interpretation of the class struggle and which linked the international and socialist country elements of this concept to conditions on the ground in Third World countries. Soviet scholars and policymakers had to pay close attention to the class formations and class struggles internationally and in Third World countries in particular. The significance attributed to the class struggle had a critical impact on the Soviet Union's conduct of its foreign policy. As Karen Dawisha puts it, for the Soviet Union international relations was concerned with the interaction not primarily between states and governments, as in the Western conception, but between class forces – socialism, capitalism, feudalism, etc. It goes without saying that interaction between these forces was often expressed in the form of state-to-state relations. But the important point here is that because the focus of the Soviet perspective was on the dialectical relationship between class forces, the USSR had absolutely no qualms about openly supporting any communist party, national liberation movement, or separatist group which helped to "tilt the balance in favor of socialism."[14]

This view of international relations in a world of often rapid change caused difficulties for Soviet policy formulation and implementation. Determining which parties in multiethnic developing societies were truly progressive was no easy task. Moreover, supporting a particular communist party or national liberation movement could jeopardize relations with a friendly bourgeois regime.[15] Reconciling support for an anti-imperialist or neutral but bourgeois regime over a local communist party as a necessary component in the global correlation of forces was equally difficult. However, these were the very kinds of calculations that had to be made in South Asia and as subsequent chapters will discuss, considerations of the global correlation of forces were often paramount.

Nonetheless, the role of the national liberation movement and class formations was key to any understanding of the concept of the correlation of forces and the Soviet view of international relations in the Third World. It was the character of those internal forces, as they interacted with the larger international environment, which purported to give Soviet analysts clues to the progress of world socialism and the prospects for its development in particular Third World countries.

The Third World and the regional environment, 1970–1985

National liberation movements. National liberation had two closely related meanings in the literature: the first had to do with the Third World's political independence from colonial rule, and the second with its independence from neocolonialism (economic independence, usually at a later date).[16] In South Asia, for example, many national liberation movements had been successful in achieving *political* autonomy, but economic independence was not yet a reality from the Soviet perspective.

In the Soviet literature of the 1970s and early 1980s, because national liberation movements had come to be considered as part of the historical process of overthrowing capitalism and ultimately, building socialism, the distinction between the political and economic phases of liberation was often blurred. Boris Ponomarev, then head of the International Department of the CPSU, reflected the melding of these two meanings when he stated that:

> liberation movements are an integral part of the natural historical process of the development and replacement of socioeconomic formations. They express the objectively arising necessity of passing to new and more progressive forms of social life, and are an inevitable result of the growing internal contradictions of an antagonistic society divided into hostile classes.[17]

The national liberation movement's immediate objective in the colonial period was political independence. Through the realization of political autonomy, the struggle for the ultimate objective, socialism, was begun.

The Soviet definition of a national liberation movement also addressed its class content. Because national liberation was seen as a step in the struggle against imperialism, national liberation movements, particularly in their first phase, required a united front of all anti-imperialist forces, including the national bourgeoisie.[18] Eventually, it was thought, the bourgeoisie would not be able to lead the movement, its influence would wane, and the proletariat, progressive intellectuals, and peasants would control the movement. Thus, as the deputy head of the International Department, Rostislav Ulianovskii stated, "Even those liberated countries which are today governed by the national bourgeoisie cannot avoid the issue of socialism as an alternative for their development in the near future."[19] Although the bourgeoisie could play a critical role in mobilizing social forces to overcome political dependence, it was the proletariat and its progressive allies that were assigned the role of directing the movement to an anti-capitalist stance.[20] Under this characterization, no country in South Asia, with the possible exception of Afghanistan, could be seen as having entered the second phase of national liberation. The key questions in South Asia and in other developing areas then were which combination of classes would act to direct this transition to socialism, which classes should be supported, and to what extent should they be supported.

In order to distinguish the class content of different phases of the revolution, Karen Brutents (International Department of the CPSU) introduced the concept of revolutionary democracy. This was to be an "intermediate, transitional" stage, neither proletarian nor bourgeois, but favoring socialism and deriding capitalism. It was often led by the peasantry, the intelligentsia, and the urban petty bourgeoisie; and while such groups were seen as having a generally negative attitude towards class struggle, nonetheless, these groups also had a strong antipathy towards class exploitation. It was, therefore, possible during this stage of revolutionary democracy to stimulate those class groupings which supported a transition to a socialist state by developing the role of the proletariat in the movement and strengthening proto-socialist institutions (e.g., the state sector).[21]

Classification of countries under this theoretical model was not a simple task however, and formulating a coherent policy using it was even more difficult. Furthermore, the transition to socialism posed some hazards both for the developing country and for the USSR. While it was theoretically possible to encourage movement towards socialism, in reality it would be difficult politically, particularly when one was dealing with a valued friend, such as India.

Many Third World countries appeared to have become temporarily (or permanently) trapped in this transition stage of revolutionary democracy; therefore, understanding this period became critical. Rostislav Ulianovskii, who was in charge of Asia and other areas of the Third World in the International Department of the CPSU, recognized the perils facing developing countries in the transition to socialism. He concluded that, despite difficulties, revolutionary democracy would nevertheless lead to scientific socialism.[22] Nodari Simoniia, then section head at the Institute of Oriental Studies, on the other hand, tended to stress the difficulties in the transition. For him, the Third World's historical development was unique insofar as the colonial period distorted the formation of the relations of production. This situation mandated that most national liberation movements would be comprised of national capitalist, colonial and pre-colonial forms, further complicating the transition phase.[23] A major implication of the difference in these two views was that for the latter, the experience of the Soviet Union and the other European socialist countries had little to offer the newly independent countries which were just as likely to stay within the phase of revolutionary democracy or be transformed to some other kind of non-socialist system as to make the transition to scientific (Soviet-style) socialism.

One thing that all scholars agreed on initially was that the possibility of making the transition to socialism would be improved if these countries received assistance from the USSR and its allies. Indeed such aid was seen as a duty:

> The international duty of the countries of world socialism is in every possible way to promote the creation of favorable conditions for the choice of the newly liberated peoples of the socialist path of development, for the achievement of full and comprehensive national independence from imperialism by the young developing countries.[24]

Of course, this "duty" was not without its perils for the Soviet Union. Even the Soviets recognized, often belatedly, that aid with strings produced distrust and tension with friendly regimes (e.g., India) or increased animosity with the United States or ex-colonial powers. It could lead to the commitment of more Soviet resources than might be wished (e.g., as in Afghanistan), or it could result in the disruption of regional stability and power balances.

Nevertheless, up until the mid-1970s, the dominant view among policymakers remained that true independence could only be assured by taking a socialist development path. Movement along this path could be slow or speedy, and the tempo could be assisted by Soviet aid, but the ultimate destination was never seriously in doubt: the transition to socialism was inevitable. By the time Gorbachev ascended to power, serious doubts had begun to emerge even amongst policymakers.

Paths of development. In response to the great variety of types of political and economic systems that arose in the Third World in the post-colonial period, Soviet scholars set out to analyze the differences between developing countries. Their aim was to distinguish features of socialist, capitalist, and non-capitalist paths of development in an effort to understand the underlying rules operating in various conditions in the Third World and the prospects for domestic and foreign policy progress in the developing countries. These efforts yielded two major theoretical approaches that gained widespread recognition in the late 1970s and contributed to the increased sophistication of policy which became more apparent once Gorbachev came to power: the first is the development of detailed typologies of Third World countries which attempted to amplify the socialist/capitalist/non-capitalist trichotomy; and the second was the concept of multistructuralism or *mnogoukladnost'*, which went beyond a strict class approach to the analysis of developing societies. These two approaches not only allowed Soviet analysts to address more adequately the complexity of the Third World, but also allowed them to revise earlier claims concerning Third World revolutionary potential and development prospects and to posit a gloomier future for much of the Third World. Furthermore, theorizing and research in these two areas raised issues about development that began to blur distinctions between capitalist, non-capitalist, and eventually, even socialist societies.

Development typologies. One of the simplest typologies was developed by Karen Brutents. He retained the distinction between socialist, capitalist, and non-capitalist orientations; however, he further delineated the capitalist group by identifying those countries dominated by imperialist monopolies and those trying to oppose neocolonialism.[25]

In addition, a far more complex and detailed set of development typologies was generated, primarily in the research institutes. Some of this literature made clear the connections between different development paths (particularly non-socialist paths) and real political conditions that seemed to attach to each type (e.g., police control and bureaucratization).[26] Others concentrated more on socioeconomic characteristics of countries. For example, the work of Nodari Simoniia focused on the differences in social and economic development in the

Third World. Simoniia listed six types of capitalist development ranging from those with well developed export sectors (the so-called newly industrializing countries or NICs) and those dominated by transnational corporations (TNCs) to broad based capitalism which is characterized by economic diversification and a relatively well developed internal market (e.g., India) to those classified as desperately poor for whom the major problem was one of survival (and by implication, not some more esoteric commitment to socialism or capitalism).[27] Another scholar, Viktor Sheinis, developed a hierarchical ranking of developing countries that was based, not on path of development as a political choice, but on strictly socioeconomic indicators such as structure and production of the economy, demographic features of the country, etc.[28]

The main contribution of this type of detailed categorization was to overcome the overgeneralization of distinguishing only capitalist and non-capitalist paths of development. As imprecise as some of the new concepts were, they reflected Third World reality more accurately than did the capitalist/non-capitalist dichotomy.

Mnogoukladnost'. A second theoretical strand in the literature which also supported this search to comprehend the diversity of the Third World was the concept of *mnogoukladnost'*, the multistructural nature of Third World societies. The term was used to refer to the coexistence of several modes of production or substructures in one developing country. One of the first scholars to use this term was the South Asianist, Aleksei Levkovskii. He argued that not only did South Asia (specifically India) have coexistent modes of production which complicated the developmental process, but there was not necessarily a leading sector (i.e., capitalism) that would dominate and transform other social structures.[29]

Levkovskii's thesis did not go unchallenged. Attacks came from sympathizers and critics. As Valkenier notes, critics at the Institute for International Economics and International Relations (IMEMO) tended to brush it off as the Institute of Oriental Studies' preoccupation with "particularistic experiences of individual Third World countries."[30] Even among sympathizers, there were questions as to whether the term ought to apply only in the phase of the transition and whether the depiction of a lack of a leading sector was accurate. However, by the early 1980s, the applicability of *mnogoukladnost'* for South Asia was recognized. The prevalent interpretation was best represented by Glerii Shirokov, India specialist and deputy director at the Institute of Oriental Studies: "The special features of India's industrialization may be seen in the fact that it is taking place in the context of a backward and multistructural economy characterized by the *predominance* of pre-capitalist structures."[31] This author extended his argument in a 1984 book where he claims that the multistructural nature of India's society laid the groundwork for its dual economy, an economy which was at once driven to develop capitalist reproduction but at the same time was restrained from modernization by the predominance of pre-capitalist formations.[32]

Impact of these approaches. With the appearance and general acceptance of these distinct but related approaches, *mnogoukladnost'* and detailed typologies, a theoretical basis was given for a less dogmatic analysis of development in South Asia and the Third World. *Mnogoukladnost'* was clearly an attempt to represent better the diversity within developing societies while admitting to the persistence and strength of the traditional sector. The breakdown of the strict capitalist–socialist dichotomy had the advantage of allowing scholars to distinguish developing countries from each other while recognizing that these newly free countries may display unique features not common to either capitalist or socialist states.

By recognizing the complexity and diversity not only among but also within developing countries, Soviet scholars and (theoretically) policymakers could better cope with the rapid changes areas like South Asia were undergoing. Although the Third World was clearly seen as being in a disadvantaged position *vis-à-vis* the world economy and even though many problems could be attributed to imperialism's workings, there was increased sophistication in the Soviet approach to South Asia and the Third World. The West would be blamed occasionally for India's problems with the Sikhs in the Punjab, but increasingly, there was recognition of the problem of political separatism as domestically generated.[33] Whereas in the 1950s and 1960s, Soviet scholars routinely decried the exploitative nature of foreign aid and trade with the West and advocated the applicability of the Soviet Central Asian development experience for the countries of South Asia,[34] by the late 1970s and 1980s, these views were tempered so that economic relations with the West were still seen as exploitative but necessary, the state sector was no longer seen as the salvation of Third World, and particularly South Asian, development, and central planning was viewed as not necessarily efficacious.

The role of the state. Just as other aspects of Third World development were being reviewed critically, the role of the state as a vehicle for socialist development was also questioned in the late 1970s and early

1980s.[35] In the 1950s and 1960s, Soviet writers often portrayed the role of the state in the Third World as long-range planner, banker, nationalizer of industry, employer, and ultimate guarantor of political and economic independence. By pursuing relations with the USSR, the state sector could be developed. The expansion of the public sector in developing countries was anxiously observed by the USSR, but by the 1970s, Soviet scholars began to temper enthusiasm for this sector because of disappointing performance in terms of efficiency and productivity. This did not mean that there was agreement among policymakers and scholars. However, public enterprises had not made impressive gains particularly in the late 1960s and 1970s. Despite the fact that in certain cases, these enterprises operated virtually as monopolies – with no problems of market access, favorable investment terms, etc. – problems of inefficient management, institutional organization, and ministerial interference helped to decrease productivity in this area. Moreover, in the field of savings, public savings lagged far behind private savings. The state sector was an important element in the economies of South Asia, but in terms of public enterprise productivity or state investment and planning, it was conceded to have missed the mark.

Even though it was no longer viewed as the panacea for overcoming underdevelopment, the state still had a key role to play in the transformation of South Asian economies. Two 1985 articles in *Narody Azii i Afriki* set forth some reasons for the necessarily expanded role of the state in the Third World. In the first article,[36] the public sector was described as the force which helps to transform the traditional, precapitalist economic structures into capitalistic ones. The state sector also helps transform the national bureaucracy into the national bourgeoisie, and state capital substitutes for the big capital so often missing in these countries. Thus, the state sector fills in gaps in the economy and improves the country's prospects for development. In a second article,[37] O. V. Maliarov explained the expanded role of the state as a direct consequence of the lag in development and inadequate levels of national capital in the South Asian economy caused by its colonial heritage:

> This limited the direct and indirect ties of foreign capital....its role as catalyst in the formation of Indian capital, its part in the development of the private capital structure and capitalism as a whole. Together with the competition of foreign goods and capital, high investment barriers were created in the path of Indian industrial capital formation.[38]

As such, state capital was forced to take up this gap. But even though the public sector in India worked to limit the interference from foreign investment (through regulation and provision of capital), to direct private sector growth, and to expand the state sector, its activism in supporting capital formation in India also had the effect of limiting the growth potential of the state sector.

These views represented an important attempt to provide a rationale for the need for a strong state sector in developing countries, the positive effects of which had been promoted in the 1960s by policy-makers and scholars such as R. Ulianovskii and R. Andreasian. What was noteworthy was the interest of Soviet specialists in the role of the state not simply for the expansion of the state sector and public industrial enterprises, but for its general impact on planning and financing development. Sergei Kamenev, an economist specializing in Pakistan, noted that since independence, Pakistani public finance had grown to include support for branches of industry and infrastructure that private capital could not or would not enter.[39] Another Asia specialist, Nikolai Dlin, propounded similar arguments when he observed that the state functions in many spheres of the economy including state-run agricultural enterprises, public industries, etc. One of its key roles, however, was in the field of public finance which serves both the public and private sectors. He stated, "Indian monopolists welcome the role of the state sector in the development of capital finance branches."[40] If productivity and growth in the state sector were not impressive, the concomitant reduction in the amount of revenue South Asian states were choosing to devote to public sector projects did not go unnoticed by Soviet scholars. What was the reason for the shift in emphasis, particularly in India? One answer was that public finance had served to transform the national bureaucracy into the national bourgeoisie which, of course, would choose to support the private sector over the public sector.[41]

Hence, for many Soviet scholars a looser attitude concerning the role of the state was demanded by any examination of the situation of South Asia; however, as Valkenier pointed out, "Of course, no one proposed that the tenet of the leading role of the state be scuttled, only that the state not be overburdened with an unnecessary expansion of functions."[42] Indeed, for countries like Afghanistan and Nepal, where the economies were predominantly pre-capitalistic, the state was clearly seen as the best hope for modernization.[43] Furthermore, in Bangladesh, the state was seen as instrumental in supporting industrial and infrastructure development.[44] Even if the state in South Asia had not selected a socialist path of development, it *could* act to transform pre-capitalist structures in the economy. Some Soviet scholars formulated the dilemma as "how to convert the state sector into a system-molding structure within which the public interest will prevail over the private interest (without, however, eliminating the latter for the time being)."[45]

Foreign capital. Building on Lenin's reasoning that through imperialism the developing world is divided between the major capitalist centers,[46] Soviet scholars carefully explained the role of investment capital, transnational corporations (TNCs), and even Western economic aid in neocolonialist exploitation. The concern with the role of foreign investment became especially prominent in the 1970s, just after the time when Western and particularly Latin American scholars had begun to take note of the role of TNCs in the underdevelopment of the Third World. Many of these writers were very critical of the TNCs and foreign investment; however, another group (still critical of the exploitative nature of foreign investment) recognized that many developing countries required large infusions of capital to promote economic development.[47] While the foreign investment/TNC arguments were paramount in Soviet writings on Latin American development, because of the relatively smaller role of TNCs in South Asia, scholars tended to focus somewhat less on these issues. However, foreign investment, taken with development aid and loans, was seen as an important tool of economic and political exploitation in the region.

Noted economist, V. V. Rymalov, developed the theme that the worsening condition of the capitalist world economy caused the deterioration of the economic position of the Third World. Specifically, he argued that foreign investment (and its sister, foreign aid) bound the Third World to the West. "Its indebtedness has become a major channel of imperialist exploitation of the newly free countries."[48] One scholar at the Institute of Africa, V. Vasilkov, noted that foreign investment was a component of a larger strategy of Western imperialism; he lamented that "American TNCs deliberately sidetrack a vast group of the least developed countries where hundreds of thousands of people suffer from hunger and disease."[49]

Most scholars came to accept that the Third World needed capital infusion even though the infusion was viewed as exploitative. Soviet literature began to shift from emphasizing the TNC and direct investment to stressing international finance and credit as a major source of Western exploitation.[50] This no doubt was a reflection of the increased significance of credit from international monetary institutions and private finance and the mounting debt crisis in the 1970s and 1980s. One historian claimed that interest had replaced dividends and profits as the main form of exploitation in the developing countries.[51] These kinds of observations led Nodari Simoniia to conclude: "We can thus see that at the present historical juncture financial enslavement has become the main form of exploitation of the developing states by world imperialism."[52] Nevertheless, Soviet scholars, including Simoniia, began to view direct investment, credit, and aid in a more complex and interrelated way. They focused more on the problems of capital inflows of all kinds and how it distorts independent economic activities, rather than on condemning TNCs *per se*. Soviet scholars also began to accept that many countries count on foreign aid, along with other forms of foreign capital, to manage development programs:

> In many South East Asian countries fulfillment of economic develop-
> ment plans depends in varying degrees on American credits and
> subsidies. In Pakistan, for example, about 20 per cent of all revenue in
> the state budget came from American aid in the mid-sixties.[53]

The argument developed, reminiscent of Cardoso and Faletto's contention that in Latin America development does indeed occur but that it is capitalist development, that foreign investment and aid may encourage dependence but they may be useful, if not critical, in bringing about *capitalist* development in the Third World. Simoniia saw the growth in the interference of Western capital (through investment, aid, or loans) as unhealthy, but he recognized that countries needing assistance must accept it despite the often unfavorable economic and political terms attached: "It is true that the newly free countries require both financial and technological resources. The question is on what terms are these much-publicized 'benefits' going to be provided."[54] Glerii Shirokov also noted that capitalist aid was a means by which the West stimulates capitalist development in the Third World and thus rededicates these countries to the cause of world capitalism.[55]

While Soviet scholars were busy deciding what benefits, if any, derived from capitalist aid and investment, most countries in the Third World and South Asia were accepting aid and even actively soliciting investment from the West. Furthermore, the spectacular economic performance of the East Asian newly industrialized countries (NICs) did not support the views of many conservative Soviet scholars concerning the adverse impact of integration into the capitalist world economy and the prospects for revolution; however, it did prove that development, albeit capitalist development, could be stimulated by foreign investment and aid.

The role of foreign capital in the South Asian economies could not be ignored, even though foreign investment was not as significant in South Asia as it was in Latin America. In India at the time, for example, TNCs were relatively unimportant in the economy, accounting for only three of the top twenty-five firms. Nonetheless, with Rajiv Gandhi's explicit calls for increased investment for industrial development and expansion of the private sector, the situation changed, and by the late 1980s India had developed a serious debt problem. Foreign aid also had played an important role in South Asian economic development. In Sri Lanka, for example, the amount of revenues coming from aid was very high during the height of the Mahaweli Basin Project, and while this massive kind of aid was seen as tying the developing state closer to the West, it was also recognized that the capital was essential to modernization.

Agriculture and industrialization. All countries of South Asia continue to be predominantly agricultural (even though in the peripheral countries, the agricultural sector has not been extremely productive) and poor. For example, just before Gorbachev took office, GNP per capita ranged from a low of $140 for Bangladesh and a high of $380 for Pakistan in 1982.[56] Moreover, the agricultural sector in much of South Asia is influenced by pre-capitalist structures (e.g., particularly in Nepal and Afghanistan) and often is characterized by small landholdings (e.g., Nepal, Bangladesh, Sri Lanka). Given the significance of this traditional sector in the economies of the region (and elsewhere in the Third World), it is not surprising that in the 1950s and 1960s, many Soviet scholars pressed for the expansion of industry – preferably state-owned heavy industry – as key to economic development. But over time, this view was greatly modified as it was recognized that Soviet-style modernization was not necessarily appropriate for the Third World.

Partly because of the acceptance of the concept of *mnogoukladnost'* which stressed the possibility of the traditional agricultural sector playing the system-forming role in the economy, the theoretical significance of agriculture in the developing economies of South Asia was given more attention. It was recognized that the multistructural nature of the societies made for a slow transition period and that the agricultural sector was likely to remain dominant for a very long time. As one economist noted:

Agriculture is the bottleneck of the developing SSEA (South and South East Asian) countries. The demand for foodstuffs increases as a result of the general increase of the population....There is a similar growth of demand for the agricultural raw materials needed for the developing industry. In India, 40 per cent of the branches of industrial production process agricultural raw materials. Meanwhile, agricultural production in the developing countries cannot keep pace with expanding demand because of the backward economic forms and type of reproduction.[57]

For many scholars, the establishment of a capitalist agrarian sector in the countries of South Asia was seen as critical to the modernization of the economy in general.[58] Given the numbers of the population engaged in agriculture, transforming peasants into agricultural workers was imperative for the development of the economy.[59] For many scholars, the persistence of the dual economy in South Asia was possibly the biggest blockade to economic development.[60]

Summing up. The preceding discussion has attempted to show the breadth of the debates on the Third World and South Asia that were on-going in the USSR, particularly in the 1970s and early 1980s, and the important role of the Indologists in those debates.[61] The literature in a range of areas, from the national liberation movement to paths of development and development typologies to the role of the state and foreign capital, indicated important contentions and evolving approaches. The discussions about Third World and South Asian development did not directly challenge the general line on correlation of forces; however, as the debates developed into the 1980s, their relevance became clear. Under Gorbachev, these debates continued, expanded, and became more influential in policymaking. But it would clearly be inaccurate to view the late 1970s and early 1980s as a period with a monolithic approach to the developing countries, for it was in these years that the development of some fundamental rethinking on the diversity and complexity of the Third World, and the relationship of the USSR to the LDCs, took place even though the application of this rethinking to Soviet policy was not immediately apparent.

The New Thinking and beyond

The first indications of a thorough revamping of Soviet foreign policy came in 1986, most notably with Gorbachev's speech to the 27th Party Congress in February.[62] Gorbachev's report did not question any of the philosophical foundations of the official Soviet view of

international relations such as the continuing conflict between capitalism and socialism, the internal contradictions within capitalism, and
the inevitable triumph of socialism worldwide. It was, nonetheless,
innovative in its attention to what Gorbachev saw as *common human*
problems (e.g., nuclear war, pollution, world poverty, regional conflicts) facing an increasingly interdependent world and its attempt to
underscore the desire for improvement in East–West relations. That
Gorbachev also expressed his intention to remove Soviet troops from
Afghanistan at the earliest opportunity signaled the seriousness of his
intention to clear the path for renewed US–Soviet detente and to
resolve regional conflicts by peaceful means.

Foremost among the problems mentioned by Gorbachev, of course,
was the threat of nuclear annihilation, a problem which proponents of
the new approach to foreign policy saw as transcending the traditional
capitalist–socialist dichotomy.[63] Indeed, some Soviet observers
explicitly asserted that the traditional conflict between capitalism and
socialism was no longer applicable.[64] As such, what Gorbachev was
referring to in 1987 as the New Thinking, was initially most significant
for its potential impact on East–West relations, but its effects would be
equally dramatic for Soviet policy in the Third World. Without having
directly rejected a basic contradiction between capitalism and
socialism, New Thinking undermined this fundamental notion by
advocating cooperation and interdependence between capitalism and
socialism for a higher purpose, human salvation and development.[65]
War, particularly nuclear war, between the superpowers was to be
avoided at all costs, and by extension, collaborative measures (i.e.,
negotiations, agreements) should be taken by the United States and
the Soviet Union to decrease the possibility of conflict. As Gorbachev
advisor Evgenii Primakov would argue, the strategic corollary was
reasonable sufficiency – sufficient weaponry to deter attack but not to
engage in offensive action.[66]

At its core, the New Thinking became a rejection of the notion of
correlation of forces. Stripped to its barest essentials, correlation of
forces can be thought of as class-based *realpolitik* or balance of power.
Despite the fact that the inevitability of war doctrine had been slowly
eroded in the post-Stalinist Soviet Union, Soviet policy in the Third
World in the 1970s and early 1980s, as chapter 3 will show, relied
heavily on military means for achieving foreign policy goals.[67] Policymakers and scholars alike in Brezhnev's time had rationalized that
military assistance, even when it exacerbated regional conflicts, was
necessary to combat imperialism's aims and assist progressive forces in

the Third World. However, as Gorbachev noted, "Clausewitz's dictum that war is the continuation of policy only by different means, which was classical in his time, has grown hopelessly out of date. It now belongs to libraries. For the first time in history, *basing international politics on moral and ethical norms that are common to all humankind, as well as humanizing interstate relations*, has become a vital requirement"[68] (emphasis, mine). New Thinking posited that human interests were critical in determining foreign policy, and in so doing negated a fundamental presumption of correlation of forces, the necessity to evaluate international and regional environments with respect to class. If human interests could override class interests, cooperation between imperialists and socialist countries at the international level at least could be extended to areas beyond arms control, and thus, a fundamental basis for socialist internationalism could be eroded.[69] Although it was most closely associated with improving East–West relations, the impact of the New Thinking was equally critical for Soviet policy in Eastern Europe and also in the Third World: it struck at the heart of the Brezhnevite policy and theory concerning the Third World that dominated Soviet foreign policymaking from 1970 to 1986.

The focus of Soviet thinking about international relations began to shift away from its traditional preoccupation with imperialism and the contradictions between the socialist and capitalist systems. Beginning with the historian Viacheslav Dashichev's 1988 *Literaturnaia gazeta* article, the foreign policies of the capitalist states were no longer blamed for the tensions between East and West. Indeed, Dashichev's article went so far as to charge that the tensions were in large part caused by Brezhnev's expansionistic foreign policy in the Third World.[70] A roundtable discussion by scholars mainly from the Institute of World Economy and International Relations (IMEMO) and the Institute of Oriental Studies published in *Narody Azii i Afriki* in 1988 took a fresh look at the concept of imperialism, analyzing whether the traditional Leninist approach was appropriate any more and whether imperialism was really exploitative.[71] Roundtable participants, as well as other scholars, argued that Lenin's theory of imperialism may have been correct in its historical context, but that global conditions had changed as had the nature and functioning of contemporary capitalism.[72] The economist Anatolii Elianov put it very directly: the reason some countries were poor had less to do with international capitalism than with internal factors.[73] Moreover, some scholars began to argue that capitalism no longer required neocolonialism to prosper and that old notions about imperialism were completely inadequate to study contemporary international development.[74]

The issue then was not how to foil imperialism and promote socialism (an essentially zero-sum view). Instead, the issue became how to build a non-confrontational, cooperative, and mutually beneficial relationship with the non-socialist world. According to the New Thinking, an "integral world" (*tselostnyi mir*) was being created, and as the New Thinking developed, interdependence was talked about not just as fact but as a desired outcome of Soviet foreign policy. As Gorbachev would write: "And here we see our interdependence, the integrity of the world, the imperative need for pooling the efforts of humanity for the sake of its preservation, for its benefit today, tomorrow and for all time."[75] Soviet foreign policy's new tasks then were to intensify its relations at all levels with socialist and capitalist countries and to further intertwine the USSR into the global economy, an economy in which capitalism predominated. Viacheslav Dashichev wrote:

> [the turnaround in Soviet policy] will greatly expand the scope for international collaboration and the mutual influence and enrichment of socialist forces in the political, economic, theoretical, scientific, and cultural spheres. Socialist solidarity will become richer and acquire an organic nature....What has been established as the keystone of our foreign policy activity is a principle that develops Lenin's ideas: The interest of saving human civilization from nuclear annihilation takes precedence over any class, ideological, material, personal, and other interests.[76]

Interdependence was not only a necessity forced on the Soviet Union by the exigencies of the nuclear age, it was a condition that would actually benefit the development of reform socialism. Economists and other scholars also advocated interdependence, arguing that by reducing tensions between East and West and integrating the USSR further into the world economy, perestroika could succeed better.[77] Cooperation from the West, however, was necessary, as many commentators were eager to point out in criticisms of American foreign policy in the Third World.[78]

With New Thinking, the political groundwork was laid for some major changes in Soviet policy in South Asia and the rest of the world. As the first part of this chapter showed, however, the theoretical groundwork for rethinking Soviet policy in the Third World, and particularly the Afghan experience, had been laid earlier in the literature on paths of development and the national liberation movement.

By 1987, some of the implications raised by the earlier, critical thinking began to be addressed directly. Georgi Mirskii, once again, was in the middle of the debate with an important article that appeared in *Mirovaia ekonomika i mezhdunarodnye otnosheniia* (*World Economy and International Relations* [MEiMO]).[79] Building on the earlier literature on paths of development, Mirskii argued that the notion of Third World countries having a choice of development path was misplaced and that for most newly independent countries the capitalist path was the only alternative. While he was optimistic about the prospects of Marxist–Leninist vanguard party-led states, his overall assessment of the socialist orientation was the most highly pessimistic to date.[80] A year later, Alexei Kiva, was more blunt: he argued that the concept of socialist orientation had to be separated from its traditional Marxist interpretation which is overly optimistic and utopian.[81] Relatedly, Alexander Bovin writing in *Izvestiia* went beyond a criticism of socialist orientation and condemned communist parties themselves for failing to become mass organizations that would spur on socialist develop-ment.[82] By late 1989 and particularly 1990, there were a substantial number of scholars attacking even progressive interpretations of notions such as socialist orientation, transition to socialism, and imperialism. Illustrative of many scholars' frustration with past theori-zing about socialist or non-socialist development, one researcher at the Institute of Oriental Studies simply recommended abandoning dis-cussion of socialism altogether.[83]

Particularly noteworthy were the developments in analyses of the role of capital, the role of the state, and the effect of relations with the USSR on the developing countries. As this chapter has shown, earlier writings had usually portrayed the role of foreign capital in the underdeveloped economy as exploitative; however, some scholars saw foreign capital as a necessary evil. However, by 1987, Nikolai Shmelev would argue that in order to help close the widening gap between advanced industrialized countries and Third World coun-tries, more foreign capital should be made available to the under-developed countries.[84] The earlier notion that foreign capital was necessary for economic development was clearly accepted. Moreover, in keeping with the acceptance of an intertwined world economy, scholars seemed less concerned that reliance on foreign capital would precipitate exploitation or dependency. Indeed, economists such as Shmelev and Khvoinik worried more about government socio-economic plans and intensification of economic growth than about any negative consequences of foreign investment.

More than in any other area, Soviet analyses of the role of the state in economic development in the Third World seemed bound up with scholars' views of the USSR's own development. Earlier, some scholars viewed the role of the state and the state sector as essential for development, particularly in many countries of South Asia where the national bourgeoisie was seen as too weak to promote sufficient growth. Scholars might recognize that there were problems, that the state sector was not as efficient as it should be and that its industries needed to be modernized, but the leading role of the state was never completely rejected. By the late 1980s, scholars began to question that fundamental assumption, and a debate arose not only over the function of the state and the state sector, but also over the *type* of state necessary for economic growth. One of the Institute of Oriental Studies' top experts in this field, O. V. Maliarov, wrote an article in 1988, which extended his previous work on the role of the state and detailed the functions of the state sector in countries controlled by the national bourgeoisie, arguing that as it developed the state sector in these societies became less independent and more reliant on the private sector.[85]

Maliarov's article was hardly sanguine about the prospects for the state sector, but other scholars were even quicker to attack the state sector in the Third World for poor economic planning and implementation. Writing in 1988, IMEMO economist Nikolai Karagodin sharply criticized economic policies of many underdeveloped countries for being driven by short-term "political interests" rather than by long-range economic objectives; however, he also argued that a strong state could overcome short-term political interests and forge an effective development policy.[86] Two historians examining the question of the role of the state in the choice of development in Asia and Africa noted that "the interaction and struggle of the two tendencies of social development [capitalism and socialism] ... are mediated by different *cultural-civilizational bases*"[87] (emphasis, mine). Georgi Mirskii, however, took a different tack in an article on military regimes in the Third World. He reasoned that military regimes often arose because of the failure of the civilian bureaucracy to effect economic development, but he also noted the poor economic performance of some of the "strongest" Third World states, military authoritarian systems, and argued for creating conditions to accelerate the democratization process worldwide.[88]

In other words, an examination of the literature reveals an attempt to grapple not just with the question of the significance of the state sector *per se* in the Third World, but with the issues of what it meant to be a strong state, how necessary the state was in promoting economic development, and what types of states could best achieve high economic growth rates. Not surprisingly, by the late 1980s, overcentralization was seen as a key cause of economic underdevelopment in a variety of types of economic systems.[89]

Possible solutions for the problems of the state sector and overcentralization were found in several places. Maliarov suggested that the state sector could be complemented by cooperatives.[90] IMEMO's Stanislav Zhukov examined the development of the service sector (a topic that hardly had been touched earlier and when mentioned was often castigated) in the Third World, noting that it had become an important factor in Third World economies.[91] Most notable, however, was the renewed interest in the subject of small business in the developing economy – there had been considerable attention paid to "cottage industry" particularly in India in the literature of the 1960s. The characterization of small business in the late 1980s, however, was certainly not full of the earlier vitriolic against the petty bourgeoisie. Two articles in 1989 by the economist Valentin Uliakhin illustrated the new approach: both argued that small business in Asia was instrumental in fueling economic growth and that the Asian example was an important one for perestroika in the Soviet Union.[92]

From this point of view, circumstances had almost been reversed: at one time the USSR was to have served as a model of development for the Third World; even in the more skeptical early and mid-1980s, scholars and policymakers were arguing that close ties with the USSR were critical for the Third World's "independent" economic development – but now, the less developed countries were seen as a model for the faltering Soviet economy.[93] On two points at least, there was near unanimity: the USSR could not afford to finance the economic development of the Third World and economic relations ought to be of mutual benefit. Leon Zevin, for example, argued that the slowdown in the expansion of Soviet–Third World trade in the 1980s was caused by the Soviet failure to rationalize its foreign trade policy, but indicated that intensified economic ties would benefit both sides while others advocated trade along "global" lines as a means to improve economic conditions and growth in the Third World.[94]

Because of the intensity of Soviet ties in the region, South Asia was one area of the world where these reassessments of the international environment and the Third World could have had enormous consequences for Soviet policy. It was certainly a region where superpower conflict had manifested itself in regional tensions (between India and Pakistan); the need for economic development was as acute as in any region of the world, and Soviet ties with at least two countries of the region (Afghanistan and India) were important to that economic development. The most dramatic example of the effects of the New Thinking, of course, can be found in Afghanistan. By 1987, the USSR had been militarily involved in the country for nearly a decade, and an end to the conflict by military means was no closer, at least without substantial increases in the Soviet commitment there. The earlier writings which raised serious questions about socialist orientation, the prospects for a rapid transition to socialism, and so on, were certainly directly relevant to Afghanistan. But overt criticisms of Soviet policy in Afghanistan in the early and mid-1980s were not to be found in the literature; indeed, articles in conservative journals like *International Affairs* continued to focus their attention on imperialist intrigue as the main cause of the Afghan crisis. As late as 1988, an article appeared which called the Afghan civil war "an undeclared war by imperialism."[95]

Once Gorbachev referred to Afghanistan as the USSR's "bleeding wound" scholars began to assess Soviet policy and the Afghan situation more critically and directly in open publications. An interview in the magazine *Ogonek* caught everyone's attention. Major General Kim Tsagalov, a doctor of philosophy and veteran of the Afghan war, condemned the Kabul regime for precipitating the crisis in Afghanistan, and the Soviet government for sending troops in and aggravating the situation.[96] Later, Dr. Tsagalov would blame Lenin for taking an essentially political position when he asserted that countries could make the transition to socialism without necessary development of the capitalist social base, and he wrote very explicitly that the concept of socialist orientation was utopian, having no basis in real conditions.[97] Another scholar writing in *Narody Azii i Afriki* posited that the Afghan regime's policies, supported by the USSR, had been completely wrong-headed until 1986–87 when the Communist Party in Afghanistan promoted development of the private sector and a policy of national political reconciliation designed to advance Afghanistan's backward condition.[98] This kind of public rethinking of the Afghanistan experience was important, not so much for the decision to withdraw which had seemingly already been taken by Gorbachev, but for reaffirmation of the principles underlying the New Thinking and willingness to scrutinize and criticize policy decisions taken by Moscow and its allies.

As for the other countries of South Asia, only India received extensive treatment. Not unexpectedly, the analyses, coming mainly from Institute of Oriental Studies and IMEMO scholars who earlier were advocates of multistructuralism in India's political and economic development, fit well within the tendencies of the New Thinking described here.[99] There was simply very little written on the smaller countries of Bangladesh, Nepal, and Sri Lanka, and less than what one might hope to see on the region's second largest power, Pakistan. What is interesting about the literature on the region, however, is that some new and controversial topics were attacked in a more direct way. For example, the whole question of sectarianism and communal conflict was examined in some detail, and the analyses offered, once again, practically ignored class analysis and instead looked at a complex range of historical, cultural, and sociopolitical factors.[100] Similarly, scholars began to address the role of religion in the politics of the Islamic countries of the region in a less dogmatic way.[101] They were much less inclined to reduce conservative domestic and foreign policies to outside influences or crude class analyses, and instead tried to address Islam and the power of the clergy in an integrated and historical way. In South Asia, as in the Third World more generally, the prevalent approach then became one entirely compatible with the New Thinking in the international arena – scholarly views may diverge, but on the whole, the sophisticated and multisided approaches to the problems of these countries that began in the late 1970s and early 1980s were being amplified and extended.

Conclusion

This chapter has surveyed briefly the development of Soviet views of the Third World and South Asia since 1970. A reading of the literature indicates the prevalence in the 1970s and early 1980s of a core of informing images or perceptions, based on correlation of forces and complemented by an increasingly pessimistic assessment of the prospects for a rapid transition to socialism in the Third World. Within these broadly accepted images, there was some room for debate and several policy options.

By the late 1970s and early 1980s, scholars were beginning to approach issues in ways that moved away from these traditional core perceptions and further opened the debate (although still very limited in Brezhnev's days) concerning South Asian and Third World development and foreign policy. With the advent of New Thinking in Soviet foreign policy, these views, which reinforced and indeed gave concrete support to many of the tenets of New Thinking, became more widely accepted. The New Thinking then was the acceptance of a more sophisticated approach to the Third World – one that focused less on class analysis, correlation of forces, and imperialist machinations and more on the complexity and diversity of social and economic formations. That it would have far-reaching policy implications was clear, but precisely what those would be was not immediately discernable: If the multistructural nature of South Asia made it unlikely that a transition to socialism would occur in the near future, what should the USSR do? How should the USSR handle the socialist Third World countries like Afghanistan and Cuba? Should the USSR reorient its Third World foreign policy towards more politically and economically stable countries (such as the NICs)? What might the USSR be able to learn about economic development from the Third World? If the Cold War was over and if a correlation of forces approach to foreign policy was being rejected, what should be Soviet policy in South Asia – an area where the superpowers had competed vigorously over the years?

Part of the answer to these questions lies in an examination of actual Soviet policy implementation in the region (chapters 4, 5, 6), but another important part lies with a consideration of the objectives of Soviet policy and the means available to pursue those goals. That is the subject of the next chapter.

3 The Soviet Union in South Asia: objectives and instruments

Soviet views of the international environment, the Third World and South Asia, as articulated in the scholarly literature, became increasingly sophisticated in the 1970s and 1980s. Soviet analysts became more aware of the difficulties facing Third World states in completing the second phase of national liberation, freedom from economic dependence, and in undertaking a socialist path of development. The Soviet leadership was also painfully aware that it could not finance Third World development. Until the mid-1980s, however, political rhetoric and scholarly analysis continued to hold to the view of the inevitability of socialist transformation. Policy objectives for South Asia reflected the ambiguity in Soviet thinking about the Third World. On the one hand, there was recognition of limited Soviet capabilities, particularly in the economic sphere, and limited prospects for socialist transformation in the developing countries. On the other hand, there was the continued need to combat imperialism in order to promote socialism's development, first in the USSR and its East European allies, and second, globally. Political objectives then continued to reflect correlation of forces thinking and a somewhat dampened optimism about the prospects for the socialist transition in the Third World; that thinking was tempered by the realities of conditions in the Soviet Union and South Asia. Importantly, revised perceptions of the Third World and of Soviet capabilities were reflected more in changing instruments of policy than in objectives.

The widening discussion about the Third World, therefore, did not result in major policy shifts until the Gorbachev era when some of the most basic tenets of the Soviet view of international relations began to be questioned. With the triumph of human interests over class interests, the recognition that regional conflicts needed to be solved by peaceful means, and the acceptance of global interdependence, the objectives of Soviet policy in South Asia changed and there was a slow

39

move away from reliance on the military instrument of power as the primary tool of Soviet policy in the region.

In addition, the growing link between domestic policy and foreign policy objectives must be acknowledged. The New Thinking in foreign policy certainly helped Gorbachev advance the cause of perestroika within the USSR, and as domestic political restructuring progressed, foreign policy objectives became increasingly linked to domestic policy objectives. Thus, for example, if the USSR were to be intertwined with the world economy, certain domestic economic reforms would be necessary (e.g., increased opportunities for foreign investment, eventual ruble convertibility, etc.). If this kind of economic rationalization were to be undertaken within the USSR, then foreign trade would also have to be conducted on the basis of convertible currency.

This chapter will focus on the formulation of Soviet policy by examining its objectives and instruments in South Asia. It will examine Soviet objectives in South Asia first by looking at how Soviet assessments of correlations of forces in the region were supported by superpower and regional competition which influenced Soviet political objectives, and then by looking to Soviet aims in strategic terms and in the area of economics.

Objectives

Political objectives: regional tensions, superpower rivalries, and the Gorbachev era. Throughout the post-Second World War period, India had been the cornerstone of the USSR's South Asia policy. Despite some difficulties and disagreements which at times made the friendship rocky (e.g., the USSR's arms program to Pakistan in 1968–69, and its competition with India over influence in Bangladesh in the early 1970s),[1] the Indo-Soviet relationship managed to endure, growing closer and expanding from the political/diplomatic realm to cultural, economic, and military dimensions, and the consistency of that relationship affected Soviet aims and objectives for South Asia at large. By the mid-1960s, India's position as a trusted Third World comrade to the Soviet Union had risen dramatically, as indicated by the increasing importance of Soviet aid and trade in her economy and particularly the Indian military's reliance on Soviet arms and equipment. Through this alliance, the USSR could further its objective of advancing a positive Soviet image in the region specifically but also in the Third World more generally. The USSR hoped to use India to aid in the promotion of its political aims in the Third World. By allowing India free reign on the subcontinent, the USSR enjoyed the public support (or at least the lack of harsh public criticism) of one of the non-aligned movement's most influential members. With India as the cornerstone of its South Asia policy, the USSR was able to maximize its main objective of countering the United States and China in Asia.

The need to offset American influence in South Asia and the Third World was clearly indicated by both the global and regional correlation of forces; it was seen as the USSR's "international duty."[2] However, the need to minimize Chinese influence in South Asia had been made more acute by the relationship between Beijing and Islamabad that had begun to flourish by the 1970s. These ties were perhaps as troubling to India as they were to the USSR. It is no coincidence that Indo-Soviet ties warmed considerably at roughly the same time as a triangular relationship between the US, China, and Pakistan emerged to undermine Soviet influence in the subcontinent.

China's interests in South Asia did not stop with its territorial dispute with India or its friendship with Pakistan. China began to court the peripheral states of the region, Afghanistan, Nepal, Sri Lanka, and even Bangladesh and Bhutan, extending economic aid and increasing political and cultural ties. Nepal openly used its China ties to press India for aid and trade concessions while Bhutan, which had traditionally held to an isolationist foreign policy, determined to open diplomatic relations with China. Neither of these situations sat well with either Delhi or Moscow.

Sino-American detente further reinforced regional perceptions, suspicions, and the regional balance of power. Not only did the USSR have to contend with individual American and Chinese activism in South Asia, but with the US and China edging closer together in the 1970s, South Asian linkages with Beijing became more troubling. Clearly, the objective of countering the US and China was only complicated by the prospect of US–Chinese collusion in South Asia. As one scholar put it:

> The divisive activities of the Mao group objectively play into the hands of the imperialists, paving the way for rapprochement between the forces of aggression and expansionism in Asia at the expense of the vital interests of the peoples in this part of the world. Recent events in the Indian subcontinent have shown that the American imperialists and the Maoists actually acted jointly against the forces of national liberation in a vain attempt to thwart the people of Bangladesh for independence.[3]

The USSR's objectives in South Asia in the 1970s and early 1980s were thus influenced by complex yet relatively stable interrelationships between the superpowers and regional actors. The longevity and intensity of the Indo-Soviet relationship is best viewed in terms of the similarity of their policy objectives (e.g., to counter Pakistan, allied to the US, and to minimize Chinese influence) in a number of critical instances. The Soviet Union's successes on the subcontinent were also influenced by America's relative disinterest in the area. Howard Wriggins characterized US policy towards South Asia from 1965 to 1979 as one of "minimum concern .... perhaps encapsulated in the proposition 'they can do us little good, but also little harm.'"[4] With the Soviet intervention in Afghanistan, of course, the US was forced to recognize the region's significance; however, by then, the geostrategic situation of South Asia had already been transformed. China, on the other hand, pursued a more consciously active role in the region throughout the period 1970–85. Hence, regional and superpower triangles may have shifted emphasis over time, but the basic patterns of tension persisted.

The Saur Revolution in Afghanistan accentuated the contradiction between capitalism and socialism in countries of socialist orientation, and, therefore, made the objective of countering imperialism more acute for the USSR. As Alexei Kiva noted, "Socialist orientation of newly independent countries is a rather complex social phenomenon, as it features the sharpest confrontation between ... capitalist and socialist trends ..."[5] Scholars at the Institute of Oriental Studies and the Institute for World Economy and International Relations, however, had noted the challenges to this group of countries in maintaining economic and political control, let alone in making a transition to socialism.[6] With its vulnerability, it was not surprising, therefore, that the imperialist West would be interested in the outcome of the struggle in Afghanistan and would actively attempt to overturn the gains of the Revolution. But, as one writer put it, "Given the existing balance of forces in the world ... the alliance of the forces of socialism, peace and progress has resolutely blocked the way for those imperialist circles whose policy is to export counter-revolution. The events in Afghanistan are convincing proof of this."[7] The concern with the global correlation of forces and the correlation of forces in a country bordering on the USSR meant that Afghanistan would take a special place in the group of countries identified as socialist oriented countries with vanguard parties. There was clearly an overestimation on the part of Moscow of the viability of the regime in Kabul, the depth of its reforms, and the role of the global correlation of forces in securing the gains of the revolution. The Soviet leadership, despite the advice of some experts, was willing to offer its protection to a country that had not yet achieved socialism. The significance of the Soviet intervention in Afghanistan, therefore, is that it can be seen as the application of an extended Brezhnev Doctrine.[8]

The People's Democratic Party of Afghanistan (PDPA), once installed in Kabul, would be supported by the USSR; however, the Soviet Union's willingness to engage in a decade-long military intervention to establish socialism in one of the world's least developed countries was evidence of its commitment to the irreversibility of the socialist development "choice."[9] Had the PDPA regime been successful in Afghanistan, the global correlation of forces would have been tipped further to the socialist system. In terms of the struggle between capitalism and socialism, Afghanistan was a testing ground that the "old thinkers" did not want to lose. The political objective of maintaining the PDPA regime in power was therefore critical.

Nonetheless, Afghanistan presented some ideological dilemmas. What were the prospects for socialism in Afghanistan? What kind of strategy of socialist development would be possible? At what cost? These issues were implicit in the literature of the late 1970s and early 1980s, as were their implications for Soviet policy. Imbedded in the work of scholars like Nodari Simoniia who had a very pessimistic opinion about the prospects for the development of socialism in the Third World were the answers to these questions. Afghanistan, as one of the least developed countries in the world would be among the worst candidates for a rapid transition to socialism, and the costs of trying to by-pass capitalism altogether, if possible, would be very high.

No change was evidenced in Soviet policy until Gorbachev announced his interest in resolving the Afghanistan problem and improving relations with both China and the US. New Thinking had chipped away at the core of correlation of forces: regional conflicts had to be resolved, human interests placed above class interests. Then the withdrawal of troops was possible. Even after the pull-out had commenced, the writing of some commentators indicated their preference for maintaining the PDPA regime in power. One writer, for example, characterized the PDPA as a source of "social renewal," although he also added that other "forces of social renewal" existed.[10]

Security objectives. Like its political objectives in South Asia in the 1970s to early 1980s, the USSR's military objectives were determined both by considerations of its international role *vis-à-vis* the United States and China and by South Asian regional instabilities and opportunities. The region had been a sensitive one, with intense communal conflicts existing alongside the international frictions already discussed. The fact that the USSR bordered Afghanistan only served to reinforce concerns over the area's instabilities. Moreover, both India and Pakistan moved to develop nuclear capability, with India actually detonating a device on May 18, 1974, and Pakistan stepping up its nuclear program dramatically in the late 1970s and into the 1980s. Leonard Spector, writing about the escalation of the nuclear threat in 1984 said: "Although it is still possible that an active nuclear arms race in South Asia may be averted, the risk of such a race appears to be dramatically increasing."[11] The history of tensions between the two countries, and the long-standing animosity between China and India, meant there was great potential for a nuclear exchange that could spill over into other areas. Despite all this, and despite the close US ties to the Shah's Iran, Pakistan, and China, South Asia obviously was not the Soviet Union's most pressing security concern.

The region was assigned to the Southern theater of military action (TVD) which differed from other TVDs in some important ways. As Michael MccGwire observes:

> The Soviets are not faced by an in-place threat of territorial aggression across their southern borders, and it would not be easy for an opponent to mount such a threat .... This means the Southern TVD comes in a poor fifth to the other TVDs in strategic priority.[12]

But, as the Soviet intervention in Afghanistan demonstrated, it did not mean that the USSR would not project its forces into the region. Its security interests in the area fit within a set of larger political and military goals, that is, to minimize the role of Western imperialism in the Third World (in the 1970s and early 1980s) and to avoid war between the superpowers. Thus, regional tensions and superpower competition constrained Soviet policy such that, for example, the Soviet intervention in Afghanistan was possible because there was a low risk of confrontation with the US or China, while intervention in the Persian Gulf would be less likely since heavy Western interest in maintaining access to oil supplies would increase the risk of super-power confrontation.[13] Similarly, because of historical patterns of US and Chinese support for Pakistan, serious Soviet military intervention there would also carry a higher risk than Afghanistan did.

Even though the Southern TVD may not have been as critical to the USSR as the Northwestern, Arctic Ocean, or Far Eastern TVDs and even if the Soviet Union was constrained by war avoidance objectives in its ability to project its forces in this area, it still had some latitude for pursuing its regional objectives, while supporting the overall goal of limiting the US and China. This situation is illustrated by American and South Asian concerns of a Soviet naval presence in the Indian Ocean. "The initial Soviet naval presence in the MTVD [marine theater of military action] was related to the problem of sea-based delivery systems and the apparent U.S. intention to deploy ballistic-missile submarines in the Indian Ocean."[14] It was not until the late 1960s that a permanent Soviet presence in the Indian Ocean was noticed. The upgrading of facilities at Diego Garcia in the early 1980s, fueled by events in Afghanistan and Iran, further worried the USSR since, with the exception of Aden, it had no base in the area. As Geoffrey Jukes notes:

> Thus, the Soviet presence has combined antisubmarine area familiarization, assistance to local powers, shadowing of Western naval forces, and a modicum of flag showing around the area. What has been lacking, and still is lacking, has been any evidence of the maintenance of a task force designed to interfere with mercantile traffic, tanker or other, on the sea-lanes of the Indian Ocean.[15]

From the South Asian perspective, the United States was a much more serious threat to peace in the region. Indeed, India's position, particularly under Mrs. Gandhi, was to ignore or minimize Soviet naval forces in the region while criticizing the American use of Diego Garcia. Others, like Sri Lanka and India under Desai, took the view that neither superpower was welcome in the area and called for the demilitarization of the area by all external forces.

Another objective was the Soviet desire to decrease Third World reliance on the West for arms and military equipment through the export of Soviet arms.[16] This objective was supported in the theoretical literature by the interest in the military as a progressive modernizing force.[17] South Asia certainly received considerable amounts of arms from the Soviet Union. Data from both the Arms Control and Disarmament Agency and the Stockholm International Peace Research Institute indicate that the USSR was the major supplier of weapons systems to the region.[18] (See Table 1 for arms delivered to the region by the USSR, the United States, China, and others in the 1971–90 period.)

The increases by the USSR in the 1976–80 period and by the US in the 1981–85 period are due in large measure to the Afghan conflict, particularly noted in the US case where exports to Pakistan increased from 4% to 12%. Similarly, the reduced arms transfers by the United States in the late 1980s are in large part due to the Soviet withdrawal from Afghanistan. The Soviet Union, however, continued to play a

Table 1. *Shares by suppliers of major weapons to South Asia, 1971–1990*

Period		USSR	USA	China	Others[a]
1971–1975	(1)	$2,970	$55	$880	$1,485
	(2)	54%	1%	16%	27%
1976–1980	(1)	$5,076	$322	$645	$1,933
	(2)	63%	4%	8%	24%
1981–1985	(1)	$6,776	$1,506	$878	$3,388
	(2)	54%	12%	7%	27%
1986–1990	(1)	$17,934	$1,260	$1,640	$5,262
	(2)	69%	5%	6%	20%

Note: [a] Includes France, UK, FRG, Italy, and others. (1) Figure in $US million (constant 1985 prices). (2) Percentage of total.
Sources: 1971–85 calculated from Michael Brzoska and Thomas Ohlson, *Arms Transfers to the Third World, 1971–1985*, Oxford: Oxford University Press, 1987: 338; 1986–90 calculated from *SIPRI Yearbook 1991: World Armaments and Disarmament*, Oxford: Oxford University Press, 1991: 208–11. Brzoska and Ohlson's figures are based on SIPRI data.

major role in weapons supplies to South Asia, because of its commitments to Afghanistan and India.

As indicated in Table 2, Afghanistan and India consistently received virtually all Soviet arms transferred, although other countries, including Pakistan in the late 1960s, purchased Soviet weapons as well. Indeed, together India and Afghanistan were responsible for 42% of the USSR's arms exports to the Third World in the 1986–90 period.[19] Moreover, unlike Middle East purchasers, India and Afghanistan were on a clearing account system of bilateral relations and therefore did not offer the USSR the prospect of obtaining hard currency for arms. However, as of January 2, 1991, the USSR began requiring that all its foreign trade be conducted in hard currency; therefore, it was fair to suggest that Soviet dominance, particularly in the Indian market, would suffer in the future.

There was particular concern in the West about India's reliance on the USSR as a military supplier. The USSR supplied India with various types of surface to air missiles, tanks, fighter and attack planes as well as MiG fighters and interceptors, submarines and patrol ships, among others. From 1970 to 1985, India was also licensed to produce MiG-21 and MiG-27 fighters, the BMP-1 armored personnel carrier, the T-72 battle tank, and AA-2 Atoll missiles. All this pointed to an increased dependence on the USSR by India. In the late 1970s, India, while

Table 2. *Soviet arms transfers to countries of South Asia, 1971–1990 (in constant 1985 $US millions)*

Country		1971–75	1976–80	1981–85	1986–90
Afghanistan					
	(1)	$155	$894	$964	$5,460
	(2)	100%	96%	98%	95%
Bangladesh					
	(1)	$71	$0	$26	$0
	(2)	29%	0%	1%	0%
India					
	(1)	$2,730	$4,177	$5,887	$12,474
	(2)	73%	82%	68%	73%
Nepal					
	(1)	$0	$0	$0	$0
	(2)	0%	0%	0%	0%
Pakistan					
	(1)	$128	$0	$0	$0
	(2)	0%	0%	0%	0%
Sri Lanka					
	(1)	$26	$0	$0	$0
	(2)	59%	0%	0%	0%

Note: (1) Soviet arms transfers.
(2) As percentage of total arms imported.
Sources: Calculated from Michael Brzoska and Thomas Ohlson, *Arms Transfers to the Third World, 1971–1985*, Oxford: Oxford University Press, 1987: 339, 343, 346–48; 1986–90 from *SIPRI Yearbook 1991: World Armaments and Disarmaments*: 208–11. Brzoska and Ohlson's figures are based on SIPRI data.

receiving a large portion of her arms from the USSR, began to diversify military equipment sources to include France, Italy, the UK and the US, and other Western countries as well. India also began building its own arms industry in an effort to encourage military self-reliance. However, even with Gorbachev's calls to reduce regional tensions, India received a wide variety of major arms shipments in the latter half of the 1980s, including 15 Mig-29 fighter planes, 100 Mi-17 Hip helicopters, over 700 SA-8 Gecko surface to air missiles, Kilo-class submarines, reconnaissance planes, launchers and missile systems for India's destroyers, among many others.[20] In addition to continued licensed production of the MiG-27 fighter plane and T-72 battle tank, after Gorbachev's 1986 visit to New Delhi, it was reported that India would probably also receive licenses for the MiG-29; India continued to pursue this possibility into 1990.[21] It seems clear that the USSR's share of Indian procurement increased in the late 1980s as the Indian economy deteriorated. Although the USSR may have been successful in absorbing the bulk of Indian arms demands, it was not successful enough to exert undue influence on Indian policy and planning because of arms supplies, as will be shown in chapters 4, 5, and 6.

Thus, in the late 1970s and early 1980s, the USSR's main military objectives on the subcontinent were to avoid direct conflict with the United States while limiting its influence in South Asia. Soviet policy, of course, attempted to increase Moscow's own influence in military matters in the region, but strategies varied from country to country. In India, for example, the USSR used arms transfers to wean the Indian military away from the West and to increase Indian security dependence on the Soviet Union. Arms transfers to Pakistan, which occurred largely in the late 1960s, on the other hand, were designed in part to enhance the thaw in Soviet–Pakistani relations that occurred after the Tashkent conference, in part to discourage Pakistan from turning to China after losing arms assistance from the United States after the 1965 war with India, and in part to cue India that their warm relationship would not deter the USSR from pursuing its interests in other countries of the region.

Soviet objectives in Afghanistan at that time differed somewhat from those in other countries of the region because of Afghanistan's location on the USSR's southern border. Confirming the geopolitical basis for Soviet interest in the Afghan crisis in the late 1970s, an article in the journal *International Affairs* noted: "Imperialism's military interference in Afghanistan affected directly the security of the USSR's southern borders."[22] Its location then gave it importance to Moscow beyond what would be expected for a small, feudal country with few resources. As a contiguous state, the USSR generally wanted Afghanistan to conduct a nominally neutral but Moscow-leaning foreign policy and to maintain relatively stable internal conditions so that there would be no chance for spillover into the USSR's Muslim republics. Soviet objectives also included minimizing Western and Chinese influence, increasing Kabul's reliance on the USSR for weapons, military training and technology, and building up pro-Soviet sentiments in the armed forces.[23] After the 1978 Saur Revolution, the USSR's goals included the protection of the socialist revolution in Afghanistan by whatever means. With the dissolution of Hafizullah Amin's control over the country in 1979, the second and third of these basic prerequisites were threatened, and with rumors that Amin was seeking closer ties to China and his earlier demand for withdrawal of the Soviet ambassador to Kabul, circumstances did not bode well for Moscow's first requirement.

The advent of New Thinking and the modification of political objectives in South Asia brought a reorientation of the USSR's security interests. As one Soviet scholar put it, "in the absence of reduced international tensions in Asia it will be impossible to succeed in setting up a comprehensive international security system in any area, including Europe."[24] Improved relations with the United States and China required an end to Soviet intervention in Afghanistan. Thus, the military objective of protecting the Saur Revolution's gains would be sacrificed and Soviet troops withdrawn, although Moscow would continue to provide arms to Kabul well into 1991.

Economic objectives. The optimism generated during the Khrushchev period about the prospects for socialism in the Third World had been muted in the 1970s. Elizabeth Kridl Valkenier has observed that by 1965 Soviet economic policy in the Third World had shifted in favor of Soviet pursuit of "economic advantage," although the USSR still paid close attention to prospective political alliances with progressive regimes.[25] In the case of South Asia, aid extended in the early 1960s to build the state sector and encourage central planning had not led to a diminution of the private sector (nor of feudal and semi-feudal elements in the economy). Although the state sector was seen as having positive effects on the economy at large,[26] it began to be recognized as inefficient in Moscow and in Delhi.[27] The USSR's ability to compete with the West throughout the Third World in terms of development aid (and some might argue, in terms of trade as well) was clearly inadequate. Even if its geopolitical goals in South Asia had been relatively successful, the Soviet Union was forced to recognize that its capabilities might not allow its economic aims to be implemented. This recognition was bolstered by the work of scholars like Simoniia and Kim that portrayed the difficulty of the transition to socialism and of the states of socialist orientation in Asia, and the work of scholars like Maliarov which underscored the dilemmas of the state sector in the developing countries. Thus, conditions in South Asia and limitations of the Soviet economy forced a narrowing of Soviet economic objectives in the region.

As elsewhere in the Third World, the USSR carefully selected countries in which it would target its economic efforts, and economic activities centered on the promotion of trade rather than aid. Scholars such as Valkenier and Smith have noted an economic slump in the mid-1970s which further affected Soviet interests throughout the Third World in general and South Asia as well.

Despite Soviet reticence to finance Third World development, South Asia nonetheless fared well in terms of Soviet aid. The region ranked second only to the Middle East in aid given by Moscow during the 1970–85 period. However, there was a wide discrepancy between what Moscow gave to its primary economic partners, Afghanistan and India, and what was given to other countries of the region. While India received more economic assistance than all other non-communist Third World countries, aid to the rest of South Asia, with the exception of Afghanistan which by 1978 was led by a communist party, was relatively limited. Table 3 illustrates the disparities for 1970–85. For example, from 1970 to 1979, total aid received at this time by Afghanistan was $586 million; India – $695 million; Pakistan – $641 million; Bangladesh – $231 million; Sri Lanka – $56 million; and Nepal received almost none.[28] In some cases, low levels of aid were the result of the recipient country's inability or unwillingness to use credits as stipulated;[29] hence, the receiving state might have preferred to obtain aid from the West or China. More often, Soviet aid offered was simply quite limited, or in the case of Nepal, non-existent, and could never really compete with Western aid.

Gorbachev's New Thinking certainly did not stress the provision of large amounts of economic assistance to any country; however, as in keeping with past patterns, assistance continued to flow to Afghanistan and India. In 1987, for example, the USSR gave economic assistance to four countries in South Asia: Afghanistan received $396 million; Bangladesh – $85 million; India – $1,117 million; and Sri Lanka – $77 million. By 1988, only two countries were receiving any aid: Afghanistan – $776 million and India – $3,960 million.[30] The Afghan aid, of course, was tied to the survival of the Kabul government while aid to India was reaffirmed during Gorbachev's visit to New Delhi in 1986. In fact, the USSR's aid offers to India in 1986 alone exceeded assistance granted in the previous thirty years. As the Soviet economy continued to deteriorate, it was expected that aid to Afghanistan and India would suffer too.

Trade patterns in South Asia mirrored aid patterns insofar as the USSR's biggest aid recipients, Afghanistan and India, were also its biggest trade partners (see Table 4). In fact, India was second only to Cuba in the Soviet Union's trade with the Third World. India's relations with the USSR differed not only in terms of volume of aid/trade but also in other important respects.[31] India was one of the few Third

Table 3. *Soviet aid to South Asia, 1970–1988 (in $US millions)*

Total	$15,822
Afghanistan	4,121
Bangladesh	600
India	9,829
Nepal	10
Pakistan	1,210
Sri Lanka	70

Source: Derived from US Department of State, *Warsaw Pact Economic Aid to Non-Communist LDCs: Holding Their Own in 1986* (August, 1988) and *Warsaw Pact Aid to Non-Communist LDCs, 1984* (May, 1986); Gu Guan-fu, "Soviet Aid to the Third World, and analysis of its Strategy," *Soviet Studies*, vol. 35, no. 1 (January 1983): 79; and W. Raymond Duncan and Carol McGiffert Ekedahl, *Moscow and the Third World under Gorbachev* (Westview, 1990: 36. Comparable data for the late 1980s is not available.

World countries which had a clearing system of payment for goods, that is, hard currency payment was not required.[32] (Afghanistan also used this system.) Furthermore, under this system, India was permitted to import petroleum. As Santosh Mehrotra points out: "From the Soviet point of view, the supply of crude oil, the opportunity cost of which should be measured in hard currency, is a considerable gesture."[33] India and Afghanistan also had a number of joint production and large-scale industrial projects which required not only substantial capital commitments from the USSR but also long-term economic planning and cooperation.

Thus, for these two countries, unlike the other countries of South Asia, Soviet economic objectives appear to have had a more highly politicized component, that is, considerations of economic advantage may have entered the picture, but ultimately, it was the history of Soviet commitment to these countries and their geopolitical significance that drove Soviet policy. This situation was reinforced by the fact that decisions taken in the 1950s and 1960s (i.e., to support Afghanistan or India) for political reasons engendered a range of economic relations which were valued by both Moscow and the South Asian countries and which took on their own agendas.

Under Gorbachev, the imperatives of economic benefit to the USSR (begun under Brezhnev) and rationalization of foreign trade became more important. Trade with many of the countries of South Asia

Table 4. *Soviet trade with South Asia, 1970–1989*
(in millions of rubles)

Country	1970	1975	1980	1985	1989
Afghanistan	66.9	132.2	504.7	873.2	583.8
Imports	30.9	64.3	257.0	323.0	504.5
Exports	36.0	67.9	247.7	550.2	79.3
Bangladesh	–	52.2	53.7	76.4	77.1
Imports		26.5	34.9	51.3	51.3
Exports		27.2	41.5	25.8	25.8
India	364.9	685.6	1,739.8	3,072.2	2,917.8
Imports	242.6	393.5	878.6	1,499.6	1,147.2
Exports	122.3	292.1	861.2	1,572.6	1,770.6
Nepal	1.3	5.5	14.4	20.9	–
Imports	0.7	0.5	5.2	5.2	–
Exports	0.6	5.0	9.2	15.7	–
Pakistan	60.4	60.7	176.6	117.6	150.2
Imports	28.3	23.6	50.4	59.1	77.1
Exports	32.1	37.1	126.2	58.5	73.1
Sri Lanka	17.0	22.4	30.3	38.1	13.6
Imports	12.0	10.4	25.7	29.8	0.7
Exports	5.0	12.0	4.6	8.3	12.9

Source: Vneshniaia torgovlia SSSR, various years, and *Vneshnie ekonomicheskie sviazi SSSR*, 1988 and 1989.

suffered as the USSR cut back its economic commitments that were based on political objectives. Thus, in the case of the small countries of South Asia, trade either held steady (the case of Bangladesh) or decreased dramatically (Nepal and Sri Lanka), indicating that the USSR would not waste economic resources for unnecessary (or unwanted) imports. Even the long-time allies, Afghanistan and India, which had extensive and beneficial contacts with the USSR, felt the effects of New Thinking. The USSR continued their extensive connections with India into the 1980s. Indeed, although the ruble amounts of Indo-Soviet trade indicated a decrease in trade turnover in the late 1980s, Soviet commitments to expand trade with New Delhi after Gorbachev's visit to New Delhi in 1986 resulted in trade increases: from 37 billion rupees in 1986 to 71 billion rupees in 1989.[34] However, whatever increases occurred must be considered in the context of rapidly expanding Indian exports. There then remained questions about the limits to expanding trade. The problem for Soviet–South

Asian economic relations was that perestroika in the domestic economy helped shift economic objectives in foreign policy, and there were few countries, other than India, in South Asia that could offer the USSR much for its own economic development.

Conclusion. The old core values of the Soviet regime (e.g., protection of the homeland, promotion of international socialism) had always been an important aspect of the formulation of India policy objectives. They helped give Soviet foreign policy direction and justification. But policy objectives in South Asia between 1970 and 1985, as elsewhere, were also influenced by Soviet perceptions of the international and regional correlation of forces (i.e., the competition between Beijing, Moscow, and Washington, and relations between regional actors [and superpowers] and the national political, military, and economic circumstances of the countries of South Asia).

There was a clear mutuality of interests which promoted Soviet ties with India (and Afghanistan) over a long period of time. Soviet friendship with India served one of the USSR's main objectives in South Asia, that of countering Chinese and American influence in the region. India, as leader of the non-aligned movement and significant adversary to China and Pakistan, fits the bill of counterweight more than adequately. This did not mean, however, that *rapprochement* between China and India was precluded. As Rajan Menon points out, "New Delhi has not in any direct sense served as an instrument of Soviet diplomatic strategy against China and has kept open the option of normalizing ties with Peking."[35] Indeed, Sino-Indian relations improved in the late 1970s and 1980s. It also did not mean that Moscow would sacrifice its relations with other countries of the region to its friendship with Delhi. The fact that Soviet trade with Pakistan, for example, was not insignificant (more than 120 million rubles in 1984) and that the Soviet Union extended military and economic aid to Pakistan at various times suggests the lengths to which Moscow would go to cultivate "good neighborly relations" with all countries of the region. Nonetheless, the USSR's overarching objectives for nearly two decades promoted its ties with India, which in turn constrained Moscow's activities in other countries of the region. That constraint from Moscow's perspective, however, was a bearable one, given that the other countries of the region had little to offer the Soviet Union. Even with the Soviet intervention in Afghanistan, the political and military hierarchy on the subcontinent remained stable since the early 1970s, as did the international alliances. In 1985, it seemed likely that the USSR would not have minded a continuation of the South Asian status quo in the second half of the 1980s and into the 1990s.

The New Thinking changed that assessment. As Georgi Mirskii put it, New Thinking "means that Soviet foreign policy from now on should be, so to speak, classical great power policy of the normal kind, devoid of Messianic notions and pretensions."[36] Thus, in order to achieve other policy goals (i.e., *rapprochement* with the West particularly but also China, withdrawal of troops from Afghanistan, rationalization of foreign trade) and to establish the kind of "normal, non-Messianic" approach to Third World countries that was supported by New Thinking, the Soviet Union's objectives in South Asia also had to change.

Instruments of power

Soviet foreign policy objectives broadly reflected the values and interests of the USSR. In the 1970s and early 1980s that meant its need to limit the role of the US, China, and imperialism in the Third World through support of national liberation movements and to promote the USSR's political, economic, and military interests which in turn would strengthen Soviet domestic security, whereas in the latter half of the 1980s and early 1990s, it meant to improve relations with the West and China, find negotiated settlements to regional conflicts, develop a realistic approach to its ties with the Third World, rationalize economic relations, and so on. Policy objectives also reflected the constraints placed upon the pursuit of these interests by circumstances on the ground in South Asia. The effectiveness of Soviet instruments to accomplish these objectives was also affected by domestic requirements, superpower relations, and regional circumstances. The mix of instruments (e.g., political/diplomatic, economic, military) which the USSR decided to employ reflected priority of objectives, perceptions of the relative strength of particular instruments, domestic political considerations, and images of the country or region in which the instrument was to be used.

In many respects, the political/diplomatic instrument in South Asia was perhaps the most important in the Soviet foreign policy arsenal, partially because its use was prevalent to all countries of the region, whereas significant economic and military ties were limited to only a few countries. Just as Soviet objectives towards various countries of the region differed, the USSR found some instruments of policy (or combinations of instruments) more effective than others in individual states of South Asia.

The political/diplomatic instrument. Diplomacy is characterized by the formal establishment of state to state relations and usually marked by an exchange of ambassadors and is the most traditional of all the instruments of power. Although the highly secretive and personal interactions that typified Russian and early Soviet diplomacy in South Asia gave way to a diplomatic and political style which made ample use of public and international fora, the diplomatic instrument proved to be one of the most effective tools in the Soviet foreign policy arsenal.

In the Brezhnev era, Soviet diplomacy was claimed by Soviet policy-makers to be scientific. By understanding the objective laws of historical development, Soviet foreign policy and Soviet diplomacy were bound to be successful in the long run. The foreign policy of Western states, on the other hand, was characterized by miscalculation and failure, because it did not take into account these objective laws.[37]

Through diplomacy, the USSR was able to achieve one of its principal objectives in South Asia: that of establishing and maintaining friendly relations with all countries of the region. Even though its South Asian policy was highly Indo-centric (a situation which certainly did not please all countries of the region), diplomatic contacts allowed Moscow to develop relations with various countries, although these relations were not always close.

There was a diminished reliance on personalities in diplomacy which resulted from the growth of foreign policy bureaucracies and the dispersion of decisionmaking, the increased demands for technical expertise to administer the multiplying economic and military agreements, and the broad interests and interdependencies that developed in relations. Nonetheless, personalities continued to play an important role through summitry, crisis diplomacy, party-to-party relations, and the general tenor of bilateral relations.

Personal diplomacy was also important in times of stress or downturn in relations. In the early 1980s, as the Congress regime in India sought to diversify arms acquisitions, the USSR sent Defense Minister Ustinov to New Delhi in 1982 and again in 1984.[38] Similarly, Soviet anxiety over the foreign policy proclivities of a new Indian Prime Minister, Rajiv Gandhi, was somewhat relieved by having him visit the Kremlin in May of 1985, and the positive consequences of that visit were further reinforced when Gorbachev first ventured into the Third World the following year on his well-publicized trip to India.

Crisis diplomacy: the 1971 India–Pakistan war: The USSR had a highly successful venture into South Asian crisis diplomacy at the Tashkent Conference which settled the 1965 war between India and Pakistan.

Although Tashkent was the high point of Soviet diplomacy in the region, the USSR would continue to try to play a role in crisis diplomacy in 1971, although with much less success.

Unlike Tashkent, where the USSR was the honest broker to the highest level officials of two countries which by and large wished to settle their disputes, actions taken during the Bangladesh crisis reflected the Soviet inclination to support the Indian position. Thus, diplomacy during this crisis was directed mainly at the Pakistani leadership in an attempt to get them to refrain from escalating the crisis in East Pakistan. As Chapter 4 will show, contacts during this crisis were carried out mainly on the ambassadorial level, although ex-Foreign Minister Arshad Husain acted as a special representative for Pakistani President Yahya Khan in Moscow.

Another facet of the diplomacy was the public position taken by each side. The USSR, while largely supportive of the Indian position, was careful not to advocate the dissolution of Pakistan early in the crisis nor to draw too much attention to Pakistani atrocities in Bangladesh.[39] The key actions, however, again involved communication at the highest levels, coming in the form of a letter from President Podgorny to Yahya in April, 1971 and a blustery response by Yahya. Soviet–Pakistani relations may have reached a nadir in late 1971, but as the war ended with an Indian victory, Bhutto made an official visit to Moscow in March, 1972. The two sides naturally discussed the situation on the subcontinent. In July, 1972, the Simla Agreement was signed, the terms of which were highly favorable to India, and so, to the USSR.

Communist party links: Another means of promoting Soviet positions in the region was through relations with the national communist parties; relations, however did not always proceed smoothly. The decade following independence witnessed no clear-cut move toward socialism and brought repeated questioning of whether Soviet-style socialism was correct for South Asia. These tactical questions combined with the Maoist alternative offered to the Third World by China led some parties to break with Moscow. The division of the Indian Communist Party into the pro-Soviet Communist Party of India (CPI) and the pro-Chinese Communist Party (Marxist) in 1964 was largely due to Chinese influence in the international communist movement.[40]

Nonetheless, the USSR was able to consolidate ties with some important local communist parties (e.g., the Communist Party of India (CPI), the Sri Lankan Communist Party, and the Parcham wing of the People's Democratic Party of Afghanistan). These parties often accepted Moscow's lead, especially on issues of foreign affairs, but also on questions of domestic strategy: where the bourgeois democratic option existed, they opted for a position of collaboration with so-called principled opposition. Sometimes local communists were reluctant to accept the USSR's preferences. For example, Moscow was generally supportive of Mrs. Gandhi's imposition of emergency rule in 1975. The CPI initially supported that view, but with their members bearing the brunt of emergency rule, later reversed that position, saying their support for the emergency had been misplaced all along.[41]

The USSR was able to maintain good relations with parties of the region nonetheless, and particularly in India and Sri Lanka where coalitions with, or at least support for, ruling parties was possible, the USSR would try to use these ties to the benefit of political relations between the countries. In Afghanistan in the 1970s, for example, the Soviet Union used its good connections with Babrak Karmal, then head of Parcham, to press Soviet concerns with Daoud, who in the mid-1970s allowed some participation by leftist forces in his government. In particular, Parcham (and the USSR) wanted Daoud to effect more far-reaching economic reforms (some of which had been supported by Daoud when he took power in 1973) and to continue to open his government to the opposition. As has been well documented,[42] Daoud's response was instead to crack down on the Left, thereby foiling chances for collaboration with his opposition and annoying the Soviet Union at the same time.

In India, the CPSU's International Department kept close ties with the Communist Party of India, making frequent visits for consultations. On the domestic front, the Communist Party of India, as an opposition party that participates in the Indian democratic process, pressed hard for continued support of state sector economic development and worker's rights. In foreign affairs, they were actively involved in the Soviet-inspired reunification of Afghanistan's communist parties, Khalq and Parcham, in 1977, inviting representatives of both factions to India for discussions.[43] As Henry Bradsher, quoting an anonymous CPI source notes, "the invitation to the 1977 discussions was issued 'with the knowledge and consent of [the] Communist Party of [the] Soviet Union; otherwise [the] CPI would not have undertaken it. Possibly, the suggestion for such an initiative on the part of [the] CPI also came from Moscow.'"[44] Despite the close links between the CPSU and the CPI, Soviet policy in India was focused more on the Indian government and the Congress Party than on any communist party. Indeed, with the exception of post-1978 Afghanistan, the same can be said for Soviet policy throughout South Asia.

Naturally, with the dissolution of the CPSU's power in Soviet policymaking in the late 1980s, party-to-party links became less important to Soviet diplomacy. The control of the International Department, the Central Committee section that had been responsible for Soviet relations with communist parties in the Third World, had been slowly stripped away by reorganizations of the party, and eventually the party's control throughout the government was abolished, thereby divorcing party-to-party links from state foreign policy.[45]

The economic instrument. In the 1950s and 1960s, the economic instrument was used in South Asia to compete with the West, particularly the United States, to secure friendships begun through diplomatic ties, to increase Soviet influence in the region, and later, to pursue Soviet economic objectives. The economic instrument is usually divided into two types: aid and trade. Aid and trade together as an economic instrument not only served the political objectives mentioned previously. They also had the effect of serving Soviet economic objectives. The economic objectives which aid and trade could serve included the acquisition of goods needed by the USSR at prices favorable to the USSR and an increase in hard currency reserves. Thus, even though *political* considerations may have been paramount in the use of the economic instrument, particularly in the 1950s and early 1960s and particularly with regard to aid-giving, there arose from these economic relations, *economic* interests and objectives which would become more important in the 1970s and 1980s. Finally, the economic instrument was used to support security concerns in that aid and trade were encouraged with states of varying social systems contiguous to the Soviet Union in an effort to maintain relatively stable, friendly regimes on their border (i.e., Afghanistan).

With the signing of the 1971 Treaty, India and the Soviet Union would rapidly expand their economic relations in a wide variety of ways. Trade between the two increased from 354.9 million rubles in 1970 to 3,072.2 million rubles by 1985 (see Table 4). It is also significant that after repeated requests from Indira Gandhi, the USSR began shipping oil to India in 1976. Delhi paid for this oil in rupees, and it became the USSR's largest single export item to India. Also important were the bilateral planning commissions that were established and charged with coordinating the economic development of the two economies. Through the many agreements signed as a result of deepened relations brought about by the Treaty, the USSR pledged to continued its commitment to the development of the Indian economy through both aid and trade. When Gorbachev visited India in 1986, this pledge to expand economic relations was reiterated. The USSR promised more than $1 billion economic aid (to be added to the $700 million offered in 1985),[46] and the two sides agreed to increase trade by 250% by the early 1990s.[47] The USSR remained India's main trade partner in the late 1980s; however, the United States ran a close second to the Soviet Union.[48]

Economic ties with Afghanistan, on the other hand, were less straightforward. Soviet–Afghan trade began the decade at 66.9 million rubles; it rose to 79.9 million rubles in 1971, but then dropped off to about 68.5 million rubles in 1972 and 1973. With the coup that forced out the Afghan monarch and established a republic with former Prime Minister Daoud at its head and support from the left, trade between Afghanistan and the USSR nearly doubled in 1974. Between 1974 and 1978 (the year of the Saur Revolution), bilateral trade grew from 122.4 million rubles to 215 million rubles. The pace quickened between 1978 and 1980 (when trade reached more than 500 million rubles), with a pro-Moscow communist regime in power in Kabul and the introduction of Soviet troops into the civil war there. The types of goods being traded during the 1970s remained remarkably stable: the USSR imported natural gas, cotton, and fruits; Afghanistan imported machinery and equipment, refined sugar, and in the late 1970s, oil.[49] As the civil war raged on in Afghanistan and the Afghan economy deteriorated, there was evidence of difficulties in the "mutually beneficial" economic relations. After Gorbachev assumed power, the Soviet Union's trade with Afghanistan decreased, from 873.6 million rubles in 1985 to 776.7 in 1986, 771.9 in 1987, 663.2 in 1988, to 583.8 in 1989. Furthermore, by 1989, almost 87% of that trade was comprised of Soviet exports to Afghanistan,[50] indicative of the dire state of the Afghan economy.

Soviet trade with Pakistan had always been problematic. At the beginning of the decade, of course, South Asia and the world witnessed the birth of the nation of Bangladesh. Despite some Soviet efforts to insulate Soviet–Pakistani relations from the national liberation movement in East Pakistan and to press for a negotiated settlement to the hostilities between India and Pakistan, relations between Moscow and Islamabad suffered. Soviet trade with Pakistan declined from 60.4 million rubles in 1970 to 36.2 in 1972; by 1974, trade had picked up to 54.8 million rubles and stabilized at 55–60 million rubles until 1977–78, when it reached 90 million rubles. The late 1970s and early 1980s then saw a dramatic increase in trade, with total turnover reaching a high of 176 million rubles in 1980.

What is particularly interesting about this is the composition of total trade: exports exceeded imports by at least three-fold in the late 1970s and early 1980s. Soviet trade statistics indicate that the USSR's main exports since the 1970s were machinery and equipment while its main imports were textiles, clothing, and other finished cloth (mainly cotton) products. This pattern continued even in the Gorbachev period when there was an up-turn in trade as tensions diminished somewhat over Afghanistan. Total trade dipped to 85 million rubles in 1986 but recovered to approximately 115 million rubles in 1987 and 1988, with imports exceeding exports in each of those years. In 1989, trade further increased to 150 million rubles, with imports and exports approximately equal.[51] The relationship improved not only because of the improved political climate, but also because the USSR was able to sell its favored exports (machinery and equipment) and import from Pakistan some badly needed consumer goods such as clothing.

The distinguishing characteristics of Soviet trade with the other countries of the area were its relative paucity (in large part, because they had so little to offer the USSR) and the consistency of types of imports and exports. In the case of Bangladesh, the USSR was initially very supportive of the new state created by the Bangladeshi national liberation movement. Trade relations were established in 1972, with the Soviet Union reporting 8.8 million in trade that year, rising to 43.5 million in 1973. Early exports from the USSR included machinery and cotton fiber while imports to the Soviet Union were comprised mainly of jute and finished cotton products. By 1975, total trade turnover stood at 58.1 million rubles, with oil replacing machinery as the Soviet Union's number one export to Bangladesh while jute remained the USSR's leading import. Trade stagnated in the late 1970s and early 1980s, hovering at an average annual total turnover of 50 million rubles. The trends in exports and imports continued through the late 1970s and into the 1980s; however, machinery and equipment regained their premier position in the 1980s and retained it even in the late 1980s. Furthermore, Soviet exports consistently exceeded imports.[52]

Soviet trade with Nepal grew from a mere 1.3 million rubles in 1970 to 14.4 million by 1980. In 1980, as in the 1960s, the USSR imported jute and semi-processed leather and exported oil and machinery. However, even this limited amount of trade suffered in the late 1980s. From a low of 1.3 million rubles total trade in 1986, trade crept to 3.5

million rubles in 1987 and to 6.6 million in 1988, but in 1989, there was no trade at all between these countries. Sri Lankan trade showed a similar trend. In the 1970s and early 1980s, trade with the USSR increased at a slow rate, from 17.0 million rubles in 1970 to 30 million in 1980, with the Soviet Union exporting a variety of products to Sri Lanka (such as machinery, rolled metal, veneer, and others) and importing primarily tea and rubber. By 1985, trade with Sri Lanka had inched up to 38.1 million rubles only to drop back to 25.1 million rubles in 1986. Reductions in total trade continued in each of the following years, with a slight up-turn in trade (to 13.6 million rubles) in 1989.[53] These patterns demonstrated the USSR's reluctance under Gorbachev to expend even minimal resources on countries that were of little geopolitical or economic value to the Soviet Union.

As for India and Afghanistan, the situation was somewhat different. If economic relations with Afghanistan were an expensive political necessity for the USSR in the 1970s and 1980s, it was at least somewhat ameliorated by the natural gas which made up by far the largest share of Afghan exports to the USSR. It was sold at below market prices[54] and provided the USSR with a cheap source of natural gas for its Central Asian republics.

In the case of India, the USSR's main imports in the early 1970s were tea, jute, textiles, and other raw materials and semi-finished goods. By the 1980s, the major import from India was machinery. This rather remarkable situation, where the Soviet Union purchased machinery and equipment – which had always been of principal importance in their own exports to the Third World – raised concern in Moscow. And the damage was compounded by the sales of oil to India that accelerated in the mid-1970s.

As economically disadvantageous as this trade may have been to the USSR, the Soviet Union nonetheless derived some benefits from its trade with India. For example, the USSR imported increased quantities of consumer goods, particularly from the Special Export Zones (SEZs), where they could acquire drugs and cosmetics from multinational makers such as Ciba-Geigy and Hoechst at competitive prices. In 1982, Rank Xerox and an Indian firm, Modi, agreed to enter into production of photocopiers for export to Moscow.[55] This looser attitude about the private sector reflected the rethinking about development and international economic relations that was going on in the theoretical literature. The economist Leon Zevin, for example, had been arguing since the mid-1970s that the USSR could reap benefits from economic contacts with developing countries, including those of non-socialist orientation.[56] As this argument developed, the implication was that the private sector, even in the Third World, had something to offer the socialist countries. As Gorbachev's New Thinking took hold, the USSR faced the prospect of being able to acquire high quality goods from India's SEZs without paying hard currency for them.

Another critical consideration, however, is the level of Soviet penetration of the South Asian economies. Although Soviet trade turnover with India, for example, increased considerably over the decade of the 1970s and the USSR became India's major trade partner, the actual impact of that trade on the Indian economy was not as dramatic as might be expected. An examination of the ratio of Soviet trade to GDP (of the individual South Asian countries) indicates that by the end of the decade none of the countries of South Asia – not even India which had extensive trade with the USSR – was overly dependent on the Soviet Union. Trade ratios in 1980, for example, were 0.011 for India, 0.003 for Pakistan, 0.005 for Bangladesh, 0.016 for Nepal, and 0.010 for Sri Lanka.[57]

India, however, had some vulnerabilities in certain areas. For example, approximately 90% of the total Indian output of knitted goods was exported to the USSR.[58] Furthermore, by the 1980s, oil products constituted some 80% of Soviet exports to India.[59] Those oil imports were paid for under India's barter arrangement and not in hard currency, meaning that a Soviet decision to cut back those supplies could have hurt the Indian economy. The susceptibility of the Indian economy was pointed up in the first few months of 1983 when the USSR suddenly slowed down its imports from India in consumer goods such as knitwear, cashews, and oilcake.[60]

At the same time, the USSR had considerable difficulty in the late 1970s and throughout the 1980s in selling its preferred exports to India (i.e., machinery and equipment), largely because India saw the quality of many of these products as substandard and technologically unsophisticated and because India was able to produce many of these products on its own. India's import preference therefore was for Soviet oil, which put some strain on Indo-Soviet economic relations in the 1980s, and resulted in a persistent trade imbalance that favored India, described by at least one Soviet scholar as "negative developments."[61] However, even if the USSR was not pleased by the situation, it was one they were willing to tolerate for the sake of overarching geopolitical objectives. Once those objectives had shifted in the late 1980s, however, the Indo-Soviet economic relationship was more severely stressed.[62]

The military instrument. In South Asia, the military instrument con-
sisted primarily of weapons supplies, training of military personnel,
the licensing of Soviet weapons production in the case of India, direct
military intervention, and force projection. The instrument was used
not only to support Soviet security objectives in the region but also to
support economic objectives such as gaining hard currency and using
arms as part of Soviet trade with countries of the region. Additionally,
the instrument was used to serve the political objectives of countering
the US/West and China, supporting allies in regional conflicts of
concern to the USSR (e.g., the Sino-Indian border dispute), and
increasing the prestige of Soviet weaponry and technology in the
Third World. Not surprisingly, this instrument was used earliest and
most effectively in Afghanistan and India.

Like most newly independent states, the countries of South Asia – to
varying degrees – sought to augment the stature of their armed forces.
Despite the popularity in much of South Asia of Nehru's calls for
peaceful coexistence and Gandhian non-violence, India and Pakistan
found themselves at war over Kashmir in 1947 and in need of military
equipment and training. This conflict created demands by policymakers from all branches of government to deal with a direct external
threat to their national security and served to enhance the status of the
armed forces which in turn put pressures on for added military
capacity to meet future threats. While these pressures in South Asia
were clearly not as fierce as they were in other Third World countries,
particularly those with military dictatorships such as pre-1983 Argen-
tina, the regional security situation made immediate the need to
consider the demands of the military. In addition to these *international*
tensions, the states faced internal problems as well. As Karen Dawisha
observes in her study of Soviet policy towards Egypt:

> In developing countries . . ., where state boundaries are often incon-
> gruent with ethnic and historical divisions, the incidence of conflict
> within and amongst states is unusually high, with the result that a
> steady supply of arms is perceived to be vital for defence against both
> external attack and internal disintegration.[63]

The ferocity of the struggle surrounding the subcontinent's independence and the population transfers at the time of partition point to the
internal tensions facing many of the countries of South Asia. Building a
military force that could help hold such disparate ethnic and religious
groups together became a critical task for the new regimes. Finally, the
military in South Asian states represented independence from colonial
rule, despite the fact that the armed forces retained its British legacy in

terms of much of the structure and style of the military. Thus, as the
Soviet Union began to use the military instrument to implement some
of its objectives in South Asia, many of the countries of the region were
interested in securing the arms and training the USSR was offering.

Arms transfers. One of the most significant uses of the military
instrument in South Asia occurred through the transfer of arms and
weapons systems. Although arms were used in the 1950s to advance
Soviet policy in the region, there was a spurt in the growth of arms
shipments in the 1970s (see Tables 1 and 2). In one sense, Soviet arms
supplies to South Asia (India specifically) in the mid to late-1960s were
a harbinger of burgeoning exports elsewhere in the Third World in the
1970s. This increase corroborates observations by scholars of Soviet-
Third World relations that the military instrument gained importance
in the Soviet policy arsenal over the 1970s.[64]

Until the 1986–90 period, the region as a whole ranked second only
to the Middle East in Soviet arms transfers to Third World regions; in
1986–90, however, it overtook the Middle East in Soviet arms transfers,[65] reflecting the increased demands for arms by India and the
importance the USSR placed on its friendships with India and
Afghanistan. In India, the USSR used arms transfers to wean the
Indian military away from the West and to increase India's security
dependency on the Soviet Union. In Afghanistan, arms were also used
to minimize Western influence but more importantly, they also helped
to build up pro-Soviet sentiments in the armed forces and to increase
their reliance on the USSR for weapons, spares, and military technology. No major weapons systems were transferred to Pakistan from
1970 to 1990.[66]

When the liberation movement in Bangladesh sought external aid in
its efforts to secede from Pakistan, Soviet–Pakistani relations had
already begun to sour, and the USSR along with India was happy to
supply arms to the Bengalis. Up until 1974, the USSR was Bangladesh's
main arms supplier, accounting for about 55% of arms imports. From
the mid-1970s onward, Dacca continued to receive arms from the
USSR, but China became its main supplier.[67] Other countries of the
region (Nepal and Sri Lanka) were outside these geopolitical concerns,
purchased limited amounts of arms, and usually relied on other suppliers (e.g., Nepal on Britain and France, Sri Lanka on Britain and to a
lesser degree, China) and as such, Soviet arms transfers were virtually
nil.

India and Afghanistan, on the other hand, received significant
amounts of arms from the USSR (see Table 2). From 1970 to 1990,

almost all of Afghanistan's arms came from the USSR and its East European allies.[68] India had more diversified arms acquisitions, but a large proportion of its arms (ranging between 68% and 82% in the 1971–85 period) also was from the Soviet Union. India, however, received the USSR's most sophisticated weapons systems during this time, including Atoll and Styx missiles, Mi-17 Hip helicopter, MiG-27 and MiG-29 fighter aircraft, Kashin class destroyers, and the An-32 Cline transport craft, among others.[69] When India turned to the West, beginning in the late 1970s, to diversify arms acquisitions, the USSR stepped up its efforts to ensure that the Indian military would continue to rely on Moscow in a major way for its weapons needs. Indeed, after India began serious negotiations with France for the highly sophisticated Mirage-2000 fighter in 1981, Defense Minister Ustinov led a high level military delegation to New Delhi with offers of the MiG-29 and other weaponry in hopes of luring India away from France. Despite intentions to diversify arms suppliers, India's reliance on the Soviet Union as a source of weapons increased to 73% in the 1986–90 period (up from 68% in the 1981–85 period), helped along by the clearing system of payment.

Gorbachev's rejection of military means to solve international disputes and advocacy of reducing arms transfers to Third World "hot spots" had serious repercussions in South Asia. The September 1991 decision to halt arms supplied to Najibullah's regime in Kabul underscored those commitments. Similarly, the decision to require India to pay in hard currency for its arms probably ensured a reduction in Soviet arms exports to India.

Licensing of arms production. As early as 1961, the USSR began a new form of military cooperation with India with the agreement for licensing production of the Soviet MiG-21. What is remarkable about the deal is that the Soviet Union had denied the same manufacture license to the Chinese.[70] Although Sino-Soviet relations were shaky at this time, the step in offering licensing permission to a non-socialist Third World state that also was involved in a bitter border dispute with China was unprecedented, but it reflected one of the USSR's developing objectives in the region – to use India as a counterbalance to an increasingly outspoken and independent China. In addition to this objective, the licensing agreement also demonstrated the importance of Indian friendship to the Soviet Union and the lengths to which Moscow was willing to go in securing the good will of the leader of the non-aligned movement. The decision also served to increase the ties between the Indian and Soviet military establishments. On India's part, the ability to produce sophisticated weapons of an international standard helped emphasize its sovereignty and growing technological capabilities while potentially making it less dependent on outside sources (East or West) to defend its security interests, particularly against Pakistan and China where there were always fears that Soviet or Western suppliers might fail to complete delivery in a crunch.

Having acquired the MiG-21 license so early on,[71] India continued to receive licenses for other arms production from the USSR through the 1970s and 1980s, including modernized versions of the MiG-21 in 1970, 1974, and 1976. In 1980 India was granted license to produce the An-32 Cline transport aircraft and the T-72 battle tank. The MiG-23 went into production in 1983, just one year after agreement was reached for licensed production of the MiG-27.[72] As previously mentioned, India and the USSR continued into 1990 to explore the possibility of licensing MiG-29 production, and when India received delivery of Tarantul Class Corvettes in the late 1980s, an agreement was made on Indian production as well.[73]

These licenses gave India what it believed was much needed, up-to-date and technologically sophisticated weaponry at acceptable prices *and* the advantage of working weaponry at acceptable prices *and* the advantage of working towards military industry independence, that is, to be able one day to satisfy its own security demands. For the USSR, the offering of these additional licenses were clearly attached to India's moves in the late 1970s and 1980s to diversify arms supplies in the West. As Jyotirmoy Banerjee points out, "Moscow simply does not want New Delhi hobnobbing with Western military men or coveting their equipment."[74] However, to the extent that New Thinking tried to inhibit arms transfers to the Third World, licensing arrangements between Moscow and New Delhi would become more unusual.

Training of military personnel. Another advantage of transferring sophisticated arms, from the Soviet viewpoint, was that along with the equipment came the need for trained weapons specialists, and the USSR, of course, could provide the necessary training. Indeed, in 1984 for example, there were some 2,025 Soviet military advisors in Afghanistan, about 50 in Bangladesh, and about 500 in India.[75] Obviously, training was not only for effective use of weapons systems; more important was general training of personnel in strategy and tactics, operations, and command and control.

In addition to Soviet advisors in the South Asian countries, the USSR accepted a substantial number of South Asian military officers for training in the USSR in order to increase the general level of preparedness of the armed forces and to train them in specific tactical maneuvers and in strategic doctrine. In the period from 1955 to 1984, some 12,360 South Asian military personnel were trained in the USSR, with the lion's share coming from Afghanistan (12,360) and India (3,480).[76] While the figure for Afghanistan represents a significant Soviet impact on training of the military, for India the figures should be considered against the potential pool of trainees (over 1,000,000).[77]

The net effect of these efforts was threefold. First, training enhanced the skills of the officer corps. Second, it ensured that Soviet equipment would perform adequately in local conflicts and, so, increased the likelihood that Soviet allies like Afghanistan and India whose geopolitical interests were similar would be successful in regional conflicts, and made Soviet weaponry a realistic alternative to prospective Third World buyers. Finally, it instilled in the leaders of the armed forces a certain loyalty to or affinity for the Soviet Union, thus reinforcing Soviet influence in the military arena (e.g., increasing the possibility that the USSR would have some control over the ally in making decisions about whether and how to fight).

Direct military intervention. Because Soviet strategic interest in South Asia was thought to be a low priority when compared to other theaters such as Europe or the border with China, the reluctance to use direct military force in the region was not surprising. The 1979 intervention in Afghanistan had a profound impact on international perceptions of the Soviet Union as a global power and of their interests in the southern TVD: it forced a reexamination of Soviet Union military objectives in the area and of the prospective use of military force as an instrument of Soviet policy elsewhere in the region (and globally).

In 1979, the USSR felt that political, economic, and other military instruments were no longer effective on their own to maintain a reliable ally in Amin's Afghanistan and to assure, if not the success of the Saur Revolution, then the denial of the counterrevolution to Islamic forces. Faced with instability on the border of their Central Asian republics in both Iran and now Afghanistan, the USSR took the cataclysmic decision to intervene directly, sending in some 100,000 troops on December 27. Ironically, if protection of the Soviet homeland was of primary importance for Soviet foreign policy, the 1979 invasion had a negative impact on the security of the Soviet southern border. The intervention was intended to protect the Saur Revolution and give the USSR a Moscow-leaning neighbor, but it did not offer Moscow stability on its southern border, as will be discussed in subsequent chapters. Obviously, the withdrawal of troops from Afghanistan, particularly in the context of Soviet military retraction from Eastern Europe, signaled the end of the use of this instrument of power under New Thinking.

Force projection. In addition to direct military intervention, the USSR was able to increase its force projection capabilities in South Asia as a consequence of its invasion of Afghanistan. There has been considerable discussion of the effects on Soviet force projection capabilities reaped through their presence in Afghanistan, but notwithstanding deliberations of costs and benefits to the USSR's southern strategy, the move gave them some tactical advantages in their southern TVD.[78] Perhaps more important was the increased geopolitical influence of the USSR. Even if the USSR's aircraft (with the exception of the Su-24 Fencer) could not reach the Persian Gulf, the Soviet presence on the boundaries of the subcontinent clearly was disturbing firstly to Pakistan (and Iran) but also to India. As Alvin Z. Rubinstein stated, "its diplomatic options and political leverage have been enormously increased, unquestionably making its policies crucial to the region's future stability."[79] Not only did its position in Afghanistan offer Moscow the prospects of increased intelligence gathering capabilities, but it also allowed the USSR far more access to groups within Pakistan whom Moscow wished to influence, perhaps to the detriment of the Islamabad regime (e.g., the Baluchis).

Another factor in the USSR's military instrument in South Asia was the naval presence in the Indian Ocean which, as already mentioned in the preceding chapter, first became a factor in the late 1960s. Throughout the 1970–85 period, however, the use of naval power projection in South Asia by the USSR was limited.[80] Geoffrey Jukes explains that the primary role of the Soviet navy was to counter the forces of other major powers, particularly the American SLBM program. Believing that the US would deploy missile submarine forces in the Indian Ocean by the late 1960s or early 1970s, the USSR began its own deployment of naval power. Finding that the expected American missile deployments did not occur, the USSR found other tasks for its navy.[81] Objectives then shifted to include surveillance and intelligence functions and the support of allies in need. For example, the Soviet naval presence in the Indian Ocean was stepped up in 1971 in order to support India in its war with Pakistan and to ensure that there would be no outside interference. The Soviet navy was also used in 1971–72 to clear harbors for the newly independent Bangladesh.

The main reason for the Soviet naval presence in the Indian Ocean, however, was that countering the United States demonstrated that the

USSR was indeed a global power, and a regional force in South Asia.[82] When the Carter and Reagan administrations became committed to expanding the facilities at Diego Garcia and upgrading the US military capability there, the Soviet Union attempted to meet the challenge by increasing its forces in the area; however, it seems that this did not mean the introduction of strategic submarines into the Indian Ocean, in part because of cost constraints (since there was no question of Soviet national security being threatened from this area and deployment would have been expensive, it was not done).

Conclusion. This chapter has tried to give an overview of Soviet political/diplomatic, economic, and military objectives and instruments of power. Although it has not examined other Soviet tools of policy such as the cultural instrument, propaganda and public diplomacy, or clandestine activities, which were effective if not in promoting specific Soviet policy objectives in countries of the region then in promoting the Soviet Union's general influence in the region (particularly India), it has analyzed the three most important and most widely used instruments of power. These instruments were used, in various combinations, to support a range of Soviet policy objectives in South Asia. The effectiveness of these instruments along with an assessment of the feasibility of Soviet objectives will be addressed below.

Soviet capabilities in South Asia were influenced by the convergence or divergence of Soviet interests with those of the particular country, and too, Soviet policies had differing impacts depending on the receptiveness of the South Asian country to the goals of the policy (e.g., moves to promote state industry were, of course, more strongly supported in India where Nehru had expressed interest and where parts of the economy were already relatively well developed, than they were in Sri Lanka under the United National Party). The effectiveness of Soviet policy, especially in the economic and military fields, was also constrained by the ability of the South Asian states to absorb Soviet technology and their commitment to developing ties with the West and other non-aligned countries. In other words, as Soviet scholars had been arguing for some time, circumstances on the ground in South Asia were complex, and even the best-laid superpower policies would be constrained by the socioeconomic and political conditions in the individual countries of the region.

The USSR's policy objectives in South Asia remained relatively stable in the 1970s and early 1980s. As chapters 4 and 5 will demonstrate, the dominant image informing Soviet policy was correlation of

forces, which of course was consistent with geopolitical considerations: as the balance of power between India and Pakistan remained
more or less unchanged throughout the 1970s and 1980s, Soviet policy
remained stable. The instruments which it used to pursue those objectives, however, shifted over the 1970s: although the political/diploma-
tic instrument was relied on consistently, the USSR put more emphasis
on the military instrument in the 1970s to achieve its goals. And, as
others have observed,[83] it was in the area of military capabilities that
the USSR could most effectively counter the United States and the
West in the Third World. Furthermore, even if the USSR could not
compete economically across the board with the West, it continued to
use aid and trade on a selective basis (in India and Afghanistan). It also
began a more flexible approach to economic relations, one that did not
reject the benefits of the private sector.

Soviet policy in South Asia under Gorbachev, however, demonstrated that the USSR would rely less and less on the military instrument as a means of achieving its foreign policy goals. Its direct
intervention in Afghanistan was terminated; its force projection capabilities were not augmented; arms sales did not increase, and with the
decisions to stop arms supplies to Afghanistan and to make India pay
in hard currency for its arms acquisitions, it appeared that arms
transfers would in all likelihood also diminish. According to the New
Thinking, the USSR would continue to use the political/diplomatic
instrument to serve its policy and additionally, would turn to the
economic instrument. However, its own economic weakness inhibited
the effectiveness of the economic instrument, and therefore, a shift to
economic means presaged a Soviet retraction from South Asia.

4 Stability and change in Soviet–South Asian relations, 1970–1978

Introduction

Although the broad outlines of Soviet policy in South Asia were conditioned by Soviet views of their national interests and security demands, the USSR's objectives in the region varied according to whether the country was geographically contiguous, as in the case of Afghanistan, raising the stakes for Soviet domestic security; whether the state was an important international and regional actor, for example, India; what the role of other major powers (i.e., the United States and China) in the country was; whether the domestic sociopolitical circumstances in the country were progressive; and what the prospects for a transition to socialism were.[1] If the proviso formulated under Khrushchev that the USSR should counter imperialist forces in the Third World with economic aid/trade and political support had been tempered by the realities of Soviet capabilities in the 1970s, there was also less necessity for Soviet policy to be as activist: the United States under Nixon had diminished the American desire to compete for India, and the international power alliances (e.g., between the USSR and India, Pakistan–China–United States) were well entrenched by this time. Concerns about China, on the other hand, were another matter. The Chinese had proved themselves eager and willing to enter the foreign aid game, giving assistance to virtually every country of the region except India, and their close relations with Pakistan and growing interest in the US were also of concern.

With the US–Soviet detente and the American retraction from South Asia, the USSR might have had less worry objectively about the direct effects of America's imperialist foreign policy; however, as Boris Ponomarev pointed out, "detente and peaceful coexistence do not signify the status quo."[2] With the growing prospect of Sino-American *rapprochement* in the early 1970s, many Soviet policymakers and commentators saw a real need for vigilance in South Asia. At the same time, with Indira Gandhi in power in India, the election victory of the United Front in Sri Lanka, and the ouster of the monarchy in Afghanistan, there were also reasons for optimism. Despite the fact that in the early 1970s no country of South Asia seemed on the brink of making a transition to socialism, the Soviet leadership could find some consolation in the global and regional correlation of forces in the 1970s.

Basic Soviet objectives for South Asia by the 1970s then centered on the following: (1) maintaining a stable, Moscow-leaning regime in the bordering country of Afghanistan; (2) decreasing American and Chinese influence in the region; (3) developing workable diplomatic ties, and if possible, friendly relations with all countries of the region; (4) expanding relations with India and using its close relationship with Delhi to press its positions in the non-aligned movement and other international fora; and (5) promoting the national liberation movement in progressive states of the region.

In operation, these objectives often conflicted. For example, an attempt to decrease Chinese or American influence in a particular country did not necessarily increase Soviet influence. The decision to pursue the relationship with India constrained Soviet moves in Pakistan and elsewhere. Indeed, although its close relationship with India effectively allowed the USSR to counter the US and China in the region, it had the effect of contributing to the domination of the subcontinent by non-socialist India as well. Hence, the USSR, while upholding these basic objectives, had to modify its strategies in their pursuit and had to use various mixes of instruments to promote its goals.

The three categories of instruments that have been discussed are the political/diplomatic, the military, and the economic instrument. Within each of these categories exist more finely tuned instruments: for example, within the political/diplomatic instrument are personal diplomacy, crisis diplomacy, regional and multilateral diplomacy, and communist party linkages; the economic instrument is composed of aid and trade; and the military instrument includes arms transfers, training of South Asian military personnel, and the direct use of force.

What discussions of objectives and instruments alone cannot tell us is their outcome as demonstrated in Soviet relations with countries of South Asia. It is therefore necessary to examine how objectives and instruments fit together in the conduct of Soviet policy in South Asia. By analyzing the dynamics of Soviet relations with the countries of South Asia, a more accurate picture will arise of how instruments and objectives interrelated, how policies as a whole functioned, how policies were modified by perceived circumstances in South Asia, and of the effectiveness of these policies.

It would be impossible to understand the course of Soviet–South Asian relations without recognizing the essentially political nature of Soviet policy in the region. Whereas the thrust of Soviet policy in Western Europe or China was primarily motivated by security concerns, Soviet policy towards South Asia has been largely concerned with the USSR's geopolitical interests, as dictated by analysis of the regional correlation of forces – specifically, the USSR–US–China triangle and tensions between India and Pakistan whose foreign policies became intimately tangled with the major powers.

Another concern is related to the USSR's general Third World policy which aimed at strengthening national liberation movements, supporting anti-colonialism, encouraging the choice of a socialist development path or at least the development of the state sector, and improving the USSR's image in and influence on the developing countries. The Soviet Union supported South Asian liberation movements through cooperation with and support of local communist parties since the days of the Comintern; later, promoting a United Front strategy, the USSR would turn its favors to the Congress Party on the subcontinent while maintaining close contacts with local communist parties. This shift in strategy was initially rejected by communists on the subcontinent, and it brought to the fore the tension in Soviet Third World policy between ideological purity (i.e., support of vanguard parties) versus political pragmatism (i.e., recognizing the need to consolidate friendly relations with the bourgeois but often anti-imperialist regimes that would take over in the post-colonial period).

Thus, Soviet policies in the region often displayed what appeared to be conflicting attitudes (between ideological purity and political pragmatism) but which could be interpreted as a reflection of ambiguities in the fundamentals of Soviet foreign policy (i.e., striving for world peace/support of national liberation movements). In order to minimize regional conflicts and disputes then, the USSR refrained from advocating redrawing international boundaries in South Asia, despite the fact that they were laid down by British imperialists. In the 1970s, they offered support in the international arena to the Bengali nationalists in East Pakistan but not to the Naxalites or Sikhs in India. Furthermore, Moscow never completely gave up on Bhutto, even in 1971, despite his opposition to the Bengali nationalists and the partition of Pakistan. The USSR sought to improve Soviet–Pakistani relations even though

Bhutto helped foment the 1971 crisis in East Pakistan by refusing to acknowledge the Awami League's clearcut majority in electoral votes and their right to form the next government. Ideology may have played a role in forming the general outlines of Soviet Third World policy, but, clearly in South Asia perceptions of South Asian conditions and of what was possible as well as wider geopolitical considerations often took precedence in the formation of policy.

The interface between geopolitical realities, on the one hand, and perceptions and ideology, on the other, was apparent throughout the 1970s both in terms of regional politics and in terms of Soviet relations with particular countries, many of whom faced severe domestic political crises. But the possibility of reconciling them was never more apparent than in the years 1971 and 1972, with the struggle for and creation of Bangladesh. It was during this crisis that the USSR skillfully used its political, economic, and military instruments to meet a number of political objectives: support of the Bangladeshi national liberation movement, which would in turn reduce Pakistan's power on the subcontinent; countering US and Chinese influence in the region; and increasing Soviet linkages (and influence) in India.

Bangladesh and the Indo-Pakistan War

Background: tensions between East and West Pakistan. When the decision was taken to create a divided state of Pakistan, it left the new state's leaders to deal with the problems not only of economic and administrative inequality (as most of the benefits of the British Empire were located physically in West Pakistan) but also of ethnic and linguistic integration. For although the areas designated as Pakistan were predominantly Muslim, there was precious little else uniting the populations. The head of the Muslim League and Pakistan's first leader, Muhammad Ali Jinnah, attempted during negotiations with the British and Nehru to obtain a strip of territory connecting the two Pakistans, but the proposal was soundly rejected. Jinnah was handed over a Pakistan of remarkable diversity.

Despite these tensions, an East Pakistani and head of the Awami (People's) League was made prime minister of Pakistan in 1956. Husain Shaheed Suhrawardy's government collapsed the following year, however, because of pressure from the religious right and from the left.[3] An interim government was overthrown in 1958 when President Iskander Mirza, in collaboration with General Ayub Khan, declared martial law and subsequently named Ayub, a Pathan, prime minister. Ayub moved the capital of Pakistan from Karachi to the newly created city of Islamabad in the northwest and proceeded to build up the West Pakistani economy. These actions naturally enraged Bengalis whose protests had by 1962 landed many, including ex-Prime Minister Suhrawardy, in jail.

By 1963 Ayub had appointed Zulfiqur Ali Bhutto foreign minister. Bhutto pressed Ayub to consolidate ties with China, and the Sino-Pakistani Friendship Treaty was signed in August of that same year. But with Pakistan's loss in the 1965 war with India over Kashmir, Bhutto resigned his post in June, 1966, leaving Ayub to cope with the mounting tensions in East Pakistan. In March of that same year, the Awami League headed by Mujibur Rahman adopted its six point program calling for autonomy in East Pakistan.[4] The arrest of Mujib and other Awami leaders, and the floods that ravaged the area that year, only added to Bengali discontent with the regime in Islamabad.

The crisis and Soviet reaction. No relief would come in the remaining years of the 1960s: riots and demonstrations continued as Mujib was about to be brought to trial; Bhutto inaugurated his People's Party and was arrested in 1967; Ayub Khan handed over power to General Yahya Khan; and Pakistan's relations with the United States deteriorated because of the instability in Islamabad and the situation in East Pakistan. Finally, in 1970, elections were held with Mujib's Awami League headed for a landslide victory in East Pakistan, while in West Pakistan Bhutto's People's Party received more than half the total seats available. Despite Mujib's victory, Bhutto refused to acknowledge him as the new prime minister, and the opening of parliament was delayed. On March 25, 1971 talks between Mujibur Rahman and Yahya Khan to end the crisis broke down, and all pretext of a united Pakistan was lost.[5] On that same day, Mujib was again arrested, declaring that West Pakistan was engaged in genocide in Bangladesh.[6]

Once again refugees flooded into India, and the Indian government responded to the crisis. In their superb study, Sisson and Rose observe that Mrs. Gandhi claimed India wanted a political solution to the Pakistan problem, although in May she stated that India would take "all measures as may be necessary to ensure [its] security."[7] Burke on the other hand points out that "within a week of the final break between Yahya and Mujib both houses of the Indian Parliament unanimously assured East Pakistanis that their struggle would receive the wholehearted support of the people of India."[8] Naturally, India's position was not welcomed in West Pakistan, and in East Pakistan, the Bengali nationalists were thus assured of Indian support for their cause. Furthermore, Indian backing was not to be limited to public statements: India began training and aiding Bengali guerillas, the Mukti Bahini (Liberation Force).[9] This further infuriated the government in West Pakistan whose troops had been notoriously vicious, particularly towards the civilian population, in the conduct of their military activities.[10]

The refugees who rushed into India caused severe problems in shelter, food, and social services. UN estimates put the number of refugees as some 2 million; the USSR, and Bangladesh's Mujib, put the figure at 10 million.[11] Indian reaction was as expected: parliament adopted a resolution on March 31 calling on Pakistan to desist in its use of force in East Pakistan.[12] While making every effort to take care of the flood of refugees near Calcutta, India also stepped up aid to the Mukti Bahini in the hopes that they would be able to fend off the West Pakistani army themselves.

The Soviet reaction was considerably more circumspect at this juncture than was the Indian. Prior to the events of March 25, 1971, reportage in the major newspapers was limited to occasional articles written in a factual style, simply noting that Yahya's decision to postpone the opening of the Assembly had angered the East Pakistanis. Immediately after the March 25 massacres, the Soviet press expressed concern over the situation and observed that armed force had been used against the population of East Pakistan.[13] A New Delhi Radio report also said that India asked the USSR to intervene with Pakistan to stop the bloodshed in East Pakistan.[14] Shortly thereafter, the Indian and Pakistani ambassadors to the Soviet Union were met by Kosygin, although Moscow Radio said this was done at their own request.[15]

If the USSR seemed to be moving quite cautiously, it was probably in an effort to continue to support India while trying not to alienate Pakistan. However, a telegram sent by Podgorny to Yahya, urging a halt to the bloodshed and promoting a political solution to the crisis, would cause Pakistan to take offense.[16] Yahya charged that he would not allow any interference in Pakistan's affairs, that no country (not even the USSR) would allow a separatist movement to tear it apart, and that the USSR should use its influence with India to help stop the conflict.[17] The Soviet Union was surprised and irritated by the bluntness of Yahya's comments. "The USSR continued to refer to 'East Pakistan' in its statements, refusing to follow the practice adopted by India in mid-1971 of using 'East Bengal,'"[18] but Pakistan worried nonetheless about Indo-Soviet collusion in East Pakistan.

Pakistan saw its relationship with China as key to its international problems: after all, the Chinese were the only ones who had been supportive of West Pakistani motives in Bangladesh. As Chou En-lai stated in a message to President Yahya Khan, "The Chinese government and people resolutely support the Pakistan government and people in their just struggle to safeguard national independence and oppose foreign aggression and interference."[19] There would also be direct accusations against both India and the Soviet Union for interfering in Pakistan's internal affairs.[20] Both Pakistan and China saw a threat to Islamabad's success in East Pakistan in Soviet assistance to India during the crisis (e.g., direct aid of medical supplies to aid the refugees) and in its warm relations with Mrs. Gandhi.

If Pakistan saw Indian and Soviet collusion fueling the fires of Bangladeshi nationalism, India and the USSR also saw China's hand pushing the Pakistanis. One Indian newspaper reported ominously that Yahya Khan warned India that if it dared to attack, Pakistan would not fight alone.[21] The USSR approached the situation cautiously: indeed, before agreeing to sign any Indo-Soviet treaty, particularly one that included a consultation clause on military matters, Moscow wanted assurances from India that it would not be requested to intervene on India's behalf should the Chinese become involved.[22] The specter of possible Chinese involvement in a South Asian conflict did nothing to reduce international tensions nor did the fact that Pakistan had played a key role in assisting in the *rapprochement* between China and the United States.

Other than Chinese supply of materiel and verbal support, Pakistan was virtually isolated in the world community. While India continued to receive military and other support from the USSR and elsewhere throughout the crisis, Pakistan – under sharp criticism worldwide for the viciousness of its attacks on the East Pakistani citizenry – faced delays in deliveries of military equipment even from the United States, although US aid was never completely cut off. Indeed, the US announced that it would discontinue all aid, economic and military, immediately after the events of March 25, although arms in the pipeline still were shipped in early summer and the issuing of arms licensing continued.[23] The Senate Foreign Relations Committee then voted on May 7 to discontinue all aid, prompting Yahya to accept UN aid to East Pakistan which Yahya had disallowed up to that point. Despite the wishes of a large number of congressmen to use US military and economic influence to achieve a negotiated settlement on East Pakistan, the Nixon administration was reluctant to sever links with Islamabad.[24] Thus, arms and economic assistance continued well into 1971. The USSR, too, shipped arms after March 25, although according to Sisson and Rose, these were arms ordered and shipped prior to March 25 that arrived in April.[25]

The Indo-Soviet Friendship Treaty. From June 6 to 8 of 1971, Swaran Singh, then Indian Minister of External Affairs, paid an unofficial visit to Moscow where he held talks with Gromyko and Kosygin. Just two months later, on August 9 during a visit to India, Gromyko and Singh signed a Treaty of Friendship and Cooperation. The significance of this unprecedented step in Indian foreign relations was made more pronounced by the fact that it came right in the midst of the crisis in East Pakistan.

The treaty repeatedly underscored that one of its main purposes was to maintain Indian non-alignment while promoting world peace; however, Indian opponents of the treaty and foreign observers worried that it indicated a decisive shift in policy towards the Soviet Union, one that threatened the foundations of non-alignment.[26] Articles One through Seven of the treaty invoked the usual calls for non-interference in domestic affairs, mutual undertaking to pursue peace, security, and global disarmament, condemnations of colonialism and racialism and promotion of economic, technological, and cultural ties.[27]

The first of the articles of the treaty dealing with military ties called for the parties to refrain from entering into alliances which might work against the security interests of the cosignator. Article Ten required the parties not to enter into other contracts incompatible with treaty. The real cause of concern was Article Nine which required the parties to abstain from giving assistance to any third party involved in an armed conflict with the cosignor and called for consultations between the parties in the event of conflict involving either.

> In the event of either party being subjected to an attack or a threat thereof, the High Contracting Parties shall immediately enter into mutual consultations in order to remove such threat and to take appropriate effective measures to ensure peace and the security of their countries.[28]

To many observers this clause suggested a military alliance between India and the USSR and a reduction of Indian sovereignty in military affairs. Despite the assurances of Indira Gandhi that there had been no change in India's policy of non-alignment,[29] Jana Sangh members and other political opponents charged that with the treaty, Soviet influence in India had destroyed non-alignment.

Reaction from all international corners came swiftly. Pakistan, of course, was particularly incensed not only by the fact of the agreement but also by its timing: had there been any doubts about Indo-Soviet collusion in East Pakistan specifically but against Pakistan more generally, worst fears were now confirmed. Matters were not helped by comments from India reinforcing the view that the signing of the treaty and Gromyko's visit were meant to warn Pakistan that its actions in East Pakistan would not be tolerated: "India's relations with China and the Soviet Union's with Pakistan will now develop insofar as they do only in light of Article 9 and Article 10."[30] Both the Soviet and Indian governments declared that the treaty was not aimed at any third party (although India specifically mentioned China, leaving Pakistan to conclude that it was indeed the target).[31] Indeed, Bhutto expressly stated that the Indo-Soviet Treaty was contrary to Pakistani and Chinese interests.[32] Some went further still, seeing the treaty not only as pressure for Pakistan to negotiate a settlement on Bengal but also as a threat against Pakistani interests in Kashmir.[33]

Many Western analysts at the time viewed the treaty as a warning to Pakistan not to intervene in the refugee camps in India. Some also saw it as Soviet recognition that whatever influence over Pakistan it wielded at Tashkent had deteriorated and therefore, the USSR would now shift completely to India in its pursuit of a South Asian policy. The treaty was seen as denoting

> a major turn in Soviet diplomacy on the subcontinent. Since its successful mediation of the 1965 Indo-Pakistani war at Tashkent, the Soviet Union has sought to maintain neutrality in its dealings with New Delhi and Islamabad. But its efforts to exert a restraining influence on Pakistan President Yahya Khan in the East Bengal crisis went unheeded. Now it has shifted its whole weight to the other foot.[34]

But also, the treaty from the Soviet perspective was viewed as a means to off-set Chinese influence in Pakistan and to reduce the impact of US–Chinese detente:

> Russia has thus taken a dramatic lead in Asian politics by seizing the opportunity presented by India's isolation and Pakistan's truculence; the timing has only been hastened by such events as the East Pakistan civil war, the U.S. military and diplomatic support of Pakistan and the impending Sino-US detente.[35]

The Indo-Pakistani War of 1971. Meanwhile, the situation in East Pakistan continued to deteriorate and the likelihood of war between Pakistan and India seemed imminent. At a November 6 speech at the Kremlin, Politburo member and First Secretary of the Moscow City Party Committee, V. V. Grishin, issued a warning to Pakistan, saying that "the situation in the Indian subcontinent has become more acute. The tension is a consequence of the well-known events in East Pakistan.... The Pakistan authorities must stop repressions against the population and create conditions for the refugees to return home."[36] An article in *Novoe vremia* also placed the blame for the situation solely on Pakistan but noted that the conflict found its roots not in any Indo-Pakistan conflict but in the events in East Pakistan.[37]

Apparently, the USSR felt that the Indo-Soviet Friendship Treaty might even decrease the chances for war on the subcontinent by making Pakistan more circumspect in its behavior.[38] There was evidence of Soviet attempts to negotiate a solution. A report in *The Times* of New Delhi, for example, noted that Soviet Deputy Foreign Minister, N. Firiubin, had met with Awami League representatives in order to work out a deal that would give Bangladesh autonomy "within a single Pakistan."[39] Clearly the USSR was not idealizing the implications that a successful Bangladeshi secessionist movement might have for the rest of South Asia. The signing of the Indo-Soviet Treaty, however, only served to exacerbate international tensions in the region.

In late September, Prime Minister Gandhi visited the USSR for talks on "subjects of Soviet–Indian bilateral relations as well as important current international problems of mutual interest."[40] On September 29, Mrs. Gandhi held talks simultaneously with General Secretary Brezhnev, Supreme Soviet Chairman Podgorny, and Council of Ministers Chairman Kosygin. Their joint communique demonstrated the Soviet Union's appreciation of India's difficult position with regard to the Bengali refugees: "The Soviet side highly appreciated India's humane approach to the problem created by the influx of these refugees from East Bengal and expressed its understanding of difficulties confronting friendly India in connection with the mass inflow of refugees." However, the USSR went no further than to reiterate its position put forth in an April 4 letter from Podgorny to Yahya Khan, urging Pakistan to end the repression and bloodshed in East Pakistan. Mrs. Gandhi, of course, had hoped for more unequivocal support of India's position, but the USSR was still playing the role it had established at Tashkent, of a mediator urging restraint. Thus, the USSR would not openly endorse Mrs. Gandhi's position that no negotiations were possible until Sheikh Mujibur Rahman was released from prison by Yahya Khan.

In October, Mrs. Gandhi left for a whirlwind diplomatic tour of the West, visiting a number of countries including the United States, apparently to appraise world leaders of the situation in East Pakistan, to drum up support for the Indian position, and to reassure the West that India's treaty with the USSR would not harm its bilateral relations with Western countries. In Washington, she met with President Nixon. Her relatively warm reception in the US was troubling to Pakistan which realized that its policies in Bangladesh were not receiving support in the West. However, Mrs. Gandhi's visit seemed to create some misunderstandings. The US was surprised to find the Prime Minister telling audiences in Paris that Bangladesh's independence was inevitable and that in order for a peaceful solution to be achieved, Sheikh Mujib had to be released. The US had understood that India would practice more restraint and allow the US time to pursue, yet again, a negotiated settlement with Yahya Khan, who had flatly rejected any notion of releasing Mujib.[41]

Indeed, Mrs. Gandhi had left for her tour of the West in a strengthened position. Just two days before her departure, Soviet Deputy Foreign Minister Firiubin arrived in Delhi for consultations under the infamous Article Nine of the Indo-Soviet Friendship Treaty; the two sides agreed that they shared a common perception of tensions on the subcontinent.[42] Moreover, while the arms shipments to Pakistan from the US and China and to India from the USSR during 1971 probably did not significantly shift the regional balance of power, which had been in India's favor since 1965, the surface to air missiles and modern rockets (for India's Russian Osa-class missile boats) certainly cushioned India's military position.[43]

Further confounding the international situation was the continuing possibility of Chinese intervention which was heightened with the visit of Bhutto to China on November 5; but China was not to be lured into the crisis. Despite constant denials that the Pakistanis expected more help from the Chinese, it was widely reported that China was restrained in its support of Pakistan, much to Pakistan's chagrin. Indeed, at a banquet to welcome Bhutto's delegation, acting Foreign Minister Chi Peng-fei said that while China was deeply troubled by events on the subcontinent, "the internal affairs of any country must be handled by its own people," suggesting that Pakistan's problems were its own. He continued, however, by offering China's support in the event of external intervention: "Our Pakistan friends may rest assured that should Pakistan be subjected to foreign aggression, the Chinese government will, as always, resolutely support the Pakistan government and people in their just struggle to defend their state sovereignty and national independence."[44] Such comments did not go unnoticed in India, of course. However unlikely the threat of Chinese intervention, it did nothing to restrain Indian actions in Bangladesh. Indian forces had begun to move forward to its East Pakistan border in late September, as the Pakistanis forwarded troops in the West. In October, Pakistani troops in East Pakistan went into a defensive mode, attempting to stop the growing attacks by the Mukti Bahini. India too had been stepping up support of the Bengali insurgency, resulting in an increased number of border clashes, of ever-growing intensity. President Yahya proposed force withdrawals, but they were rejected by the Indian side. Throughout November, the active incursions of Indian troops into East Pakistan increased. On November 21, Indian tanks crossed into East Pakistan near Jessore. From this point, the two sides were catapulted towards war. The USSR, which had most influence with India, had given up its role of restrainer after Firiubin's visit at the end of October. As Jackson points out, "the Russians played no part in the effort to prevent the growth of tensions in the subcontinent, and Soviet influence helped decisively to exclude the United Nations from the role cast for it in Islamabad and Washington."[45] Finally, Pakistani air forces attacked India in the west on December 3, thus broadening the conflict from the east front to the west. India moved with lightening speed towards Dacca, trying to consolidate its position before international pressures for a ceasefire could congeal. Fighting was fierce on the western border, but initially the two sides seemed deadlocked. Meeting with success in the east, India recognized independent Bangladesh on December 6, 1971, thus dashing any hopes for a negotiated end to the war. By December 10, India had achieved a breakthrough in the west. The US aircraft carrier Enterprise moved into the Bay of Bengal on December 15, ostensibly for the purpose of evacuating Americans from East Pakistan. Although the Enterprise arrived there too late to have any impact on the course of the war, the Soviet ambassador to India reassured Mrs. Gandhi that the Soviet navy would not allow the US fleet to intervene in Bangladesh.[46] Indian troops took Dacca on December 16, and by the evening of December 17 both sides had declared ceasefires. The war was over.

In addition to materiel assistance, the USSR played an important role in pleading India's case in the court of world opinion. The Soviet Union was instrumental in efforts at the UN to delay a ceasefire until India had vanquished its opponent and taken East Pakistan. First, on December 4, the Soviet ambassador to the United Nations, Jacob Malik, proposed that a representative from the government of Bangladesh be allowed to speak to the Security Council. This proposal was strenuously objected to, particularly by the Chinese. Next, an American proposal was tabled: a ceasefire should be imposed and both sides should withdraw troops to their own territory with UN supervision.[47] The USSR vetoed the motion. On December 6, the USSR made another resolution, which was never voted on: imposition of a ceasefire and Pakistani recognition of East Pakistan's will as expressed in the December 1970 elections, which would have brought Mujib to power.[48] On December 8, the General Assembly supported a resolution calling for a ceasefire and withdrawal of forces to home territories. Pakistan agreed to comply with the resolution, but it was clearly not in India's interest to do so. Mrs. Gandhi therefore insisted on Pakistan's withdrawal first. The Soviet Union had managed to delay moves in the Security Council until India's military superiority had negated the utility of a UN–sponsored settlement. On December 15, Foreign Minister Bhutto of Pakistan had come to the UN to plead Pakistan's case but tore up his notes and walked out when he realized that there was nothing he could do to restore the divided nation.[49]

The aftermath. As a result of rising Bengali nationalism, West Pakistani intransigence, and Indian support of East Pakistan, the new state of Bangladesh was created with a population of 75 million. In the aftermath of the Indo-Pakistan War, Moscow's relations naturally reflected its position during the war: relations with India were very close; Bangladesh was appreciative of Soviet support during its struggle for independence; and relations with Pakistan were strained even though the Soviet Union had been careful throughout the conflict to maintain open diplomatic channels with Islamabad. The spirit of Tashkent, however, had suffered a large setback, and it would take some time for the USSR to regain its status as trusted intermediary on the subcontinent, at least in Pakistani eyes.

For the time being, the USSR would have to be content with the elevated stature of its main ally in the region. The warm political/diplomatic and military ties that were cemented with the Indo-Soviet Treaty in August would continue to develop. In 1972, the USSR and India signed an agreement, as per Article Six of their 1971 treaty, requiring both sides to coordinate plans and take into consideration mutual needs. This agreement was followed up in November 1973 by the signing of a fifteen-year Indo-Soviet agreement to increase cooperation in the fields of industry, power, agriculture, personnel training, trade and other economic sectors, and an agreement on Gosplan–Planning Commission Cooperation. The result of these agreements was to associate India's economic development for the immediate future to the Soviet Union. By 1975, the USSR had become India's main trade partner. The two countries undertook to coordinate economic planning, but mainly the Soviet Union provided planning assistance to India.[50] Thus, the political and military ties that were strengthened by the Indo-Pakistani War of 1971 were complemented by increased economic linkages.

Understandably, relations with Pakistan fared much worse. Although Pakistan would try to steer a new foreign policy course under Bhutto in the 1970s, one that was less tied to the United States, and would reorient determination to build socialism in Pakistan, Soviet–Pakistan relations never quite regained the closeness engendered by Tashkent. In the immediate period after the war, the two countries would try to fit the pieces of their broken relationship back together and try to reach accommodation, but economic ties particularly suffered because of the 1971 war.

Part of the reason for the drop in trade between the USSR and Pakistan had to do with the fact that the USSR now was trading with Bangladesh. Sheikh Mujibur Rahman had preceded Bhutto in a visit to Moscow in March 1971. Meeting separately with Brezhnev, Podgorny, and Kosygin, Mujib had sought economic aid for his struggling new nation. The Soviet Union was eager to offer emergency aid and long-term assistance to Bangladesh, even going so far as to suggest the training of administrative cadres. Moreover, the USSR agreed to clear Chittagong harbor, Bangladesh's main port. Thus, by 1973, total Soviet trade with Bangladesh had reached 53.3 million rubles, 43.5 million of which was exports. Pakistan's trade with the USSR in the same year was only 36.4 million rubles.[51] Thus, the use of Soviet economic aid/trade and technology demonstrated to many South Asia watchers the USSR's intention to bring Bangladesh under Soviet influence, and, to a lesser degree, to bolster India in its efforts to influence Bangladesh.

The immediate aftermath of the war in South Asia presented the USSR with a very favorable picture: a truncated Pakistan, albeit one still clinging to its alliance with the US and friendship with China; an independent Bangladesh with close ties to India and a hardy left-wing movement and friendly relations with Moscow; relatively stable situations in Afghanistan, Nepal, and Sri Lanka and the maintenance of the USSR's good-neighborly relations in all cases; and the region's political, military, and economic giant – India – firmly in the Soviet corner. Events in 1971 seemed to reinforce Soviet thinking about the correlation of forces. But the 1970s also brought new challenges and problems to Soviet policy in the region: if the international situation in South Asia was now stable, the domestic situation in the countries of the area was anything but tranquil.

Constancy amid disarray

It is tempting, with the benefit of hindsight, to assess the USSR's position in South Asia as unthreatened throughout the decade of the 1970s; clearly the political turbulence of those years did not allow policymakers the leisure of assuming that international ties would remain intact despite marked changes in domestic political circumstances. Every country of the region, with the exception of Nepal, faced coups or changes of government which portended a fundamental reorientation of foreign or domestic policy. The USSR was forced to reconsider at least its short-term objectives and strategies in order to cope with the uncertain political climate, for while there was much to argue for a continuation in foreign policy outlook in each of the South Asian countries, maintenance of the status quo (which was to the USSR's liking) was not a certainty.

Political instability had served to bring about the new countries of the region in the late 1940s, and the early 1970s saw a similar process creating the state of Bangladesh. But the forces for independence which were victorious in East Pakistan were the same forces which could tear the national fabric of any of the multinational states of the area. Thus, the Soviet Union had to be careful in its assessment of the Bengali national liberation movement and its prospects for progress after the war in order to avoid fueling the fires of nationalism in unwanted areas (e.g., the Indian Punjab). Furthermore, the USSR had to exercise caution in its bilateral relations with state and non-governmental actors in the region. After all, yesterday's reactionary could be tomorrow's ally (e.g., Bhutto seemed to have made a dramatic turnabout in Soviet eyes). And as always in South Asia, there were the pressing problems of economic development and debates about the most effective ways to achieve economic growth and independence. This did not mean that the Soviet Union was paralyzed in the exercise of its foreign policy; instead, circumspection about opposition political forces in South Asian countries was often required.

The USSR and India. Despite Mrs. Gandhi's Congress Party victories in the 1971 and 1972 elections and the popularity of her policy in Bangladesh both in parliament and among the public, by 1973 she began having domestic political problems. These were the result partly of the government's left-leaning socioeconomic and foreign policies which alienated conservatives and the middle classes, and partly of Mrs. Gandhi's increasing megalomania which disturbed even members of her own party. According to the Congress Party platform in 1971, and supported by the left (including the Communist Party of India [CPI]), Mrs. Gandhi introduced a number of important laws. Constitutional amendments allowed the government to limit private property rights without compensation. The government nationalized a number of insurance companies and some industrial enterprises; moreover, the government's rhetoric on their progressive social programs ran high. Their positive assessments of developments in the Indian economy were largely supported by Soviet academics and policymakers: in particular, the state sector, which the USSR felt partly responsible for helping to build, was seen as the key to Indian economic development. At the same time, the economy was experiencing a downturn: agricultural productivity was down and inflation was on the rise, and many observers were cautioning against over enthusiasm for the achievements of the state sector. As one commentator noted, "However, the role and place of the public sector in India's economy should not be overrated."[52] By 1973, with the oil crisis, the government began to face increasing demands not only by traditional conservative opponents but also by the Left. Unions, supported by the CPI, began to strike for better wages and job security. The Congress' commitment to Mrs. Gandhi's left social program seemed to be in question. As one group of Soviet scholars observed:

> On the basis of the people's broad discontent with the worsening economic situation and the Congress' nonfulfilment of its vaunted program of economic and social transformations, the activity of various nationalistic petty bourgeois and bourgeois opposition parties intensified.
>
> A large segment of the urban and rural bourgeoisie, dissatisfied with the ruling party's policy of further strengthening the state sector and its unsuccessful attempt at introducing a state monopoly on the grain trade in 1973–1974, began to support the opposition. Misgivings were aroused in certain circles by the government's putting several hundred unprofitable coal mines and textile enterprises under state control.[53]

At the same time the Prime Minister pursued the quest of socialism in India, she also became more insulated within her own party and relied more and more heavily on a small group of supporters (most notably, her son, Sanjay) for advice.

The immediate cause of the decision to impose emergency rule had to do with the well-publicized judicial proceedings against Mrs. Gandhi. An opponent from the 1971 election, Raj Narain, took Mrs. Gandhi to court charging that she had bribed voters and used her political position to influence the election outcome. The High Court went against Indira, removing her from parliament and banning her from running for office for six years, but the Prime Minister was given a twenty-day stay to appeal the judgment. The Supreme Court issued an ambivalent ruling, allowing Mrs. Gandhi to continue as Prime Minister but disqualifying her as a member of parliament. The opposition came together to protest and insist on her resignation. Ostensibly because the opposition-organized demonstrations were a risk to national security, a state of emergency was declared on June 26, 1975.

Mrs. Gandhi's actions were heavily criticized in the West, in Pakistan, and in China. Stephen Cohen and Richard Park describe the period of emergency rule, from 1975 to 1977, in the following way:

> Most of the opposition leaders (and some from her own party) were in jail; upwards of 100,000 citizens ultimately were imprisoned; the press was censored so rigorously that even the government was uninformed about conditions in the country; Sanjay Gandhi, Mrs. Gandhi's son, behaved like a *goonda* (thug); the courts were shackled by draconian limitations on their normal constitutional powers, limits approved by a pliable and irresponsible Parliament; enforced sterilization policies to limit population growth led to extreme excesses by cowed or brutalized administration officers; and trade unions were locked into pay and work policies without access to grievance procedures. Economically, there were some advances under more orderly if toughly policed conditions, but the advantages were given to the well-off, rather than the down-and-out.[54]

This assessment was naturally not shared by the Soviet Union. The USSR reacted with support for the PM's actions. The opposition, which was portrayed as having forced Mrs. Gandhi to declare emergency, was seen as reactionary.[55] The Soviet Union was clearly pleased with the new directions in social and foreign policy that Mrs. Gandhi had been pursuing and took her to be a close and reliable ally. Her opposition, on the other hand, had soundly renounced her foreign policy as being imbalanced and too Moscow-leaning, her domestic politics as too socialistic. Thus, the prospects for a change in regime were not welcomed in Moscow. It was not surprising, therefore, that the USSR had come out in favor of Mrs. Gandhi's actions in imposing the state of emergency.[56]

Throughout the emergency rule, Indira moved further left on the political spectrum and relied more and more heavily on the Communist Party of India and the USSR for support as critics in the West and political opposition even within her own party became more vocal. Indeed, the extraordinary number of high level meetings between CPSU leaders like Boris Ponomarev and the CPI leadership indicates that the CPSU actively encouraged the CPI to cooperate with Mrs. Gandhi during the emergency, even when CPI members were imprisoned. A message of congratulation sent by the CPSU to the CPI on the occasion of their fiftieth anniversary said:

> In the struggle against imperialism and internal reaction and for carrying out social and economic reforms in the interests of the people, the CPI consistently works to rally the country's Left and democratic forces, including such forces in the Indian National Congress, in support of the progressive and patriotic course of the government headed by Premier Indira Gandhi.[57]

Throughout the period of the emergency, the USSR refrained from any criticism of Mrs. Gandhi's domestic politics. When she visited the USSR in June of 1976, the Prime Minister received a particularly warm welcome, and the joint declaration issued by the Soviet Union and India made no mention of the emergency at all and said only that "the Soviet side expressed its full understanding of the efforts of the government and the people of India aimed at solving the complicated socio-economic tasks facing the country." Instead, it praised India's role in striving for world peace and regional tranquility on the subcontinent.

Moreover, the support was not all talk. During the emergency period, Soviet trade with India increased from 685.6 million rubles in 1975 to 926 million rubles in 1977, and a number of important new projects were undertaken including the establishment of coalmining enterprises, increasing the capacity at the Bhilai and Bokaro steel plants, and others.

In an effort to legitimize emergency rule, Mrs. Gandhi called a parliamentary election in March, 1977. Her decision to hold elections was apparently taken in the mistaken belief that she and the Congress would win.[58] The Soviet evaluation of her chances for success may have differed from Mrs. Gandhi's; as the election approached, the

USSR was unusually reserved on the political events in India. Indeed, an article in *Izvestiia* just before the elections warned that although the Congress Party and the CPI had defeated the reactionary forces in 1975, the strength of the right wing (the Janata Party) should not be underestimated.[59]

And the prospect of a Janata victory did not sit well in Moscow. Mrs. Gandhi's ever-closer ties with Moscow during the emergency, of course, resulted in still more criticism at home and abroad from those who believed India's neutrality was being scrapped. Morarji Desai, one of the leaders of the Janata coalition, was quoted by Moscow Radio as saying he would cancel the Indo-Soviet Treaty if the Janata won the election.[60]

The Prime Minister was defeated even in her own constituency by the coalition Janata (People's) Party led by Morarji Desai and Jayaprakash (J.P.) Narayan. As Myron Weiner notes, "In the 1977 elections turnout soared in some areas. Evidently the restrictions on political participation and the repressive acts of government motivated those who had not previously taken part in electoral politics."[61] Turnout was particularly high among scheduled castes and Muslims who had born the brunt of some of the most serious human rights violations by the government (e.g., forced sterilizations, destruction of shantytowns). Unfortunately for Mrs. Gandhi, the increased turnout did not work in her favor.

The Soviet reaction was understandably one of disappointment since Desai was a conservative who had been one of Mrs. Gandhi's most vocal critics, in the realm of her foreign policy as well as that of her domestic policies. *Izvestiia*, reporting on Gandhi's defeat, noted that errors had been made during the state of emergency. Particularly troublesome were landowner opposition to land reform, the alienation of the working class because of wage freezes, and the disunity of the left.[62] Radio Moscow commentator, A. Bovin, blamed Congress' defeat in part on its lack of resolve to implement policies and in part on the state of emergency, which, while necessary, "was accompanied by abuse by the bureaucratic civil service."[63] But Moscow did not waste time lamenting the loss of Prime Minister Gandhi. Kosygin sent a congratulatory message to Desai on his election on March 25. The message expressed his belief that the two countries would continue as before, and indeed, the new Minister of External Affairs, Atal Behari Vajpayee (a leader of the Jana Sangh Party), confirmed that the new government would honor all India's international commitments.

Thus, despite considerable lip-service by the Janata regime to a renewed dedication to neutralism and initial Soviet fears that the new government might abrogate the friendship treaty, relations between Moscow and Delhi did not suffer, although the warmth and intensity that they enjoyed under Mrs. Gandhi was muffled. Within a month of Desai's swearing in, Moscow announced that Gromyko would visit India at the end of April. During that visit, Gromyko had discussions with both Desai and Vajpayee and, at a luncheon, heard Desai comment that the Indo-Soviet friendship was strong enough to survive the demands of divergent systems, or the fate of one individual, or the fortunes of a political party.[64] Gromyko and Vajpayee signed agreements on economic and technical cooperation, trade, and telecommunications cooperation. Gromyko's visit was followed up in May by brief visits by Foreign Minister Firiubin and Deputy Defense Minister General Pavolovskii. On the Indian side, Prime Minister Desai agreed to visit Moscow later in the year. His visit in October of 1977, although lacking the flowery compliments that characterized Mrs. Gandhi's visits to the USSR, was nevertheless successful.

In fact, a joint communiqué indicated that the two countries had agreed to establish in 1978 a long-term program of integrated economic planning and cooperation. Santosh Mehrotra has described the kind of planning cooperation set out in the 1978 protocol as a "profound process of linking the national plans of partner countries in the fields of investment, production, and trade conducive to the growth of complementarity ... largely confined to the less-developed members of the CMEA and to some extent Yugoslavia."[65] In 1979, when Kosygin visited India, such a long-term agreement on planning was signed. In 1977, total trade between the Soviet Union and India was 926 million rubles; in 1978 it had dropped off to 771.4 million rubles; but by 1979, the amount had risen to 1,035.1 million rubles worth. This increase might not have been expected in early 1977 when the Soviet Union could not be sure that if Janata were elected, the coalition and Desai might not abrogate the treaty.

While Desai's regime clearly tried to reduce the international image of India as being tied to the Soviet Union (e.g., taking a more even-handed approach in public statements concerning the superpowers, moving to diversify India's arms supplies), it did not pursue this aim to the extent that it would shake the basic foundation of the Indo-Soviet relationship. Despite the international turbulence in the region in the early 1970s and the domestic instability internally in India, the international forces which motivated India and the Soviet Union to seek accommodation in the 1950s and 1960s were still active in the 1970s.

That is, the USSR's concerns about China and the US and Indian concerns about China and Pakistan were unabated in the 1970s. Furthermore, the geopolitical considerations which had led to the close Moscow–Delhi relationship had translated into economic and military policies which drew the two nations closer together and which created their own interdependencies. These interdependencies proved strong enough that even the assumption of power by the "reactionary right wing" in India in 1977 could not substantially weaken the links.

The USSR and Bangladesh. Despite the fact that the USSR played a significant role in the success of the Bengali national liberation movement, Soviet enthusiasm for the new state was not to be particularly long-lived. Mujibur Rahman's visit to Moscow in March 1972 had shown Bangladesh's appreciation of Soviet efforts during the Bangladeshi national liberation struggle and the USSR's interest in developing closer ties to the new nation. The Soviet Union undertook to assist the bankrupt Bangladesh economy and began by clearing Chittagong harbor. But amidst all the "good neighborliness" were reports that Bangladesh was suspicious of Soviet motivations in clearing the harbor.[66] The USSR was also to have cleared Chalna, but it was subsequently decided that the Bengalis themselves, aided by the Dutch, would take care of it. Furthermore, although it appreciated the assistance provided by the USSR for its economic crisis, Bangladesh had received far more economic aid from the West and India than had been offered by the Soviet Union. Still, the situation in Bangladesh was generally approved of by the USSR, and relations between the two countries were friendly. As one commentator noted, Bangladesh's "fundamental principles are democracy, nationalism, secularism, and socialism ... "[67]

However, even though relations started on a positive note, by the mid-1970s, the internal politics of Bangladesh, its relationship with the regional hegemon (India), and the expectations of the USSR would take a toll on Soviet–Bangladeshi relations. The USSR's concern over Bangladesh's instability was expressed as early as the 1973 elections. As one TASS report observed, "Exploiting economic difficulties and the fact that many domestic problems are still unsolved, the anti-government opposition, which is represented primarily by right-wing and left-wing extremist elements, is attacking the Bangladesh government and trying to undermine its prestige."[68] Mujib, however, won the election easily, prompting the following comment in *Pravda*: "The people of Bangladesh declared themselves for the progressive course, for independence, nonalignment and neutrality ... "[69]

In April of 1974, Mujib made his second trip to the Soviet Union, a combination holiday and rest.[70] Despite a cordial welcome in the USSR, Mujib was a leader in trouble. Bangladesh's economic situation was dire: it was sustained largely by aid from the United States and the West, India, and the Soviet Union. Politically, Mujib faced considerable opposition at home. He was pressed for an immediate transformation of the economy at the same time as his government had not proved successful in integrating the nation. The personal army that he created, the Rakkhi Bahini, was not able to quash anti-Mujib sentiments in the countryside and alienated the army. As Lawrence Ziring points out, "If 'Mujibism' had any chance of developing in Bangladesh, it apparently died amid the burned villages and broken hopes of the Bengali peasantry."[71]

Unable to control the situation, Mujib declared a state of emergency in December, 1974. The dissolution of the parliament had the effect of destroying the Awami League as a potential unifying force. Soviet reaction, as in the case of Mrs. Gandhi's emergency which would come the following year, was positive. Journalist Alexander Filipov, for example, noted that Bangladesh had launched a "far-reaching campaign ... against political terrorism and economic subversion by right wing reactionary forces and extremist organizations."[72] Even if the USSR disapproved of Mujib's actions, and there is no indication that they did, they would not allow the domestic situation in Bangladesh to come between Moscow and Dacca. In January of 1975, the Soviet Union granted Bangladesh a 35 million ruble loan for projects such as the reconstruction of a steel mill and oil refinery in Chittagong.[73]

Mujib was overthrown by the army, led by Khondakar Mushtaq Ahmed in April, 1975. Soviet reaction decried the slaying of Mujib but was cautious in not issuing outright condemnation of the new regime.[74] Thus, by the end of 1975, with Mushtaq Ahmed in power, martial law in force, and Bangladesh on the verge of normalizing relations with China, the Soviet Union began to question the stability of its ties to Bangladesh. It also questioned the stability of the Mushtaq Ahmed regime. Newspaper and journal commentaries hinted at trouble to come and indicated that Chinese and reactionary forces were at work in Bangladesh.[75]

Ahmed was overthrown in December, 1975, by Major General Ziaur Rahman who moved forcefully to establish a minimum of stability and order in Bangladesh. With the arrest of communist and other left-wing leaders in 1976 and as relations between India and Bangladesh continued to sour over water rights in the Farakka dam, the Soviet appraisal of the internal Bengali situation took a turn for the worse.[76] Soviet concern for the rights of persecuted communists was no doubt sincere, but the USSR's real contentions with Bangladesh probably had more to do with concerns over Chinese influence in the region and the diminution of Indian influence in Dacca.

With Mujib dead, Bangladesh's relations with India deteriorated and would not recuperate until the election of the Janata Party in India in 1977. Also in 1977, Ziaur Rahman received over 98% of votes cast in a referendum on his rule, and he improved his international stature with successful trips to India and Pakistan. These domestic and foreign achievements spurred Zia to hold a presidential election in June, 1978, which he won with nearly 80% of the votes. By then, however, the Soviet–Bangladesh relationship had lost much of its luster. Bangladesh's relations with China improved as did her relations with the Janata regime. Thus, Soviet–Bengali relations remained cordial and correct in spite of these problems, but if the USSR had hoped in the early 1970s to isolate Pakistan and its Chinese mentors with a Moscow-leaning India and Bangladesh, its objective would not be met in that decade.

The USSR and Pakistan. Soviet–Pakistani relations were at an all-time low at the beginning of 1972. From the Pakistani perspective, the USSR, along with India, had been instrumental in the separation of East and West Pakistan, and the fact that the USSR had vetoed a UN ceasefire until India had time to vanquish Pakistan in the war did not help matters. The rhetoric of the "spirit of Tashkent" was long gone. However, Pakistan was also not pleased with US actions during the war. There had been excesses by West Pakistani troops in East Pakistan, but the more important issue was one of international justice: the United States, by diminishing its support to Pakistan just when it was most needed, had allowed a violent separatist struggle, aided and abetted by India and with the intervention of Pakistan's arch-rival, to succeed.

Post-war Pakistan then tried to steer a moderate course. Zulfiqur Ali Bhutto took the reigns of power from Yahya Khan and by March of 1972, he was in Moscow on an official visit for the purpose of smoothing out problems in the relationship with Moscow that had resulted from the Bangladeshi crisis. He met with Kosygin, and the two sides issued a joint communiqué which reaffirmed their commitment to the development of good-neighborly relations and of "measures aimed at restoring Soviet–Pakistan trade, economic, scientific, technical and other relations that were interrupted as a result of the events in the area in

1971."[77] In addition to his Moscow trip, Bhutto also announced that Pakistan, having lost its eastern flank, would withdraw from SEATO. Bhutto continued to steer a foreign policy course that was somewhat more independent from Washington by also recognizing North Vietnam and opening diplomatic relations with North Korea.[78] These steps were welcomed in Moscow, but they did not bring about automatic reconciliation. Pakistan under Bhutto was determined to continue to build its relationship with China, and Bhutto was interested also in reorienting Pakistan's foreign affairs away from the subcontinent and towards the Muslim Middle East. Moreover, in February, 1973, Soviet-made weapons were found in the Iraqi embassy in Islamabad, weapons apparently intended for use by Pakistani opponents of the regime.[79]

Thus, Soviet–Pakistan relations faced ups and downs in the immediate post-war period. The Soviet Union was naturally pleased with the shift in Pakistan's foreign policy. An article in *Izvestiia* on March 22, 1973, noted, "Among the symptoms of the country's positive course in international relations were such acts as the recognition of the GDR and the DRV and the raising of diplomatic relations with the Democratic Republic of Korea to a higher level." Moreover, it was known that Bhutto was interested in immediately recognizing the new nation of Bangladesh, but internal opposition and debate forced him to delay recognition. Despite Bhutto's interest in cultivating these good impressions, however, in an April *Foreign Affairs* article, he noted that "it was to a large extent the Soviet Union's involvement in the subcontinent which made possible India's invasion of East Pakistan."

Such bitterness aside, Soviet–Pakistani relations generally were helped by the determination on both sides to improve matters and also by Bhutto's rhetoric and proposals concerning the development of socialism in Pakistan. Bhutto ushered in far-reaching land reform programs and nationalized the banks. P. Kutsobin and V. Shurygin, writing in *International Affairs*, noted with satisfaction that:

> the democratization of the country's socio-political life creates favorable conditions for implementing the socio-economic measures set out in the ruling party's policy-making documents: radical land reform, restrictions on the operations of local and foreign capital, and improvement in the conditions of the poorest section of the population.[80]

Economic relations between the two countries had deteriorated substantially during 1971. Commitments taken during Bhutto's visit to Moscow to return economic ties to their pre-1971 level were enacted with Soviet largesse in late 1973 at the steelworks in Karachi.[81] Between 1972 and 1977, trade between the Soviet Union and Pakistan had increased from 36.2 million rubles to 92.3 million rubles worth.

All this might seem to point to the regeneration of the "spirit of Tashkent" in Soviet–Pakistani relations; however, in addition to the bitterness over 1971, there was still the matter of China. Bhutto had made no moves to downplay the Beijing-Islamabad connection, and Soviet reaction to the continued Sino-Pakistani friendship was understandably cool. Despite the fact that Moscow did not approve of Bhutto's ties to China, the USSR preferred to paint China as the villain rather than risk further alienation of Pakistan. Thus, when Bhutto visited Beijing in 1976, *Pravda* reportage concentrated more on the negative aspects of Chinese influence rather than on the incorrect approach of Pakistani foreign policy.[82] The Pakistan–China link became even more critical as Bhutto announced his intention to give Pakistan nuclear capability. This not only provided a morass of problems *vis-à-vis* the transfer of Chinese nuclear technology to Pakistan but also strategic concerns *vis-à-vis* India.

Even if Soviet–Pakistani relations were not back to their 1966 highpoint, they still had improved much from 1971. By 1977, the USSR seemed genuinely pleased that Bhutto had been reelected. As one journalist observed, "By showing preference for the Pakistan People's Party, the voters, thus, spoke out for the promotion of vital progressive reforms in various spheres of the life of the country ... "[83] However, the March elections were followed by months of severe internal strife in Pakistan: the election results were contested and there were mass demonstrations and rioting. Bhutto and the opposition were unable to negotiate an agreement that would stop the disorder and schedule new elections.

Soviet satisfaction with Bhutto's election then was to be short lived. In the summer of 1977, Bhutto was overthrown in a military coup led by General Zia ul-Huq. Although Zia pledged a timely return to civilian rule and democracy, he also announced that Pakistan would undergo an "islamicization" because of the socialist and secular ideas that Bhutto had introduced. Zia had Bhutto arrested, ostensibly to protect Bhutto. (He was later tried and executed against great international protest.) The USSR was clearly not happy with the situation in Pakistan, and this situation was not helped by the fact that by the end of the year, Zia had made his first trip to China where he was well received. Obviously, the new regime had no intention of abandoning or minimizing their now longstanding relationship with China. The

USSR, nonetheless, tried to maintain cordial relations with Islamabad, but Soviet–Pakistani ties would continue to deteriorate under Zia, especially after the Afghan revolution in 1978.

USSR and Sri Lanka. The Soviet Union's ties with Sri Lanka fared well in the 1970–78 period. The election of Sirimavo Bandaranaike and the United Front brought a dramatic improvement in Soviet–Sri Lankan relations. Mrs. Bandaranaike was personally and politically close to Indira Gandhi; hence, the defeat of the United National Party was not only a progressive move for the island but also one that could increase Indian influence in the region. The political coalition that she headed, the United Front, was composed of Bandaranaike's own Sri Lanka Freedom Party (SLFP), socialists, and communists. Their platform professed a commitment to building socialism in Ceylon and opposition to imperialist aims in the region. Mrs. Bandaranaike's policies to expand the state industrial sector, distribute agricultural land, and nationalize the tea plantations were applauded by academics and policymakers alike in the USSR.

Moreover, the United Front allowed the direct participation of communists and socialists in the cabinet. This coalition was welcomed by the Soviet Union. One commentator called the election results "a big victory for democratic forces" and said they signified the people's support for "progressive regimes, for greater sovereignty and radical social change in the interest of peace and democracy."[84]

In fact, Mrs. Bandaranaike and the United Front had won a stunning victory for the left (taking 121 of 156 seats in the parliament). It therefore surprised the government when in 1971 the radical left party, Janatha Vimukthi Peramuna (JVP), staged an insurgency. On April 5, ninety-three police stations were attacked by the JVP and its supporters, mainly young, rural, Sinhalese Buddhist students. The revolution failed primarily because the JVP tried to seize power without taking control of the center, Colombo. It was poorly organized in the capital and its plan to kidnap Mrs. Bandaranaike and other government leaders failed. Finally, the JVP was factionalized and ill-organized.[85]

Left-wing members of the United Front tried to blame the insurgency on CIA and UNP instigation. The immediate response of Soviet observers echoed this analysis. One article in the *New Times* pointed to right-wing UNP and CIA collusion in the insurgency, and a Moscow radio report, trying to cover all contingencies, claimed the plot was laid by "ultra-Leftist terrorists and reactionary forces."[86] In fact, the JVP drew its following from lower-class Sinhalese Buddhists in the southern part of the country, Sinhalese who, unlike the well-educated

Trotskyists and Communist Party members, had little contact with the West. These were predominantly 18 to 25-year-old students who had suffered the ignominy of unemployment, despite their university education. The oversimplified analyses of the political situation by some Soviet analysts and the Sri Lankan communists, however, did not mask the fact that Sri Lanka's domestic tranquility was very fragile and that the United Front faced some extremely difficult tasks in terms of economic modernization and political integration.

The United Front's reform of the constitution in 1972 was hailed in Moscow as a positive step to fulfilling some of the country's needs. The constitution abolished the governor generalship and the Senate (half of which had been appointed by the governor general) and changed the name of the country from Ceylon to the Socialist Republic of Sri Lanka. Other steps taken by the government included nationalization of foreign owned tea plantations and the establishment of ceilings on private landholdings. These were welcomed by the USSR:

> All the healthy forces in Sri Lanka visualize their country's economic development as follows: continued advance along the road of progressive reforms, broader measures to nationalize private capitalist enterprises, enlistment of industrial and office workers into production management through workers' councils, and promotion of mutually beneficial relations with friendly countries, in particular such as neighboring India and also the Soviet Union and other states.[87]

These progressive measures, however, were off-set by persistent economic difficulties and the doggedness of the "reactionary opposition" (UNP), whose actions "forced" Mrs. Bandaranaike to crack down on the opposition, banning meetings and prohibiting publication of UNP-leaning, independent newspapers.[88]

In 1974, Mrs. Bandaranaike made a trip to the USSR. The years from 1970 to 1974 had been tough ones for her and Sri Lanka. Despite progress made in implementing her party's program, she had faced an insurgency and three years of emergency rule, trying to quiet the situation (and her opposition). The successful, if uneventful, trip came at a relatively peaceful time and was a boost to Mrs. Bandaranaike in holding the United Front, which had always been wracked by dissent, together. Its major outcome was to provide for a trade agreement that would be finalized the following year. In January of 1975, a trade protocol was signed that provided for a 50% increase in Soviet–Sri Lankan trade from 1974. Despite what the USSR had viewed as positive steps in the development of the Sri Lankan economy, the volume of Soviet–Sri Lankan trade remained unimpressive. In 1970, total trade turnover was 17 million rubles and by 1974 it was 34.2 million; however, with the agreement in 1975, trade sank to 22 million rubles. The trend was not to improve by 1977: in that year, Soviet–Sri Lankan trade totaled only 26.2 million rubles.[89] Furthermore, Sri Lanka was not overwhelmed by Soviet aid. According to the Department of External Affairs of the Government of Sri Lanka, the USSR offered a trade credit of some 13 million rubles in 1970 (before the SLFP took office), but even as late as 1983, very little of the credit had been used. Government aid officials blamed this on the fact that the credit had been tied to the purchase of Soviet industrial products and machinery for which spare parts were difficult to obtain; this prompted some Sri Lankans to observe that Soviet aid benefited the USSR more than Sri Lanka.[90]

It appeared that Soviet–Sri Lankan relations were more a matter of form than substance. Mrs. Bandaranaike, like Mrs. Gandhi, seemed to get along well with the Soviet leadership, but unlike Mrs. Gandhi, Bandaranaike was unable (or unwilling) to pursuade Moscow to lend some financial weight to its public statements of support. This was not the case, however, in Sri Lanka's relations with China. Although Sino-Sri Lankan trade did not account for a substantial portion of Sri Lankan trade, Chinese aid was valued in Colombo. Chinese aid was not tied to the purchase of products that Sri Lanka did not want, and most important, China had enhanced its position with the construction of Sri Lanka's major conference center, the Bandaranaike Memorial Center and Institute (after Sirimavo's assassinated husband) in Colombo. While the USSR was careful not to criticize the Sino-Sri Lankan friendship, in light of Chinese links to other countries in the region in the 1970s (Afghanistan, Bangladesh, Nepal, Pakistan), the USSR probably would have preferred China to be less popular in Colombo.

Soviet–Sri Lankan relations would remain fairly stable and consistent in the 1970s, until the 1977 elections. The United Front collapsed in early 1977, causing a splintering of the left. The United National Party was able to capitalize on this disunity to capture 139 of 168 seats in the parliament. The election was a disaster for Mrs. Bandaranaike's SLFP which took only 8 seats, one of which went to Mrs. Bandaranaike herself. *Pravda* pointed out that the UNP's dramatic victory was caused by voter's frustrations over Mrs. Bandaranaike's inability to cope with economic problems.[91]

The weeks after the election Sri Lanka witnessed some communal violence. Jayewardene's government asked two Soviet trade union officials to leave the country, because he believed them to be inciting the conflict.[92]

Thus, Soviet relations with Jayewardene's Sri Lanka were not off to a particularly auspicious start. Although the USSR was careful not to offend the new regime, Jayewardene's plans to stimulate the economy through foreign capital, privatization, and the creation of free trade zones, was not seen as progressive by Soviet analysts.[93] Ideologically, the Soviet Union was closer to the United Front of Mrs. Bandaranaike than to the UNP and Jayewardene, but it was still not clear what direction Soviet–Sri Lankan relations might take. The general tenor of public statements was more reserved and trade was down (from 26.2 million rubles worth in 1977 to 15.4 million rubles worth in 1978). On the other hand, the USSR was proceeding with the construction of a hydroelectric power plant at Samanalawewa, and diplomatic channels were open and cordial.

The USSR and Nepal. Unlike other countries of the region, Nepal in the period 1970–78 faced no major domestic upheaval or political change of regime. The monarchy was pressed by internal opposition to broaden popular participation and establish a true constitutional monarchy, but it remained firmly in control throughout the 1970s. Nepal's left-wing opposition was largely attracted to China. Therefore, while the 1970s allowed the USSR to be somewhat complacent about Nepal, from the Soviet perspective the years also brought no hope of progressive change in that country.

Although the USSR and Nepal have had diplomatic relations since 1956, their relations have been somewhat contained. In part, this is due to Nepal's preoccupation with India and China, and in part, it has to do with the USSR's interest in India and her problems, which has left Nepal on the periphery of Soviet concerns in South Asia. Nepal had been economically and politically dependent on India since colonial times, and these ties were not substantially reduced in the post-colonial period. Virtually all of Nepal's foreign trade went through India, and India had a near monopoly on arms sales to the Himalayan kingdom. In an effort to reduce Indian influence in Kathmandu, Nepal turned to her other giant neighbor, China, in the 1960s. However, there were limits on the effectiveness of "playing the China card." The Indian military build-up in the Himalayas which continued after the 1962 Sino-Indian border war left Nepal vulnerable, and India, angered by Nepal's China strategy, could retaliate during negotiations over economic agreements so vital to Nepal's economy. As Leo Rose and

John Scholz put it, "The hard-line positions adopted by the Indian government in most negotiations with Nepal since 1970 have been, in part, a reflection of this attitude, and Kathmandu has found the China connection of limited utility under these changed circumstances."[94]

That Nepal sometimes had difficulties in managing its relations with the bordering Asian superpowers does not seem to have had any direct effect on Soviet–Nepalese relations which remained throughout the 1970s cordial but restrained. King Mahendra visited the Soviet Union in June of 1971 for talks with Podgorny, Kosygin, Gromyko, and other Soviet leaders. It was posited that the reason for the visit was Nepal's interest in obtaining Soviet aid in the construction of a fertilizer factory;[95] however, an offer of such aid was not forthcoming. (The USSR had granted limited amounts of aid to Nepal in the past: for the Kanti Hospital in Kathmandu, the Panauti hydroelectric station, a cigarette factory, a sugar refinery, and some road construction.) Soviet commentary earlier in the year stated that Soviet–Nepalese cooperation had helped to "liquidate the survivals of feudalism" in Nepal.[96]

King Mahendra died later in 1971 and was replaced by his son, Birendra Shah Dev. The main thrust of Nepal's foreign policy continued to be India and China, but Birendra also began to develop Nepal's image in the international arena with his proposal to make the Himalayas a zone of peace. China and Pakistan readily accepted the idea. Both the USSR and the US, waiting for India to endorse the plan, were non-commital; however, China anxiously noted that the USSR had tried to link Birendra's plan with Brezhnev's proposal for an Asian collective security system.[97]

Some tensions between the USSR and India and China were evident in Nepal. When King Birendra visited China in June of 1976, Sergei Malin, a Moscow radio correspondent commented, "Loud words about peace and solidarity were heard in the speeches but many Nepalese statesmen and political figures are beginning to feel the ever greater pressure of the iron hand under the velvet glove of their northern neighbor."[98] Of particular concern to both the USSR and India was the road the Chinese had constructed to connect Tibet to Nepal, a road that ended not far from the Indian border. Not to be out-done, the USSR invited the king to visit later that year.

Thus, King Birendra visited the Soviet Union for talks with Podgorny in November. As a result of their meetings an agreement on economic and technical cooperation was signed which provided for Soviet aid, particularly in building projects in the food industry. In May of 1976, this visit was followed up by Deputy Foreign Minister

Firiubin's visit to Kathmandu. Soviet trade with Nepal was of minimal importance to both countries: in 1970, total trade turnover was valued at only 1.3 million rubles, with Nepal importing oil and machinery and the USSR taking skins and jute; by 1975, trade was up to 5.5 million rubles, a healthy increase but still of little significance even to Nepal. With the newly signed economic agreement, Soviet–Nepalese trade totaled 7.4 million rubles in 1978.

It appeared that the Soviet Union was content to conduct polite and cordial diplomatic relations with Nepal but was not willing to finance Nepal's economic development. Although the USSR seemed concerned about the negative effects of Chinese influence in Nepal, especially vis-à-vis India's security, relations with the monarchy were not critical to Moscow in geostrategic terms nor in terms of political/ ideological affinity. Thus, the USSR's relations with Nepal remained stable, but they were probably the set of South Asian ties with which the USSR was least concerned.

The USSR and Afghanistan. With the exception of India, there is no country in South Asia with which the USSR has had more extensive ties than Afghanistan. The RSFSR established relations with Kabul in 1919, and the two countries have maintained a remarkably close relationship, albeit with several tense periods, since that time. Because of its location on the Soviet southern border, Afghanistan was at one and the same time the country most crucial to the USSR's geopolitical interests and most peripheral to the South Asian regional political system. It is at once Middle Eastern and South Asian, being a Muslim country to the east of Iran and yet sharing ethnic and historical ties with Pakistan and the British Empire. The geographic factor which placed Afghanistan at the interstices of three major systems (the South Asian, Middle East, and Soviet) also made this country of strategic interest to the USSR.

Moreover, it is a country whose modern history is replete with instances of political upheaval. Indeed, the 1970s saw two major regime changes in Kabul, both of which were of particular interest to the Soviet Union, although Soviet–Afghan relations were never fundamentally challenged by them.

Relations with the regime of King Zahir Shah had been quite friendly. Zahir Shah understood well the nature of his relations with the Soviet Union and did little to offend his mighty northern neighbor. Under Zahir Shah, Afghanistan practiced a neutralist foreign policy known as *bi-tarafi* (without sides). Whatever their ideological interests in seeing a more progressive government in Afghanistan, the USSR not only tolerated but also cultivated relations with the monarchy. On the occasion of the fiftieth anniversary of the Soviet–Afghan Friendship Treaty, Podgorny sent a message to the King saying that Soviet–Afghan relations were long-standing and served as a bright example of the peaceful coexistence of states with different social systems.[99]

Indeed, ties between the Soviet Union and Afghanistan were strong. In the early 1950s, Afghanistan sought arms from the United States but was refused. The then Prime Minister, Mohammad Sardar Daoud turned to the USSR and its Eastern bloc allies in 1956 for military supplies. Since that time, the Afghans relied on the Soviet Union for weapons and training needs.[100] The USSR had also been Afghanistan's main trading partner since the mid-1950s. In 1970, total trade between the two countries was valued at 66.9 million rubles, with the Soviet Union buying natural gas and skins and selling machinery and oil products, among other items. Thus, by the beginning of the 1970s, Afghanistan, one of the world's least developed countries, had a trade turnover with the USSR higher than that of Pakistan. Furthermore, according to Soviet sources, the Soviet Union accounted for 54% of all Afghanistan's foreign aid in the period 1956–61.[101] The *Economist* also noted that the USSR had contributed about 60% of Afghanistan's foreign aid.[102] Afghanistan had benefited considerably from her *bi-tarafi* foreign policy and by the open competition in economic aid between the USSR and the US in the 1950s and 1960s.

However, this Soviet and American largesse did not insulate Afghanistan from the kinds of political and economic upheaval that other countries in the region had experienced. As Gankovskii *et al.* point out, "Political instability in the country increased as the economic situation deteriorated following two successive severe droughts (in 1970/71 and 1971/72) ... "[103] Dissatisfaction had been growing among students (particularly graduates of secondary schools who had difficulty finding suitable employment) and among the armed forces. The inability of the monarch's regime to cope with the economic situation and the political opposition resulted in a coup by the army, led by the King's brother-in-law and former Prime Minister (1953–63), Sardar Daoud, in July 1973.

While he was Prime Minister, Daoud had been active in cementing Afghanistan's relations with the USSR. Significantly, he included representatives and supporters of the left in his government; however, not long after consolidating power, he began ridding his cabinet of the left. In the first half of 1974, Pacha Gul Wafadar, Minister of Frontier Affairs, was appointed ambassador to Bulgaria; Abdul Hamid Mohtad,

Minister of Communications, was dismissed; and Parcham supporter Faiz Mohammad, Minister of the Interior, was eventually sent as ambassador to Indonesia.

The Parcham had been closely identified with the Soviet Union through the person of its leader, Babrak Karmal. With Daoud's elimination of the left from his government then, the Soviet Union could not have been very pleased. There was very little negative comment made in the Soviet press about the Daoud regime's move to the right. In fact, the Soviet press continued to report on the progressive nature of the Daoud government. A *Pravda* article by South Asia analyst, Alexander Filippov, noted the "progressive measures" being taken by the republican government. Particularly important were the land reform, industrialization plans, and the policy of a guided economy. "For a state such as the Republic of Afghanistan all these progressive measures, carried out in a relatively short time, are of cardinal importance. They testify to the country's determination to proceed on the course of radical changes."[104] Another article went so far as to say that the land reform (which really never got under way) had removed the conflict between peasants and feudalists.[105] It appeared that Moscow believed that the Afghan left still had some influence at this time and that Daoud could be pursuaded to continue with his professed course of action. According to Henry Bradsher, at Daoud's first visit to Moscow in June 1974, Soviet leaders Brezhnev, Kosygin, and particularly Podgorny, urged Daoud to stay the leftist course with the support of the "broad popular masses."[106]

There were a few positive signals that might have encouraged Soviet leaders to believe they could influence Daoud. By June 1975, Afghanistan had nationalized all private banks, a move which the Soviet press applauded.[107] Furthermore, Soviet–Afghan economic relations continued to develop. In February 1975, a major economic and technical cooperation agreement was signed providing Afghanistan with a 308 million ruble loan to be used for a variety of economic development projects. Interestingly, one of the projects to be financed with the loan was the construction of new gas installations and a new gas pipeline from Afghanistan to the Soviet Union, all designed to increase the volume of natural gas flowing to the Soviet Union.[108] At the same time as the agreement was signed, a protocol was also finalized that postponed the repayment of 100 million rubles worth of loan and interest payments from 1975 to 1980. The Soviet Union also extended an additional $428 million in development aid.[109]

The signing of these economic agreements was followed up in

December 1975 by a visit of President Podgorny to Kabul. The principal reason for the visit was the signing of another protocol, this one extending the life of the Soviet–Afghan Treaty of 1931. The visit was accompanied by a flurry of coverage on Soviet–Afghan cooperation and Soviet aid to Afghanistan. The Soviet press noted that the USSR had assisted with some 124 projects in Afghanistan and was responsible for building about 70% of all Afghanistan's hard surface roads, 60% of its energy capacity, and two large irrigation works, among other projects.[110] When Daoud took the reigns of power in Afghanistan in 1973, Soviet–Afghan trade stood at 68.1 million rubles. By 1975, total trade had increased to 132.2 million rubles, with the USSR importing natural gas, fruit, and cotton, and exporting machinery, geological equipment, oil, and refined sugar.[111]

Outwardly, relations between Moscow and Kabul looked ideal, but in fact, Soviet–Afghan relations had begun to sour. By the time of Daoud's and Podgorny's visits in 1975, it was clear that the left had been permanently eliminated from policymaking in Kabul. Also important, Daoud had begun to pursue a friendship with the Shah of Iran and to improve Afghan relations with Pakistan, all of which was interpreted by the left in Kabul as instigated by American imperialism. Thus, Daoud moved further right, both in terms of domestic Afghan politics and international ties; Afghanistan's *bi-tarafi* might no longer be as sympathetic to the Soviet Union.

Conclusion

By the late 1970s, the USSR faced some difficulties in virtually every country of South Asia. In Afghanistan, Daoud had shut the left out of his regime and was beginning to turn to the Shah of Iran for support; in Pakistan, Bhutto whose troubled regime had paid lip service to socialism was deposed by an Islamic general; in Sri Lanka, the socialist SLFP was replaced in elections by the conservative UNP; and in India, Mrs. Gandhi's handling of emergency rule, which had been supported by the USSR, brought the more conservative Janata to power. Despite these changes in South Asian politics, however, the 1970–78 period proved to be successful for the USSR's South Asia policy from a geopolitical perspective.

The USSR could point to the Bangladeshi national liberation movement and claim success for having supported that progressive cause. While the USSR was concerned about the destruction of international borders and the prospects for other successful separatist movements in the region, the dismemberment of Pakistan was not an unwelcome event to the USSR's biggest regional ally, India. Furthermore, although Afghanistan's Daoud was courting the Shah of Iran, he maintained fairly close ties to Moscow, and Moscow continued to provide him with economic and military support. The objective of maintaining a pro-Moscow tilt to Afghanistan's foreign policy had not really been seriously challenged. Another of the Soviet Union's objectives in the region, to conduct friendly relations with all countries of the region, also was largely successful. Relations with Sri Lanka were a bit cooler under Jayewardene than they had been under Mrs. Bandaranaike, who after all was a good friend of Mrs. Gandhi, but there was no dramatic change in political and economic ties. Relations with Pakistan that had been so badly damaged by the 1971 war had been painstakingly repaired by both sides, and although Moscow did not achieve the kind of close ties with Bangladesh that it had originally hoped for, its relations were cordial. Most surprisingly, Moscow's relations with the new government in Delhi, which had campaigned promising a more "neutral" policy than Mrs. Gandhi had pursued (the implication being that India would loosen its ties to the USSR), remained stable. Janata more vigorously pursued policies to promote the private sector and diversify arms acquisitions, but did not abrogate the Indo-Soviet Friendship Treaty. Trade and other ties then continued to develop, securing the success of another of the USSR's policy aims, the expansion of ties with India.

Its achievements were less obvious in the area of curtailing US and Chinese influence in the region. The USSR gained almost by default in the US case: American influence in the region, which had been primarily through Pakistan, had declined because of the 1971 war and did not recover well under Bhutto. The Chinese, on the other hand, had managed to develop their links to Colombo, Islamabad, Kabul, and the new capital of Dacca. Only in New Delhi was little headway made. However, in no case, with the possible exception of Pakistan, did the increase in Chinese activities actually diminish Soviet ties with any country.

In other respects, this period was somewhat illustrative of the less simplistic, less optimistic thinking about the Third World that was emerging in the literature. If, as many analysts believed, the class structure in Pakistan was deemed less progressive than that in India,[112] there was no euphoria about the prospects for a rapid transition to socialism in any of the countries of South Asia, including India. Although Soviet observers believed firmly in the superiority of planning and the state sector in promoting economic development and social progress, there were indications that even in the early and mid-1970s, they were aware of the many difficulties facing countries like India, Bangladesh, and Sri Lanka, which at certain points were characterized as preferring socialist development.[113] In keeping with the selectiveness exercised by the Brezhnev regime elsewhere in the Third World, there would not be wholesale financial sponsorship of the "progressive" regimes in Bangladesh (prior to 1975) and Sri Lanka (before 1977), which were less established and less central to the overall struggle against imperialism globally than India was. Events in the countries of South Asia in the 1970s, like other areas of the Third World, were demonstrating to the Soviet Union that backsliding was always a danger for these fragile, young regimes. Thus, the first inklings of a more complex view of the Third World can be seen in Soviet policy in the 1971–78 period; however, the major concerns were about balance of power and correlation of forces.

5 Soviet–South Asian relations in the wake of Afghanistan, 1978–1985

Introduction

The early 1970s saw the USSR concentrating its efforts in South Asia on the subcontinent proper: the decade began with the Bangladeshi national liberation movement and another Indo-Pakistani war. International concerns about the region were heightened once again by India's detonation of a nuclear device, which had repercussions not only for the tensions between India and Pakistan but also for China. By the late 1970s, however, the USSR was forced to shift its focus away from concerns about Indo-Pakistan enmity and domestic politics in the southern states of the region to the rising instability in southwest Asia. Despite the fact that there was no fundamental realignment of Indian foreign policy, the USSR's relations with the Desai regime were not as close as they had been with Mrs. Gandhi. Political conditions in Pakistan had deteriorated in 1976 such that by 1977, Bhutto had been ousted in a military coup led by Zia ul-Haq who promised to reinvigorate Islam in Pakistan. The USSR and the rest of the world watched with concern as Bhutto was put on trial, convicted, and sentenced to death, despite heavy international protest. In 1978, the regime of the Shah of Iran also came under heavy pressure from a variety of opposition groups; the 1979 revolution brought to another country in southwest Asia a movement to "re-Islamicize" society. There were also downturns in relations with post-Mujib Bangladesh and J. R. Jayewardene's Sri Lanka as well.

Furthermore, the political situation in the country that bordered the USSR also deteriorated. As Mohammed Sardar Daoud's position in Afghanistan began to weaken in 1977, the question became not whether he would be overthrown, but by whom. Although the answer to that question was not clear in 1977, there was reason to believe that the leadership of the People's Democratic Party of Afghanistan might be successful in unseating Daoud. The USSR had continued to maintain the close contacts with Karmal and the Parchamis that it had nurtured in the 1960s and 1970s. However tenuous the agreement by Khalq and Parcham to restore unity to the PDPA,[1] the Soviet Union was ready to take advantage of its ties to the small Afghan communist movement, should they be successful in overthrowing Daoud.

The Saur Revolution and the Soviet invasion

The demise of Daoud's republic came on April 27, 1978, but its downfall began much earlier. As Louis Dupree notes:

> The turnaround began in March 1977. The Republic of Afghanistan, after four and a half years of on-again, off-again, mostly ineffectual reforms, waited for President Mohammed Daoud to appoint a new Cabinet. Most observers hoped the Cabinet would include moderate leftists. Instead, at this crucial point, Daoud reverted to the behavior of an old-style tribal khan and appointed friends, sons of friends, sycophants, and even collateral members of the deposed royal family.[2]

Daoud inaugurated a one party system (Hezb-i-Inqelab-i-Meli [National Revolutionary Party]), promulgated a new constitution, and was elected President in 1977. Soviet scholars later argued that it was the increased inequalities generated by Daoud's policies that exacerbated the class conflict and brought about the revolution;[3] however, the immediate cause of the revolution was the assassination of Mir Akbar Khyber, a PDPA leader, in April. His funeral turned into a demonstration which prompted Daoud to imprison leftists such as Nur Mohammed Taraki, Babrak Karmal, and others. Taraki's right-hand man, Hafizullah Amin, apparently was only under house arrest, however, and managed to direct the PDPA's army supporters to launch a coup.[4] Daoud, his family, and other close supporters were killed, and the PDPA became the new masters of Afghanistan.

The Soviet Union was the first country to recognize Taraki's fledgling regime, with official recognition coming on April 30, 1979. Although initial press comments were limited to reportage of the events of the coup and the assumption of power by the PDPA, within a month of the coup Soviet analysts took on a more positive attitude toward the revolution and began writing that Taraki's government would be a progressive force in the development of the country: "the work-loving and freedom-loving people of Afghanistan have entered one of their most important states of development."[5] Bradsher points out that within two and one half months of the revolution, the USSR had signed "some 30 new aid and cooperation agreements" with the new Afghan government;[6] however, Dupree notes that most of these agreements had been negotiated during Daoud's reign.[7]

Despite the flush of success over Afghanistan's left government, Moscow soon had to face the internal divisions that were tearing apart the PDPA.[8] The Soviet Union had close ties to Parcham, but the new regime was being headed by Taraki, a Khalqi, generally conceded to be an Afghan nationalist as well. However, while Khalqis held the highly visible positions of prime minister (Taraki), and deputy prime minister and foreign minister (Amin), Parchamis, or Parchami sympathizers, headed the important ministries of planning (Sultan Ali Keshtmand) and interior (Nur Ahmad Nur), and Karmal was also appointed deputy prime minister.[9] Their mid-1977 reunification notwithstanding, these factions of the PDPA had many differences between them. Taraki and Amin began to eliminate Parchamis from policymaking, at first by sending leaders to serve as ambassadors (e.g., in July, deputy Prime Minister Karmal was sent to Czechoslovakia, Anahita Ratebzad [a long-time communist, rumored to be Karmal's lover] to Yugoslavia), and later by imprisonment. In August, General Abdul Qader, the nationalist Parchami-allied Minister of Defense, was arrested for treason. It would be revealed a month later, with the arrest of other Parchamis, that the regime had foiled a coup attempt.[10] In September 1978, plagued by further fears of a Parchami coup, Amin and Taraki ordered all banished Parchamis home, "but instead of going home the ambassadors had all disappeared – presumably with Soviet help, because the first reappearance was when Karmal returned behind smoking Soviet guns more than a year later."[11]

Background to the invasion: Even if the Saur Revolution did not come as a surprise to the populace of Kabul or foreign observers of Afghan politics, the communist regime soon faced animosity from a number of quarters of Afghan society including tribal leaders, clergy, the educated elite, and even other Marxist organizations such as the radical, left-wing, Tajik party, Setem-i-Melli. Soviet commentators conveniently labeled the growing opposition to Taraki's government "reactionary" and attempted to link them to foreign intrigue.[12] Unfortunately for the USSR, the numbers of these reactionaries grew rapidly as Taraki and Amin instituted a reign of terror and ill-planned reforms.

Taraki's role was primarily that of "Great Leader"; his strength was his ability to act as father to the revolution, but his interest in interpreting events and devising proper Marxist positions to advance the revolution meant the government often lacked concrete direction and, more significantly, took up policies which served to aggravate the growing tensions in the country. Amin, on the other hand, accepted that an aggressive stance was necessary to consolidate the revolution but was more skilled at practical matters than Taraki. Thus, from early on, Amin was a key force in policymaking and implementation for the new regime.[13]

Under the guidance of Amin, police and military organizations rounded up Parchamis and other left-wing opponents or potential opponents as well as former supporters of Daoud and members of Afghanistan's small educated class. According to the party program that had been promulgated just weeks after the PDPA took power, military tribunals were set up to adjudicate the cases of those deemed to be anti-revolutionaries, although the result of the "trial" was usually known at its outset.[14] There are estimates that executions even during these early days of the revolution ran at approximately fifty per day at the Pul-i-Charki prison in Kabul.[15]

At the same time that the PDPA was engaged in its active campaign of political terror that was targeted primarily at urban politicos and intellectuals, it also undertook a number of agricultural and social reforms which would serve to alienate rural Afghanistan. Shortly after the PDPA took power, it promulgated its thirty-two "basic lines of revolutionary duties," twenty-three of which pertained to domestic restructuring. Among the most significant of the proposed reforms were those banning usury, promoting sexual equality, and mandating land reform.[16]

The first reform, on usury, was implemented in July, 1978. Its purpose was to free the peasants, who desperately needed credit to finance purchases of seed for farming, from the high rates of interest charged by landlords and moneylenders. The reform provided that all such debts (and mortgages) contracted prior to 1973 would be null and void, thus relieving the debtor of his obligations. The law understandably angered the landlords and propertied middle class; moreover, it contained no provision to assure peasants of government loans. There was also widespread abuse of the law, with debtors claiming non-farming related debts (such as dowries) as agricultural debts.[17] It had, in effect, destroyed the traditional moneylending system of the rural areas without introducing a viable replacement.[18]

In October of the same year, the reform on sexual equality was promulgated. Its target was the traditional marriage contract which exacted a very high payment by the family of the groom to the family of the bride, known as the "bride-price" or *shir-baha* (in Dari). the "bride price" could place an extreme burden on poor families. The law, therefore, set a low amount for the "bride-price"; it also raised legal marriage ages to 18 for males and 16 for females; and required voluntary consent of both parties to marry. However laudable these aims, the law created many problems. First, the family of the groom not only paid money to the bride's family but also received an often sizable dowry from the bride's family. More important, the traditional marriage contract and the *shir-baha* provided financial security for the woman in case the marriage should be terminated due to divorce or separation. With the new law, that security had been removed.[19] Furthermore, the weak government in Kabul had no way of regulating and policing its new law. Its language and aims had the effect then of further alienating the traditional rural population while having little real impact on marriage customs and relations between the sexes.

Even though its other reforms had met with little success, the regime introduced what was possibly its most controversial reform in November: land redistribution. Its objective was to destroy feudalism in Afghanistan; its method was a radical redistribution of land that was to be completed by July, 1979 and accomplished by limiting the amount of land that any owner could hold. Excess holdings would be expropriated and redistributed to landless or land-deficient peasants by Khalqi-manned teams of inspectors who would travel the countryside.[20]

The PDPA naturally claimed that virtually all of Afghanistan's peasants would benefit from the land reform; however, it faced problems. One of the principal defects of the land reform was its failure to realize that land is but one component of agriculture. Lacking other resources (seeds, water, etc.) to exploit the land, it was not surprising that peasants were not as appreciative of the redistribution as the regime might have expected. Furthermore, many peasants would not accept land that they had not paid for, particularly when that land came from wealthier neighbors whom they had known for years. Anthony Hyman, commenting on the failure of the reform, states that "It offended the popular sense of justice or right conduct, completely failing to mobilise the rural poor for their Khalqi state, and contributed to the chaotic conditions of civil war which overtook Afghanistan in the summer of 1979."[21] Less drastic versions of all these reforms had failed under the rule of Amanullah (1919–29) and under Daoud's republic, but the PDPA attempted to enact them vigorously nonetheless. Initially, the Soviet Union, for its part, was outwardly supportive of the general goals of the "basic line of revolutionary duties." Soviet reports seemed to favor many of the steps advocated by Taraki such as liquidating of feudal and pre-feudal relations, strengthening the state sector, promoting industrialization, and effecting universal education.[22] These views resonated in the academic literature by analysts such as Ponomarev who had a more optimistic view about the capacities of vanguard parties to effect progressive changes.[23] However, as it became apparent to all observers that the reforms were meeting steadfast resistance not only from their natural opponents (i.e., religious leaders and landlords) but also from their intended beneficiaries (i.e., poor rural peasants), Soviet commentary became less effusive, reminiscent of the more cautious, complex views of Simoniia, Kim, and others. As opposition increased, Soviet commentators began to focus their attention on the precise role of foreign influences in the growing conflict.[24] It appeared that in the debate over the nature of development in the Third World, and in Afghanistan particularly, the proponents of correlation of forces had the upper hand.

While the Soviet press blamed external intrigue for Afghanistan's internal problems, Soviet policymakers were reevaluating the Saur Revolution and the policies of the Khalqi regime. It was no secret that Karmal and the Parchamis had largely argued for slower reforms that would at first appeal to nationalistic sentiments. Karmal from his position of official exile in Czechoslovakia, and later in the USSR, could take some small comfort in knowing that his analysis was at least more correct than Amin's had been.

In September, 1979, Nur Mohammed Taraki visited Moscow on returning from a non-aligned conference in Cuba. It was apparently on this occasion that Brezhnev advised Taraki to slow-down the pace of reform and concentrate on national unity.[25] That the USSR was not pleased with the situation in Afghanistan was indicated by a Soviet press release which stated that Taraki and Brezhnev had held talks in a "cordial, comradely atmosphere."[26] Taraki returned from his meeting in Moscow to discover that Amin had relieved four of Taraki's close associates of their cabinet positions and was on the verge of having them arrested. Thus, on September 14, Taraki summoned Amin to the People's Palace where a shoot-out ensued. Taraki, the Afghan press reported, had to resign his position because of ill health.

Amin emerged from that meeting as the new leader of Afghanistan, but it was clear that he had no intention of pulling back on his programs of rapid social reform and political terror. Soviet commentary on the Afghan situation became more cautious. Without spelling out the obvious (that Amin had to go if the revolution were to survive), news commentators emphasized the need for consolidating the revolution. In addition to these more circumspect press reports, with Amin's assumption of power, a decided chill was introduced to Moscow–Kabul relations. First, Prime Minister Kosygin flew over Afghanistan from a trip to India without sending the customary greeting to Amin. Second, there were also indications that Moscow was actively seeking new opportunities in Afghanistan. Thomas Hammond writes that:

> There were rumors that Soviet officials, in desperation, had contacted the chairman of the Afghan Islamic League to see if his group would support a move to dismiss the Khalq regime and replace it with a government of national unity. There were also persistent rumors that the Soviets were planning to form a new, broadly based government that included ministers who had served under King Zahir.[27]

Furthermore, on the eve of the anniversary of the Soviet–Afghan Friendship Treaty in September, a very brief and cold message was sent to Amin: no personal message of goodwill was forthcoming. Third, Amin's Foreign Minister, Shah Wali, at a meeting of communist ambassadors accused the Soviet ambassador in Kabul, Alexander Puzanov, of harboring political fugitives and of trying to eliminate Amin in September of 1979. On top of all this, Amin then declared Puzanov *persona non grata* and demanded that Moscow withdraw Puzanov.[28]

The rumors and growing Soviet–Afghan tensions were compounded when General Ivan Pavlovskii, commander-in-chief of the Soviet Ground Forces and deputy Defense Minister, visited Afghanistan in August–October, 1979. Not only was Pavlovskii an important military figure, he was also the official who had been sent to Czechoslovakia just prior to the Soviet invasion in 1968 and the commander for the actual invasion.

Despite the fact that Moscow wanted Amin out of office, the USSR did lend assistance to Amin in combatting rebel forces in Paktia in October. Indeed, according to Bradsher, "Soviet military commanded, ran logistics, and provided air power for the Afghan army."[29] Amin, however, was not willing to relinquish total control of the army to the USSR, notwithstanding the fact that his own policies were costing him control of the country. Late in November, Lieutenant General Viktor Paputin, first deputy Minister of Internal Affairs, was dispatched to Kabul. Although the exact purpose of Paputin's visit is unknown, most analysts have surmised that his goal was to obtain Amin's invitation for Soviet troops to enter Afghanistan and to remove Amin from power, by whatever means necessary. In December another shoot-out ensued, but again Amin escaped harm. Although Paputin's mission was unsuccessful,[30] the USSR had already begun preparing for its full invasion to save the embattled PDPA regime.

At for the actual decision to invade, it was obviously taken at the highest levels. As Selig Harrison states:

> According to Yuri Gankovsky, a Soviet Afghanistan specialist at the Institute of Oriental Studies who warned against the decision to invade, Brezhnev and his ideological eminence grise, Mikhail Suslov, pushed it through by a narrow Politburo majority over the doubts of Andropov, then head of the KGB. The optimistic assumption was that Karmal could easily win back support lost as a result of Amin's overzealous reforms by pursuing more moderate policies.[31]

The Soviet invasion and the war. Soviet troops began their full-scale invasion on December 24. The first troops were the 105th Guards Airborne Division, followed by the 103rd Guards Airbourne Division and *spetsnaz* forces.[32] On December 27, *spetsnaz* forces attacked the Darulaman Palace where Amin was staying and after a pitched battle with forces loyal to Amin, entered the palace and presumably killed Amin. Meanwhile other Soviet forces took control of Radio Kabul and lines of telephone communication. By December 29, Amin and his Khalqis had been defeated, Babrak Karmal was declared president of the revolutionary council, and the USSR was left to piece together the divided country.

The number of Soviet troops in Afghanistan reached 50,000 by the beginning of January; within weeks, the number was being placed at 85,000.[33] Of those, some 50–70% were reservists, and many were Central Asians.[34] They proved to be unreliable in the struggle against their Afghan brethren and were eventually replaced by Slavic troops. Within six months of their initial invasion Soviet troops numbered 110,000.

As Jiri Valenta and others have pointed out, there were strong similarities in the invasion of Afghanistan and that of Czechoslovakia in 1968, which further suggested that the regime viewed Afghanistan as an application of an extended Brezhnev doctrine. Not only were Generals Pavlovskii and Iepishev involved in both, but the steps taken in both instances were comparable. Using a modified Czech invasion model, Soviet troops in Afghanistan took control of roads, lines of communication, and major cities; other troops were then dispersed around the countryside; and Soviet troops were used to neutralize armed forces still loyal to Amin.[35]

The invasion had succeeded in overthrowing Amin. It had not, however, had the desired effects of containing the civil war and consolidating political power behind the Parcham-led government. First, it was the Khalq that predominated in the Afghan army, and not the Parcham; therefore, the USSR faced an officer corps that would be at best unreliable. There were even Khalqi defections from the army to the *mujaheddin*. Second, although Karmal had advocated a more moderate reform package and a policy of national reconciliation, he was widely viewed as a Soviet puppet. He soon found that it would be as difficult to obtain support for his regime as it had been for Amin. Furthermore, the resistance grew. Soviet analysts largely blamed this on the intrigues of foreign actors (most notably, the CIA, Pakistan, and China) in aiding reactionary forces.

Responses to the invasion. The Soviet invasion stunned most of the world. US intelligence had been tracking Soviet troop movements in November and were aware that invasion preparations were being made.[36] The US government made its concerns known to the Soviet Union on several occasions, but Moscow vigorously denied that any such troop movements were underway. The US ensnared in the hostage crisis in Iran, might therefore have been less capable of coordinating a response to the situation than might normally have been the case.

International condemnation of the USSR after the invasion and overthrow of the Amin regime came swiftly. The United States led the charge, with President Carter condemning the action at a press conference and a televised interview within days of the invasion. China, too, strongly criticized the Soviet move, stating:

> The perverted Soviet action has already roused the Afghan people to resistance and caused the grave concern of all countries and met their strong condemnation. The Chinese government and people will work tirelessly with all countries and people who love peace and uphold justice to frustrate Soviet acts of aggression and expansion.[37]

At a banquet given by the American ambassador in Beijing on January 3, Foreign Minister Huang Hua repeated this call "to frustrate" Soviet intentions.[38]

Negative reactions, however, were not limited to the great powers. After the USSR vetoed a Security Council resolution brought by Bangladesh, Philippines, Jamaica, Niger and Zambia on January 7, calling for the withdrawal of all foreign troops from Afghanistan, the matter went to discussion on the floor of the General Assembly where 104 nations voted for the resolution.[39] Soviet press reports denounced the moves in the United Nations, saying that the United States and China had together orchestrated the actions.[40]

If the USSR believed the furor as demonstrated in the General Assembly would quickly die down, they were mistaken. Even if the Brezhnev Politburo saw Afghanistan as an area of "legitimate" Soviet interest, like Czechoslovakia, much of the rest of the world did not. Particular concern would be voiced by the neighboring countries in south and southwest Asia whose security was most affected by the Soviet invasion and coup. Iran responded on December 28, strongly condemning the Soviet moves as anti-Islamic and arguing that these actions showed that the USSR, like the USA, was intent on carving up the world.[41] Pakistan, now under General Zia ul-Huq, followed suit, denouncing the Soviet invasion, calling upon the world community not to rest until all troops were withdrawn, and asking for assistance in dealing with the many refugees who were flooding northwest Pakistan from Afghanistan.[42] Moscow's criticism of Islamabad shot back:

> Recently Peshawar has become known not so much as the transit point along the traditional trade route to Afghanistan but as the springboard for the preparation of imperialist aggression against the Democratic Republic of Afghanistan [DRA]. It has become the main base ... which the U.S. forces and Beijing are using for subversive activities ...[43]

The charges and countercharges between the USSR, the US, China, and Pakistan went on, and Moscow did not fare much better with other countries of South Asia.

Bangladesh, whose relations with Moscow had cooled considerably since 1971, Nepal, which was still under a monarchical form of government, and Sri Lanka, which was now being ruled by a more conservative United National Party, also roundly condemned the intervention and demanded the withdrawal of Soviet troops. Soviet coverage of regional reactions, however, tended to focus on the supportive comments made by local communist parties.[44]

India's reaction alone was considerably more subdued than that of her South Asian neighbors, and the rest of the Third World, for that matter. Although Prime Minister Charan Singh met with Soviet Ambassador Vorontsov and told him that India was concerned by the USSR's action and hoped that Soviet troops would be withdrawn, public government pronouncements were markedly cautious. However, Singh's government was a caretaker government only; the recently held elections resulted in a landslide for Mrs. Gandhi and Congress (I). Therefore, "even before Mrs. Gandhi was formally to assume the office of Prime Minister in mid-January 1980, he [Charan Singh] left the problem [of Afghanistan] to her" (parentheticals, mine).[45] While Mrs. Gandhi was no doubt concerned over the destabilizing aspects of the Soviet invasion and its indirect threat to India, she also believed that the USSR had taken this action for defensive reasons: that is, that Soviet national security was threatened by the instability in Afghanistan, instability which was at least in part caused by the activities of external actors (e.g., China and the US). One *Pravda* article, which endeavored to explain the Prime Minister's position on Afghanistan, quoted Mrs. Gandhi as saying, "the USSR, naturally, does that which, in its opinion, accords with its national interests."[46]

India's rather ambivalent public comments on the invasion made it the target of considerable criticism in the West and in the Third World: was India really in the pocket of the USSR? Such speculation was not reduced by the fact that India abstained from the General Assembly vote on the resolution demanding the immediate and unconditional withdrawal of troops from Afghanistan. Mrs. Gandhi was sensitive to these criticisms, and therefore, upon taking office in January took the position that her government would devise a plan to secure the withdrawal of Soviet troops from Afghanistan. While the USSR appreciated her "even-handed " approach to Afghanistan, it was not about to concede to her pleas for withdrawal, as meetings later in the year between the Prime Minister and Brezhnev would show.

In the aftermath of the invasion. The USSR had succeeded in achieving one of its key short-term objectives in Afghanistan: eliminating the tyrant Amin. It was unable, however, to shore up much support for the new Parchami-led regime in Kabul, to control the rebellion in the countryside, to stop the hemorrhage of Afghans fleeing to Pakistan, or in short, to build a base for the development of non-capitalist/non-feudalist relations of production in Afghanistan. Soviet analysts in the wake of the invasion and the installation of Babrak Karmal as new leader in Kabul clearly laid out the need for national reconciliation and rallying around the new regime: "The April Revolution in Afghanistan has entered a new stage. The most important distinctive features of this stage are unprecedented cohesion of the whole people, the strengthening unity and the growing role of the People's Democratic Party of Afghanistan ..."[47] To underscore the concerns about national unity, considerable press coverage was given to the mistakes of the Amin regime in this regard, particularly its penchant for alienating most sectors of Afghan society. "Hafizollah Amin had imprisoned thousands of members of the PDPA, workers, peasants, intellectuals and clergy who had come out against tyranny and despotism ... and had practically turned the country into a huge dungeon."[48]

But despite the recognition of some past errors and the determination to overcome Amin's legacy by following some of the recommendations laid down by Karmal and Soviet analysts (i.e., to go more slowly), the USSR would face increased *mujaheddin* activity in virtually every area of the country. The Brezhnev regime had clearly underestimated or misinterpreted the obvious clues to the depths of Afghans' dissatisfaction with the PDPA, and equally, most Afghan and western scholars would add, their repugnance of foreign domination.

The invasion, of course, would have repercussions well beyond the boundaries of Afghanistan. As immediate reaction to the action demonstrated, the USSR's standing in the international community of nations had for the most part been hurt by the intervention. In South Asia, the invasion disturbed the regional balance of power in a way that had not been seen since the late 1940s and the retreat of British Empire.

The USSR's relations with all countries of the region, including India, suffered as a result of December, 1979. Under Bhutto, the USSR had managed to revive its relations with Pakistan, which had deteriorated as a result of the Bangladeshi national liberation movement and the Indo-Pakistan War of 1971, and although ties with General Zia were reserved, they were not hostile. As might be expected, the 1980s would witness a rather dramatic turnaround in India–Pakistani relations: diplomatic relations took a downturn due to heightened rhetoric on both sides, and economic relations also suffered, trade having reached an all-time high of 176.6 million rubles in 1980, dropping off to 117.6 million rubles by 1985. Nonetheless, Zia managed into the early 1980s to maintain a highly visible working relationship with Moscow.

Soviet–Indian ties certainly improved when Mrs. Gandhi assumed office in 1980, although the Soviet press had not expected her to win the election. Indeed, it appears that the USSR had overestimated the power of the Indian left and seemed to be hoping that a left coalition might lead a united front.[49] Soviet news commentator and long-time India watcher, V. Shurygin, and South Asia scholar, G. Shirokov, both noted that whatever the outcome of the election, disagreements among the contenders centered on domestic and not foreign policy.[50] The general thrust of India's foreign policy towards the Soviet Union was never really in question, having survived rather nicely through the supposedly more anti-Soviet Janata government.

Nonetheless, Mrs. Gandhi's return and her stance on Afghanistan were soon welcomed in Moscow, although the invasion did have its effects on the relationship.

Bilateral relations

The fundamental reorientation in Soviet policy towards South Asia that had occurred as a result of the invasion of Afghanistan thus had repercussions on Soviet regional policy and on Soviet bilateral relation with various countries of the region. Despite the initially rancorous South Asian reaction to the Soviet intervention, however, the 1980s witnessed no major reorientation of the foreign policies of any of the countries of the region. Why did no country of the region break off or significantly downgrade relations with the USSR after the intervention? Were Soviet–South Asian relations really so stable (so "mutually beneficial") that even a Soviet incursion into the area could not shake the ties?

Part of the answer lies in the perceived national security interests of the countries of the region. Even though the Soviet invasion was considered a threat to regional stability by the countries of South Asia, its impact was directly felt only by Pakistan. It was Pakistan which bore the brunt of the refugees,[51] and it was Pakistan whose national security was threatened by border skirmishes and occasional bombings by Afghan forces. Policymakers in Colombo and Kathmandu knew that Soviet actions in Kabul would have little impact on their national security.

Part of the answer too can be found in an examination of what the various parties wanted and expected of their relations. India's cautious reaction to the invasion and its willingness to abstain from the UN vote indicated that the special relationship with Moscow would not be sacrificed for Afghanistan. In the case of the peripheral countries (Bangladesh, Nepal, Sri Lanka), good relations with the USSR were valued but were not the primary foreign policy concern. For example, Soviet–Nepalese relations were not nearly as important to either party as, for instance, Soviet–Indian relations were to Moscow, or Indo-Nepalese relations were to Kathmandu. And no country of the region, even Pakistan, placed relations with Afghanistan as its top priority. Therefore, while Nepal (Bangladesh, Sri Lanka) might have been able to survive without friendly ties with the USSR, Afghanistan was not a sufficient reason to alter relations with a superpower. The case of Pakistan is certainly the most curious: if any country might have been expected to sever relations with the Soviet Union over Afghanistan, it was Pakistan. But a complete break or downgrading of relations with Moscow might serve to strengthen India *vis-à-vis* the USSR and would leave Pakistan with no voice in Moscow to air its concerns, which had proved effective, for example, in 1965. Zia therefore chose to maintain a highly visible, if strained, relationship with Moscow.

Furthermore, the South Asian response to the Soviet intervention also had to do with the balance of power in South Asia at the time. Pakistan looked enviously on as India remained the regional hegemon. While India and Pakistan were not at the brink of war in 1979, their relations were still marked by suspicion and tension. Pakistan had maintained its close ties with China after General Zia came to power, and this relationship, along with its longstanding ties to the United States and the continuing Sino-US friendship, did little to placate India whose relations with China had never fully recovered since the war in 1962. Furthermore, India had the added concern of rumors of Pakistan's developing nuclear capability. The policies pursued by Pakistan and India in the 1980s then were as much a product of their own relationship as their relationship to the USSR.

Finally, the inability to damage irrevocably Soviet–South Asian relations also has to be viewed in terms of the domestic problems that many of the countries faced. Unlike the period 1970–78, the period 1979–85 would see no change of regime in any of the South Asian countries that would potentially disrupt foreign policy ties or substantially alter domestic political or development strategies. All countries of the region, nonetheless, continued to be plagued by internal instability: for example, India and Sri Lanka would face serious separatist movements and Bangladesh would suffer political upheaval. Thus, relations with the USSR (which in all cases had been generally favorable) and its occupation of Afghanistan were certainly of less pressing concern than domestic problems.

While the Soviet invasion of Afghanistan did not shake the foundations of Soviet policy in South Asia, it clearly had negative consequences on Soviet bilateral relations with the countries of the region. At times those consequences could be seen less in obvious measures of economic or military relations (e.g., arms shipped, trade turnover) than in the general tone of Soviet diplomatic and political relations. This floundering of Soviet status in the region had to do not only with the security/balance of power concerns of the regional great powers (India and Pakistan) but also with the perception by all countries of the region that the USSR, like the US in Diego Garcia, was now a military force that had to be reckoned with in South Asia. The USSR could no longer argue credibly in Asian fora that the US was the main protagonist in militarizing the subcontinent and the Indian Ocean.

For the USSR then, in the 1980s as in the 1970s, the task was to try to overcome the specter of Afghanistan and to maintain friendly relations with countries of a region seemingly plagued by perpetual domestic instability. If the invasion made that more difficult, it certainly did not make it impossible. The USSR had to be an astute observer of domestic developments in the region, and it would have to adjust its policies in the region to the constraints of South Asian politics.

The USSR and Afghanistan. The already large number of Soviet advisors in Kabul was substantially increased after the intervention.[52] As Henry Bradsher has pointed out:

> Three levels of authority existed in Kabul and the limited areas of Afghanistan that it controlled ... At the bottom was the government. Above and directing it, in the Leninist pattern, was the PDPA most of whose leaders also held governmental positions. In theory the PDPA and the politburo drawn from the committee were the highest authorities. But in fact there was a layer above them of Soviet advisers who controlled everything.[53]

Although their role had been important throughout the short history of the DRA, they became indispensable to the running of the government in Kabul. The invasion had succeeded in removing Amin from power, but now the USSR and its personnel in Kabul faced several more difficult and interrelated tasks in Afghanistan.

Politically, the PDPA had to be consolidated; if factionalism could not be overcome, the regime would never stand on its own. Additionally, the regime's legitimacy had yet to be established among the Afghan people. Militarily, the mujaheddin obviously had to be vanquished, but it was also necessary to build the Afghan army into an effective and reliable fighting force. Economically, the country had to be put back on its feet: while encouraging ties with CMEA countries and building an industrial base for Afghanistan, the USSR had to worry about revitalizing Afghan agriculture. Shoring up support for the regime, eliminating resistance, and rebuilding the country (in short, accomplishing these objectives), would require a dramatic reorientation in the domestic policies of the DRA.

On the political front, the Soviet Union knew it had to control the factionalism within the PDPA, and this could not be done by simply eliminating all Khalqis. Khalqis outnumbered Parchamis, and most importantly, Khalqis far exceeded Parchamis in the army, and the USSR needed the Afghan army. Therefore, unlike his predecessor and no matter what his personal desires, Babrak Karmal did not assume office and immediately purge the Khalqis from his cabinet. The USSR, however, could not contain tensions for long. Assassinations and attacks on government officials were widely known to be the result of interparty disputes rather than the mujaheddin. Khalqi-led coup attempts were foiled several times in the summer of 1980.[54] In July, Agence France Presse reported that "lower ranks in several Afghan units had been disarmed because their loyalty was doubted." A mutiny of the Afghan 14th Division in Ghazni occurred after a Khalqi commander was replaced by a Parchami.[55]

Karmal's response to the in-fighting was the execution of several of Amin's former government officials (all Khalqis) and the imprisonment of other Khalqis. Karmal also reduced the power of the Khalqi-controlled interior ministry which was headed by the last powerful Khalqi in the government, Gulabzoy. As might be suspected, Karmal's actions did not stop the factional fighting within the PDPA, and Karmal's pleas for unity rang hollow in Khalqi ears. In 1981, the USSR decided to attack the problem again and name a Khalqi as prime minister, thus removing Karmal from the position.[56] They were unsuccessful in achieving this goal, however, for another Parchami, Sultan Ali Keshtmand, eventually assumed the position. Despite the pleas of Babrak Karmal that factionalism must be ended for the good of the PDPA and the DRA,[57] in-fighting remained one of the prominent features of the Kabul regime.

The Soviet Union faced another serious political problem in addition to the PDPA feuding: the failure of the PDPA regime to establish itself as the legitimate government of Afghanistan. Daoud's regime had lost legitimacy by the spring of 1977; whatever hopes were held out that the Taraki regime could gain the support of the Afghan people were deeply questioned by the spring of 1979 and completely lost as Amin gained control of the government. The USSR's hope was that by eliminating Amin and his henchmen and by putting in place a regime that would promote national reconciliation, abrogating or slowing down on many of the economic and social reforms undertaken by the Khalqis, the confidence of the majority of the Afghans could be won. It was curious then that the USSR should choose to support Babrak Karmal, a Parchami known by Afghans to have very close ties to Moscow and one of the key Parchami leaders banished to Eastern Europe by the Khalq in the early days of the revolution. Any Afghan who entered Kabul behind the Soviet invasion would have difficulty ruling the country, but by selecting Karmal as leader of the PDPA the

USSR did little to improve its chances of securing a government that would have legitimacy in the eyes of the Afghans.

Karmal's government faced the first critical test of its durability in February, 1980, when mass demonstrations against the regime and its Soviet supporters wracked Kabul for weeks. Bhabani Sen Gupta states:

> It began as a general strike in Kabul on 21 February, backed by almost 95 per cent of the traders, and developed into mass civil disobedience. There were reports of sporadic fighting between Afghan government troops and rebels. Soviet soldiers kept to their barracks, leaving Afghan troops and PDPA cadres to persuade the shopkeepers not to close their shutters.[58]

Other reportage puts the starting date of the demonstrations in January and continuing to the end of February.[59] Whatever the exact starting date of the disturbances, their extent and duration indicated the high level of dissatisfaction among Afghans. Afghan government news releases naturally tried to minimize the problems, calling them the work of "mercenaries" and "troublemakers."[60] Generally, the Soviet press simply reported Kabul's view; however, one correspondent, pointing to the widespread nature of the disturbances, reported that "groups of mutineers, using the reactionary clergy, were able to draw into their adventure a certain part of the confused population."[61] Interestingly, there were also reports in late February (the same time that the demonstrations were occurring) of a mass meeting of Soviet–Afghan friendship honoring the sixty-second anniversary of the Soviet army and navy. When and where this meeting was held was not reported.[62]

As soon as the demonstrations were quieted, Karmal announced the promulgation of a new constitution which was designed to shore up support for the regime. In addition to Karmal's repeated personal assertions that the regime would defend Islam,[63] the new constitution guaranteed freedom of religion for all peoples. It also provided equal rights for women and all national (ethnic) groups. Most importantly, the new constitution proposed a "mixed economy" for Afghanistan, ensuring that agriculture would not be collectivized. As Sen Gupta points out, "The economic thrust of the constitution was clearly aimed at assuring Afghanistan's one million small traders and businessmen and the great bulk of its peasants that their interests were safe and secure in Marxist Afghanistan."[64]

But a new constitution alone would not revive the faith of Afghan citizens in their government; therefore, Karmal sought to expand his political support once again by assembling the National Fatherland Front [NFF], a coalition of "national, democratic and progressive forces" in June, 1981. The meeting was preceded by months of preparation, assembling representatives of various groups who would concede to the leading role of the PDPA in the Front.[65] The NFF was theoretically overseer of the socioeconomic reforms that were being put into place, but as Bradsher points out, "It was, instead, a matter of trying to co-opt a wide range of people into what had already been decided by the PDPA under Soviet guidance."[66] What had been decided was that some of the land reform and debt policies promulgated under the Khalqi-led regime should be substantially revised. Thus, Karmal's government increased the amount of land one could own, and repealed the debt laws, but this was largely a propaganda ploy since both these reforms had by 1982 been largely disregarded anyway.

If the post-invasion regime was having difficulties in securing political support both from within the PDPA and among the population at large, things were not faring much better on the military front. Soviet plans for quick entry and departure from a quieted Afghanistan were soon dashed as the mujaheddin showed no more fear in attacking their troops than they had Afghan troops. In fact, the anti-government insurgency continued to grow, in spite of, and to a large extent because of, the presence of Soviet troops. The intervention even seemed to embolden some of the mujaheddin. Gulbeddin Hekmatyar's Hezb-i-Islami organization released the following statement: "Our aim is great and long-term. Our struggle is for creating concrete defense positions in Afghanistan for the advancement of Islam to Central Asia and Europe."[67] Obviously the mujaheddin would not be intimidated by Soviet troops. Barring the rebels' military defeat, the USSR and the DRA were forced to rely on a propaganda campaign to develop what little support was possible for the Kabul government. Thus, in the 1980s, the amount of news coverage blaming the US, Pakistan, and China for Afghanistan's civil war increased.[68] If the Kabul government was to be tainted by the Soviet intervention, the mujaheddin would be faulted for affiliation with the imperialist/anti-Islamic/war-mongering Americans, Chinese, and Pakistanis.

In order of priority, the USSR's military objectives in the early 1980s appear to have been (1) retaining control of the main urban areas (e.g., Kabul, Herat, Qandahar, Kunduz, etc.) and (2) eliminating rebel positions "at minimum costs to their own forces."[69] To accomplish these goals, the Soviet Union employed well over 100,000 troops,[70] composed mainly of the 40th army and spetsnaz forces supported by gunships, MiGs, and attack aircraft. They faced mujaheddin forces divided into about seven major groups, including fundamentalist organizations such as those of Gulbeddin Hekmatyar and Yunis Khalis, and Burhanuddin Rabbani's Jamiat-i-Islami, those of the sufi leaders Sayyid Ahmad Gailani and Sibghatullah Mujaddidi, and Nabi Mohammedi's Harakat-i-Inqilab-i-Islami. There were even a number of small, far-left-wing parties such as Setem-i-Melli (Against National Oppression) and Shu'la-i-Jawed (Eternal Flame) and Maoist groups such as Majid Kalakani's Sazman-i-Azadibakhsi-i-Mardom-i-Afghanistan ([SAMA] Afghan People's Liberation Organization).[71]

Although the mujaheddin were not well united or organized in their struggle against the USSR and the Afghan government in Kabul, they had been remarkably effective in denying Soviet troops any kind of victory in Afghanistan. While the Soviets had been able to control the major cities, they had not been able to prevent the rebels from infiltrating the urban areas, nor had they been particularly successful in regaining rural areas controlled by the mujaheddin or in destroying their strongholds. The tenuousness of DRA army positions was pointed up in November, 1981, when mujaheddin forces attacked the prison in Kandahar; Soviet commando forces were reported to have been flown in to respond.[72] Pitched battles were reported in the Panjsher valley, and as close to Kabul as Paghman. The pace of battle therefore picked up in 1982 and especially in 1983, with the USSR trying to use its technological superiority to get the upper hand in the situation.

Despite the frequency of Soviet and DRA army unit attacks on the rebels, the mujaheddin seemed to have remarkable staying power. Indicating their willingness to continue the stepped-up attacks, Karmal said in September, 1982 that the government was "unflinchingly following its principled policy for the total elimination of counter-revolution."[73] Major Soviet offensives were launched in Herat, Kandahar, Paktia, and north of Kabul in 1983. But mujaheddin operations continued. Not only were the *dushtmani* (bandits), as the Soviets called them, successful in carrying out raids on particular targets,[74] but they were also able to retain control of important tracts of territory: for example, Rabbani's and other groups managed to hang on in the Panjsher. Soviet and DRA troops were sometimes able to push the mujaheddin out of a stronghold temporarily, such as in the summer of 1983 when they were forced out of the area south of Jalalabad, but, as in this instance, the mujaheddin often reoccupied the area again. By early 1984, the mujaheddin had become so bold as to attack the Darulaman Soviet military headquarters.[75]

In short, unless the USSR was willing to suffer substantially greater numbers of casualties and to commit more troops and resources to Afghanistan, the standstill with the Western-aided mujaheddin would persist. The introduction of Blowpipe and Stinger missiles to the mujaheddin in 1986 meant that the Soviet and Afghan armies would suffer even more to hold onto their gains. The USSR would be able to maintain control of the major urban areas, albeit with incursions from the rebels, and the mujaheddin would continue to control large portions of rural Afghanistan and to deny the Kabul regime much of the countryside. As long as they could do that, they could also deny Kabul the means to rebuild the overwhelmingly agricultural Afghan economy.

This meant that economically, Afghanistan would be even more dependent upon the USSR than ever before. Soviet–Afghan trade expanded every year from 1980 to 1984, with total trade turnover of 504.7 million rubles in 1980, 655.8 in 1981, 691 in 1982, 675.2 in 1983, 898.7 in 1984.[76] Furthermore, in 1970, the USSR accounted for 34.2% of Afghanistan's exports and 38.4% of its imports; in 1975 – 23.9% of exports and 38.7 of imports; in 1980 – 52.7% of exports and 59.3% of imports.[77] With the destruction of the economy, Afghanistan had to import a wide variety of goods from arms, military equipment, and industrial machinery to foodstuffs. The USSR's top exports to Afghanistan in the early 1980s, however, consistently were machinery and equipment and oil while Afghanistan's top export had been natural gas which was sold at below-market values and piped directly from northern Afghanistan to Soviet Central Asia.

At the same time that the USSR was promoting or allowing Afghanistan's dependence, it was also encouraging Karmal to enact some of the above-mentioned socioeconomic reforms which were designed to restore the confidence of the Afghan public in the new-found moderation of the PDPA regime. The USSR was surely helping to establish industrial enterprises in urban areas, but at the same time, was supportive of the "mixed economy" approach to Afghan development. Although the Kabul regime tried desperately to assert its legitimacy and independence from Moscow in the economic as well as political and military spheres, neither Karmal nor his successor, Najibullah, was able to gain enough domestic support to implement effectively his political–economic program. Thus, in 1985, as Gorbachev was about to take office, the USSR faced a stalemated situation in Afghanistan. The Parchami-led regime, unlike Amin's, was certainly faithful to Moscow (indeed, it was dependent upon Moscow for its very survival), but unless Moscow was willing to extend its support for the PDPA even further, consolidation of the Saur Revolution would not be possible. As some scholars had warned, the difficulties of making the transition to socialism in one of the world's least developed countries should not have been underestimated, not only by the regime in Kabul but by the regime in Moscow as well.

The USSR and India. The Janata government was still in power in New Delhi in 1979 when Defense Secretary Subramaniam visited Moscow in October. Janata's explicit policy of diversifying Indian arms purchases and building India's own defense industry was a concern to Moscow: after all, under Mrs. Gandhi the USSR had become India's number one arms supplier and indeed, provided India with 80% of her defense needs. A severe cutback in this relationship would mean a loss of income and prestige for the USSR's Third World policy. Janata had already favored the purchase of the British Jaguar aircraft. Subramaniam's visit raised the prospect of India acquiring a large arms deal including AN-32 medium transport aircraft, MI-8 helicopters, and manufacturing rights to the MiG-23.[78]

With the heavy international condemnation of the invasion of Afghanistan and the prospect that Soviet–Indian relations might suffer severe setbacks because of the Soviet intervention, maintaining close Indo-Soviet diplomatic and military relations was more imperative than ever to Moscow. In an effort to assuage Indian sensibilities, Gromyko accompanied by Deputy Foreign Minister Firiubin visited New Delhi in early February for discussion of issues of mutual interest, specifically the Soviet position on Afghanistan. Their visit was immediately followed up in late February by that of Deputy Premier Ivan Arkhipov who flew to India for the twenty-fifth anniversary of Indo–Soviet economic relations.

This diplomatic pressure was supplemented by economic and scientific advances as well. The annual trade protocol, signed in February, planned for an increase of about 50% in trade over 1979 levels. In March, a three-year scientific and technical cooperation program was signed, calling for joint projects in the fields of magnetohydrodynamic power generation, solar energy, metallurgy, and such new fields as lasers, systems analysis, semi-conductors.[79] These agreements were followed up by a Soviet shipment of 30 of a projected 250 tons of heavy water for atomic power stations "without preconditions of full-scope safeguards."[80] The USSR was determined to reinforce its long-standing ties with India and, if possible, to expand into areas (such as lasers, systems analysis, semi-conductors, weapons production) where India had the research potential and possible access to markets for development. Thus, in the early months it seemed to the outside world that Afghanistan would have no effect on bilateral Indo-Soviet relations, and surely, India did not disappoint the USSR much in the international arena either. It continued to maintain its position on Afghanistan: that introduction of outside troops into the area was a negative development but that the USSR was forced into intervening, that Soviet troops would be withdrawn as soon as Kabul requested or as negotiations made their presence unnecessary. Furthermore, in July, Mrs. Gandhi's government took the unusual step of recognizing the Heng Samrin regime in Kampuchea. Although its timing was difficult for much of the world to understand, this step naturally was applauded in Moscow. Pravda correspondent, V. Shurygin, said it provided the people of Kampuchea with "moral support" in their battle against imperialism.[81]

But this Indo-Soviet lovefest was not all it appeared to be. In early June, External Affairs Minister Narasimha Rao visited the USSR for discussions on the situation in South Asia with Brezhnev and Gromyko. At a luncheon for Rao, Gromyko went on at length about Soviet actions in Afghanistan and the role of imperialism in exacerbating the situation. Rao's remarks, on the other hand, while reaffirming the closeness of Indo-Soviet relations and their desire to expand those relations in all spheres, were much more guarded, emphasizing the need for a negotiated end to the situation and elimination of all external interference in Afghanistan's internal affairs.[82] Rao's comments to the Lok Sabha concerning his visit were even more pointed:

> We are opposed to the presence of foreign troops in any country. The Soviet Union had announced that Soviet assistance to Afghanistan was limited in time, purpose and scale, and did not present a threat to the security and stability of the region. However, reports coming out of Afghanistan during the past few months, even if they are discounted for the inevitable interested propaganda element, do seem to suggest that in view of the situation there the hope that Soviet assistance to Afghanistan could indeed remain limited in time as originally intended is not very strong.[83]

India was becoming understandably frustrated in its attempts to negotiate a settlement of the Afghan problem; this failure, with the likelihood of long-range continuing Soviet presence and the build-up of troops, the realization that the USSR would remain for the foreseeable future a South Asian superpower, and its continued isolation from the mainstream of Third World opinion on Afghanistan (and Kampuchea), was a sticking point in Indo-Soviet relations as they entered the 1980s.

But there was another issue that clouded Indo-Soviet relations in the early 1980s: the prospect of normalization of Sino-Indian relations. The Janata government had made known its interest in detente with China, and in 1979, External Affairs Minister Vajpayee visited Beijing. Upon returning to office, Indira endorsed the Janata policy of normalization. Mrs. Gandhi met with the Chinese Foreign Minister Huang Hua in Salisbury in April 1980; however, the process was slowed by India's recognition of the Heng Samrin regime in June.[84] This slowdown suited Moscow which, despite Indian reassurances that improvement of relations with Beijing would have no deleterious effect on Indo-Soviet relations, had become very anxious over an impending Sino-Indian normalization.[85] One article in *Pravda* pointed out that India and China disagreed not only on their international boundaries but also on many issues of international development, including relations with the USSR. The article went on to state that China's principal interest in normalizing relations with India was to separate it from the USSR.[86]

But despite Soviet concerns and the slowdown in normalization efforts due to Kampuchea, Sino-Indian relations did not fail completely. India, for its part, continued to send delegations to Beijing and to voice an interest in solving border disputes and other international disagreements, while trying to assure Moscow that Indo-Soviet relations could not be affected. One of the effects of the normalization attempts was to prod Moscow into using its oil influence in Indian policy. In March 1979 and again in December 1980, the USSR offered to increase the quantity of oil sold to India, something which India very much wanted; both cases were tied to India's apparent interest in cultivating ties with China.[87]

Further adding to strains in the Indo-Soviet relationship were the actions of the Communist Party of India which was actively opposing most of Mrs. Gandhi's programs. Mrs. Gandhi hoped that the USSR would intervene on her behalf and pressure the CPI to take up the post of supportive opposition, but even though Brezhnev was said to have mentioned the CPI's position on the Indian government to the CPI during his December visit, CPI policies remained unchanged. Mrs. Gandhi's tactic was to try to divide the left opposition, which she had some success in doing, and to weaken the CPI, even *vis-à-vis* the USSR. One way to achieve this was to "set up a rival Friends of the Soviet Union (FSU) under the Congress (I) to counter the CPI-sponsored

Indo-Soviet Cultural Society (ISCUS) and a parallel 'world peace and solidarity' organization to the World Peace Council."[88] Clearly, the message from Mrs. Gandhi to Moscow was that the use of the CPI as an instrument of influence in New Delhi could be a double-edged sword.

If things were not going as smoothly between Moscow and Delhi as they had in the 1970s, it was not for want of the USSR's trying to resurrect once again the warm personal relationship that Brezhnev and Gandhi previously had, and it would not stop Mrs. Gandhi from landing a major arms deal from the USSR in the fall of 1980. There were reports in November that she had agreed to purchase the AN-32 and of deliveries of MiG-25s and MiG-23s[89] and renewed charges that the Soviet Union had tried to acquire naval facilities in India.[90] Additionally, in November, there was a rice for oil deal in which the USSR provided 200,000 tons of crude oil and 500,000 tons of diesel oil for 500,000 tons of Indian rice.[91]

These arms and oil shipments were followed up in December by a visit by General Secretary Brezhnev, the preparations for and significance of which were reported with great aplomb in the Soviet press. Brezhnev arrived with a sizable delegation which included Gromyko, First Deputy Premier Arkhipov, a number of members of the Central Committee, and deputy Foreign Ministers Firiubin and Vorontsov. While it was clear that Afghanistan had been an important part of the talks, the Soviet press was careful not to cover Mrs. Gandhi's comments indicating that India did not countenance external interference in Afghanistan's internal affairs. In an attempt to influence India to continue its initial interpretation of Afghanistan, Brezhnev offered to increase its oil shipments to India from 1.5 million tons annually to 2.5 million tons.[92] But the use of the oil instrument led to other problems: the USSR then tried to redress what it saw as a growing imbalance in Indo-Soviet trade (with India exporting increasing amounts of industrial goods and importing Soviet oil) through the 1981 trade protocol signed in February which indicated increased Indian exports of such products as cardamom, sugar, tobacco, and cosmetics.

The USSR entered 1981 with several sometimes competing problems in its relations with India. First, there was a growing recognition in the Soviet Union of an imbalance in Indo-Soviet trade. Second, there was a fear that the USSR might be losing influence in the Indian military due to its policy of diversifying arms acquisitions, as exemplified by Indian negotiations with the French for the Mirage fighter aircraft. Third, India's *rapprochement* with China was moving slowly forward, with the visit of Foreign Minister Huang Hua scheduled for June. Fourth, even though Indo-Soviet economic relations were faring well, Mrs. Gandhi's domestic economic policy had begun to shift. There were far-flung discussions in India concerning the dismal performance of the state sector and policies proposed that would favor the private sector. As S. Nihal Singh points out:

> The government switched from import substitution to export pro-motion, allowing liberal duty-free imports, and adopted a more favo-rable approach to the import of foreign capital and technology. Signposts of the new policy included an invitation to multinationals to explore for onshore and offshore oil, an offer to Middle East investors to participate in Indian industry with majority equity shares and the tapping of foreign private capital for the fertilizer and alumina industries.[93]

This, of course, did not help Mrs. Gandhi's position with the left, a situation that further exasperated her as left coalitions won electoral victories in the states of Bihar and West Bengal in the spring. Finally, the USSR had the persistent problem of Afghanistan and its affect on the Soviet Union's status in the Third World. The USSR clearly did not want a deterioration of relations with New Delhi at this stage, but the political situation in India was dodgy.

Despite the Congress (I) Party's flirtations with the private sector, the Indo-Soviet Planning Group signed an agreement on March 30 for cooperation in economic planning. Agreements to cooperate, however, seemed to require reinforcement by additional Soviet good-will. Thus, at the end of April, another barter agreement was signed which provided for the shipment of Soviet oil to India in exchange for Indian rice and other foodstuffs. But the main Soviet concerns in 1981 were geopolitical.

The lengthy negotiations with France indicated that India was obviously more impressed with the Mirage 2000 than with Soviet aircraft. Furthermore, in 1980 and 1981, India ordered major weapons systems from Canada, West Germany, the United Kingdom, and the United States, and received a license to manufacture the German Type 209 submarine.[94] The possibility that a licensing arrangement with the French might be worked out on top of major weapons systems pur-chases elsewhere prompted the visit of a high level military delegation led by First Deputy Defense Minister N. V. Ogarkov to India at the end of April. The Soviet counter-offer of the MiG-25 Foxbat on favorable terms was clearly made to persuade India against the Mirage. Soviet pressure concerning the Mirage was an open secret in New Delhi, causing Defense Minister Venkataraman to deny at a meeting of the Lok Sabha on February 26, "that Soviet Union was trying to scuttle India's plan to purchase Mirage aircraft from France."[95]

These efforts by India apparently to move away from her dependence on Soviet arms coupled with India's desire for normalization of relations with Beijing and the visit of Huang Hua concerned Moscow and led External Affairs Minister Rao to visit Moscow in July to reassure the Soviets about *rapprochement* with China. Rao's visit was followed by a visit in August by Deputy Foreign Minister Firiubin to discuss again Sino-Indian relations. On the occasion of the tenth anniversary of the Indo-Soviet Friendship Treaty, Gromyko also took time to comment on the ulterior motives of Beijing in seeking normalization of relations with Delhi, referring to the "great power aspirations of the Peking hegemonists."[96] Thus, Moscow could not have been pleased later in the year when Mrs. Gandhi, upon meeting Premier Zhao Ziyang and President Reagan at the Cancun Conference in Mexico, accepted invitations to visit both Beijing and Washington, or when India and China opened their first round of border talks in Beijing in December, even though very little was actually accomplished at the negotiations. Finally, in January of 1982, Indian and Pakistani foreign ministers met in New Delhi to discuss improvement of relations. One Moscow journalist covering the meeting said, "What is lamentable is the inconsistency between the words and deeds of the Islamabad authorities, which is becoming very evident, on the key issues on which the future of peace depends in South Asia."[97]

Moscow, possibly recognizing that an intensified effort would be necessary to maintain its influence in India, engaged in a flurry of activities designed to reinforce Soviet–Indian ties. It dispatched a delegation of the Supreme Soviet led by Deputy President V. V. Kuznetsov to Delhi in December. Also that month, the USSR, concentrating on its far-reaching economic relations with India, signed a trade protocol for 1982 in which over 10% of India's exports would go to the USSR, and of those exports, 60% would be manufactured and semi-manufactured goods.[98] Furthermore, a protocol was signed for Soviet assistance in constructing the Vishnakhapatnaru steel works; the agreement provided for repayment of a loan at 2.5% interest.[99] The activities in the economic arena indicated a looser attitude on the part of the USSR for India's private sector, an attitude that was shared by many academics.

Supplementing activities in the economic sphere was the visit of an extremely high-ranking Soviet military delegation in March. The seventy man delegation was led by Defense Minister Marshal Ustinov and included Chief Air Force Marshal D. S. Kutakhov, Admiral of the Fleet S. G. Gorshkov, Col. General M. A. Sergeichik, and Army General V. I. Varennikov. Upon arrival in New Delhi, Ustinov was reported to have said that Indo-Soviet defense cooperation "serves both the national interests of the USSR and India and the interests of strengthening peace in general and international security."[100] The Soviet efforts were not entirely without desired effect. During the Ustinov visit, the two sides discussed the possibility of Indian manufacture of the MiG-23 and MiG-27, and India put in an order for AN-32 transport craft.

The Ustinov delegation arrived in New Delhi around the same time as a delegation, led by then candidate member of the Politburo and General Secretary of the Georgian Communist Party, Edvard Shevardnadze, was in India for the congress of the Indian Communist Party. Shevardnadze met with Mrs. Gandhi during his stay, but the CPI congress promised to be embarrassing for her since it would oppose many of her policies.[101] At the meeting, Shevardnadze praised Mrs. Gandhi's foreign policy, saying:

> the Soviet Union values highly the Indian Government's realistic approach to the Afghan events and also the position of the CPI and all progressive and democratic forces in your country on that question ... India's foreign policy meets with the approval of many states. We know that it has the support of leftwing, democratic and patriotic forces in your country ...[102]

Varanasi, as expected, issued a resounding criticism of the government which the USSR obviously could not temper.

Mrs. Gandhi may have hoped for more Soviet influence in CPI affairs, but she had to look forward to the upcoming border talks – the second round between India and China – which were being held in New Delhi in May. Although the talks again brought no solution to the dispute, Rao dashed off to Moscow in June, again to appraise (and reassure) the Soviet leadership of the status of Sino-Indian relations. Probably just as worrisome for the USSR was Mrs. Gandhi's trip in July to the United States. No major breakthrough in relations was expected, but Mrs. Gandhi had not made an official visit to the US in eleven years, and, given her policy stances in recent years, the trip was a big event. Further cementing ties with the West, in October India and France finalized an agreement for the purchase of 40 Mirage-2000 aircraft and for the license to manufacture 110 in India. That agreement was followed up in November by a visit by General Zia to New Delhi for talks which resulted in the establishment of a bilateral commission to improve Indo-Pakistani relations. Mrs. Gandhi was clearly maintaining a high profile foreign policy, one quite different from her style in the 1970s.

She had carefully avoided turning her visit to the US into a snub of the USSR, however, by scheduling a trip to Moscow for September. Furthermore, she might have seen such a trip as advisable given the recent signs of Sino-Soviet *rapprochement*. But with her good friend Brezhnev ailing, her trip was rather uneventful. There were reports, however, that Mrs. Gandhi raised the issue of the vocal opposition of the Indian Communist Party with Brezhnev and Gromyko. S. Nihal Singh argues that one outcome of these discussions was the publication of an article by International Department deputy, Rostislav Ulianovskii, in *Asia and Africa Today* supporting Mrs. Gandhi and her fight against "right reactionary forces."[103] As the article hinted and as the CPI and other watchers of the Indian scene knew, the Prime Minister was clearly facing domestic difficulties; 1983 and 1984 would come to be known as years of great internal political turmoil.

In addition to a vociferous and increasingly successful political opposition, Mrs. Gandhi's major problem would be that of ethnic and religious conflict. While India had long been plagued by ethnic dissatisfaction and disputes, communal violence had become more acute in the 1980s. In 1983 and 1984 alone, over 3,000 people would be killed in just two episodes of rioting. "[One of] the worst cases of sectarian violence in the post-partition history of India was the 1983 widespread rioting in Assam against the 'aliens' (the Bangladeshi migrants), in which 1,200 were killed ..."[104] Another disturbance occurred as a result of government activities against Sikh separatists in the Punjab.

The Sikh Akali Dal Party had petitioned the central government for increased autonomy in the Sikh Punjab. Initially the quest for a Sikh state, Khalistan, had only a small, but fanatical, group of followers led by Sant Jarnail Singh Bhindranwale. As the battle between local interests and central government became more pitched, however, support for the separatists grew. Although the USSR supported the national liberation movement in Bangladesh, the Soviet Union appeared to have little sympathy for Sikh complaints. Soviet analysts saw the disruption in the Punjab as fueled by outside forces, particularly the United States. The US had given political asylum to Jagjit Singh Chauhan, a secessionist leader. One TASS report claimed that the CIA maintain close links with the Punjabi secessionists and that using CIA funds, a consulate of Khalistan had opened in Vancouver, Canada for the express purpose of training Sikh terrorists.[105] Why would the US want to encourage Sikh separatists? The US wanted to destabilize the situation in India to "weaken the positions of the Indian Government, which refuses to bow to Washington's diktat."[106]

Leaving aside Soviet claims about the activities of the "consulate" in Vancouver, well-armed Sikh militants under Bhindranwale were holed up in the Golden Temple of Amritsar, the most sacred shrine in the religion of Sikhism. Frustrated with police inability to eliminate the separatist militants and their terrorist activities, Mrs. Gandhi decided to attack the Golden Temple in June, 1984. The move killed not only the extremists but also innocent Sikhs who were worshipping at the temple. Her action appealed to some Hindus and colleagues favoring a strong central government, but its effect was to alienate and provoke an even wider body of Punjabi Sikhs. Thus it was on October 31, 1984, that Mrs. Gandhi was shot to death by two of her Sikh bodyguards at her residence. Not surprisingly, her assassination released a devastating round of retaliation against India's Sikh community, in which more than 2,000 Sikhs were killed.

The situation in the Punjab became the most prominent of the ethnic/communal disputes threatening to dismantle the federation, but it was by no means the only one. While Gandhi's actions had certainly contributed to tensions between the Punjab and New Delhi, her death did not solve the problem of ethnic and religious conflict or local versus central control. The country looked on anxiously as her youngest son, Rajiv, the General Secretary of the Congress (I) Party became Prime Minister, wondering if his inexperience would cause a collapse in his government and yet hoping that new blood could stabilize the country.

Rajiv may have been something of an unknown quantity to the West, but as General Secretary of the Congress, he had already visited Moscow in July, 1983 since Indira had made no secret of the fact that she was grooming her son to follow in her footsteps.[107] Moscow obliged Mrs. Gandhi's wishes. In Moscow, he met with Vice President Kuznetsov, Marshal Ustinov, International Department Head Boris Ponomarev, Foreign Trade Minister Patolichev, and Foreign Minister Gromyko. Nonetheless, neither the Soviet Union nor the United States could predict if the quiet, well educated but relatively inexperienced Rajiv would be successful, first of all, in maintaining the prime ministership, second, in being able to govern India and the Congress Party, and third, in solving the Sikh problem.[108] Rajiv and the Congress, however, had a resounding victory in the elections in December, winning 400 out of 509 seats in the Lok Sabha. Although these electoral victories helped secure his immediate political future, he still had to face difficult domestic issues such as the Punjab.

While India may of necessity have turned inward in the mid-1980s, its relationship with the USSR was not put on hold. Defense Minister Venkataraman had visited Moscow in June, 1983, and made an agreement with Marshal Ustinov for the licensed production in India of the MiG-27 aircraft. His visit was followed up by one in September by Defense Ministry Secretary S. M. Ghosh who met with Ustinov, Ogarkov, Kutakhov, and Gorshkov. The results of these meetings were a deal for the T-80 tank, the MiG-29 with license for production, and upon completion of successful testing, the MiG-31.[109] Trade too developed, although in this area, Moscow was now candid in its displeasure of what it saw as the imbalance in Indo-Soviet trade: specifically, the USSR was receiving too much Indian machinery and semi-manufactured goods and shipping too much oil to India.[110]

The USSR and India continued to maintain a remarkably close relationship throughout the 1980s, but clearly by 1983 and 1984, with Moscow having to cope with a succession and India facing domestic turbulence, Indo-Soviet relations lacked the dynamism of earlier days. Furthermore, when India took a reprieve from internal problems to address foreign policy issues, it was faced with an up-and-down relationship with Pakistan which had received sizable amounts of arms from the US, the Bangladeshi-proposed South Asian Association for Regional Cooperation, a Tamil separatist movement in Sri Lanka, and the persistent problem of Afghanistan. By the time Gorbachev took office, Rajiv had his domestic political position somewhat consolidated, and both countries were better able to address the Indo-Soviet relationship again.

The USSR and Pakistan. The Soviet invasion of Afghanistan presented Pakistan with an unusual situation. Pakistan was the single country with the most to lose after the intervention: on its border it found an occupying superpower force, a civil war, and eventually within its border, millions of Afghan refugees that had to be housed and fed, and expanded drug trafficking and arms trade that were raising communal tensions in some Pakistani cities. On the other hand, Pakistan gained considerably because of the intervention: (1) General Zia found the legitimacy he had been seeking among his own people and was able to stabilize his rule; (2) the USSR would become the international pariah in South Asia, and Pakistan could finally begin to live down the execution of Bhutto; (3) the status of Pakistan in the Third World generally, and in the Muslim world particularly, rose sharply; (4) Zia could begin to rebuild some bilateral relations (e.g., with the US) that had suffered because of Pakistan's treatment of Bhutto; and (5) Pakistan benefitted from extensions of aid from multilateral sources and from individual countries, most notably in the field of military aid from the United States.

General Zia's regime cleverly decided not to purposefully provoke the USSR over Afghanistan: they did not wish to give the USSR reason to extend their military might into Pakistan or to encourage Indo-Soviet collusion in destabilizing Pakistan. Instead, Zia cagily improved relations with the United States, which had made clear that it saw the Soviet intervention in Afghanistan as a very serious and highly destabilizing matter, while he held Pakistan out as the bridgehead against atheist communism's advance into the Islamic world. Both the Islamic world and the United States were sympathetic to Pakistan's difficult position. Pakistan, however, was wary of the US; after all, the Carter administration had charged that Pakistan was engaged in nuclear proliferation and invoked the Symington Amendment in cutting off all but food aid to Pakistan in 1979.[111] The US offered a $400 million aid deal which Zia called "peanuts."[112] To Pakistan the offer was large enough to incur the ire of the USSR, yet too small to do much good for Pakistani security. Thus, Zia decided to hold out, suspecting that the next offer from the US would be substantially larger and hoping that the Saudis would do their part and make a large contribution to the protection of international Islam.

The US was able to build some good faith is Islamabad in 1980 by supporting Pakistani debt reschedulement to the tune of $100 million and a $1.6 billion IMF credit.[113] Furthermore, during Zia's visit to Washington in late 1980, the US also raised the possibility of supplying Pakistan with the F-16.[114] While the US position seemed to be edging slowly to where Pakistan hoped it would be, the talk of multimillion dollar aid deals and provision of F-16s was a source of concern for India and the USSR. An article by *Pravda* correspondent V. Baikov charged that the US and China were making Pakistan a bridgehead to threaten Afghanistan and India. The article went on to note that the US had been trying to secure a base in Pakistan for its rapid deployment force, presumably using the offer of F-16s to lure Pakistan into a deal.[115]

The theme that Pakistan was in large part responsible for the instability in Afghanistan was a constant one in the Soviet press. While there had been charges that Pakistan was inciting the counterrevolutionaries inside Afghanistan under the Amin regime, Pakistani agitation was emphasized even more after the Soviet intervention. Most Soviet reporters focused on the use of Pakistani territory as a base for "anti-Afghan subversive activities" and training of rebels, but some went further. Soviet commentator V. Svetlov asked, threateningly, if Pakistan thought about where the US was pulling it in its hostilities with Afghanistan, and he reminded readers that their aggression was taking place "in the immediate vicinity of the USSR."[116] Similarly, a TASS dispatch from New York in February, 1980 stated, "One can see the contours of a dangerous plan aimed against Pakistan's neighbors – Afghanistan, India and the Soviet Union."[117]

A change of administration in Washington and the continuation of the Soviet presence in South Asia brought, in 1981, agreement between the United States and Pakistan on a six-year, $3.2 billion aid package composed of military and economic assistance. In addition to the fact that Pakistan got the kind of money it had been looking for initially, it also acquired forty very much sought after F-16s.[118] In order for the US to make such an agreement the US Congress had to waive the Symington Amendment. This action generated charges from the Soviet Union that the US was more concerned with its own global expansion than with nuclear non-proliferation.[119]

Both the Soviet Union and Pakistan were conducting two-pronged policy strategies *vis-à-vis* one another. Pakistan tried to increase international support among the Islamic countries and the United States while not directly provoking the USSR. The USSR, on the other hand, waged a campaign of vitriolic attacks against the Zia regime, blasting its policies of assisting the refugees, arming the mujaheddin, dealing with the US and the Chinese, and cracking down on its domestic political opposition. At the same time, the Soviet Union attempted to carry on comparatively normal diplomatic and economic relations with Zia's government. The USSR realised that Pakistan's participation in international negotiations would be essential to end the Afghan situation.

Therefore, from 1980 to 1985, the USSR and Pakistan signed economic agreements, calling for increases in trade of from 10 to 25%. While total Soviet–Pakistan trade turnover did fall between 1980 and 1985, the drop was not as dramatic as Soviet rhetoric might indicate.[120] Indeed, the USSR accounted for 2.5% of all Pakistan's exports, up from 1.6% in 1980.[121] What is particularly interesting is the composition of the USSR's trade with Pakistan: Soviet exports exceeded imports three-fold in the early 1980s. Moreover, unlike in the Indian case, in

Pakistan, the USSR had been able to continue its preferred pattern of selling machinery and equipment to its South Asian trade partner while receiving agricultural products and semi-manufactured goods. The Soviet Union, however, was not merely exploiting Pakistan's desire to avoid confrontation with a militarily superior power. The USSR actually stepped up its economic aid to Pakistan during this period.

Moscow offered an economic assistance package in 1981, which Pakistan turned down in order to accept the more substantial American deal, containing military aid; however, Moscow and Islamabad maintained their dialogue.[122] Nonetheless, smaller agreements were made such as the April, 1980 contract with a private company for the joint manufacture of tractors for which the USSR offered a $20 million credit.[123] In November, 1981, the Soviet Ambassador to Pakistan, V. S. Smirnov, announced that the USSR was ready to provide financial and technical assistance to set up export-oriented industries.[124] This was followed in December by the opening of the Guddu thermal power station which had been built with Soviet assistance. Probably most surprising was Smirnov's offer in May, 1981, for Soviet aid to build a nuclear power plant.[125] Agreements were also signed in 1983 for the purchase of Soviet oil drilling equipment and for the construction of the Multan power plant and a prefabricated housing plant to be built near Karachi.[126] Reports circulated in 1982 that the USSR would withdraw support for certain projects if the Pakistani government did not alter its policies towards Afghanistan, requiring a denial of these rumors by the Soviet deputy ambassador in Pakistan.[127] The most prominent Soviet-built project, the Karachi steel works, was, however, uneventfully completed on schedule and inaugurated in 1983.[128]

The USSR then was content to chastise Pakistan publicly while continuing to maintain a working relationship privately. Although this policy had begun to take effect in 1981, it really came to the fore with the ascent of Iurii Andropov who surprised India and others by warmly receiving Zia in Moscow during his visit for Brezhnev's funeral. There are several reasons for Soviet willingness to offer both carrot and stick to Pakistan, and these basically revolved around Soviet aims to maintain its own influence in the region (and if possible, to regain influence in the Third World more generally) and to limit US and Chinese influence. (1) Pakistan had reaped the goodwill of the international community during the Afghan fiasco and with its moves to obtain a UN-negotiated settlement in 1981, it was difficult to successfully discredit. (2) Pakistan's participation in the negotiations was a foregone conclusion, but it had expressed a preference for a coalition government that would give representation to the refugees while allowing the USSR a graceful means to leave Afghanistan. Pakistan's flexibility during negotiations might prove invaluable. (3) Although the Soviet government, like the Indian, was concerned about Pakistan's acquisition of F-16s and its seemingly unshakable commitment to maintaining a nuclear option, by using the dual approach with Islamabad, Moscow hoped to keep open lines of communication and to dissuade Pakistan from making any rash moves. (4) China remained one of Pakistan's staunchest supporters. Thus, the Washington-Moscow-Islamabad-Delhi-Beijing tangle was still very much an operative force in the region. (5) The early 1980s saw the renewed efforts at a normalization of Indian–Pakistani relations. By 1981–82, Zia's "no-war" proposal had pushed Mrs. Gandhi to accept the establishment of the bilateral commission and to counter with an offer of her own: a peace and friendship treaty. While Zia backed away from the Indian Prime Minister on the treaty and tensions still existed, the prospects for continued normalization remained, particularly through the South Asian Association for Regional Cooperation.

The USSR and the periphery – Bangladesh, Nepal, and Sri Lanka. The basic lines of Soviet policy in the peripheral countries of Bangladesh, Nepal, and Sri Lanka had been laid down in the 1960s and 1970s. Nepal, a monarchy, and Sri Lanka, a country whose foreign policy had often favored the West, were tangential to the USSR's concerns in South Asia – the India–Pakistan rivalry. The USSR had initially tried to cultivate a close relationship with Bangladesh, whose national liberation it had supported, but ran into problems with Bangladeshi domestic politics and Indian aspirations as regional great power. In all three countries, the USSR's policy was constrained by its having made India the centerpiece of its regional policy, although the USSR enjoyed friendly relations with all three countries.

There were no dramatic shifts in foreign or domestic policy in any of the countries in the 1980s that would have warranted a Soviet reappraisal of its limited objectives. Similarly, Bangladesh, Nepal, and Sri Lanka had few incentives to reorder their relations with the USSR. Thus, Soviet ties with the periphery after Afghanistan experienced no fundamental reorientation. All three peripheral countries had been developing their relations with China, with Bangladesh and Sri Lanka receiving weapons systems from Beijing in the 1980s. The invasion neither drove them further into the arms of the Chinese nor did it substantially alter the development of those relations. However, the invasion was strenuously objected to by all three countries (and of course, China), and at least in the cases of Bangladesh and Sri Lanka, there was a deterioration of relations with the USSR in the 1980s. Whether it was due to Indian interests in her smaller neighbors or to the growing Chinese presence in all three countries, the USSR seemed interested in recouping its position. Unlike in Pakistan, however, it was unwilling to use the economic instrument extensively to curry favor in the periphery.

That the peripheral South Asian countries were opposed to Soviet troops in Afghanistan had been made eminently clear. Each saw the invasion as a destabilizing event for South Asia and were not averse to making their position known to the USSR. During an April visit to Kathmandu of Deputy Foreign Minister Firiubin, for example, Nepal protested the Soviet intervention and insisted on immediate Soviet troop withdrawal.[129] While Nepal's bluntness was notable, Bangladesh was perhaps the most vociferous in its criticism of the USSR's action. As a Muslim nation Bangladesh saw the invasion as a step against Islam, but as a tiny state overlooked by India and China, it also was troubled by the implications for small, weak states elsewhere of the USSR's intervention.

As with India and Pakistan, the Soviet intervention did not substantially alter on-going ties. In February, 1980, the conservative regime of J. R. Jayewardene allowed the Soviet destroyer *Marshal Voroshilov* to dock in Colombo for several days, and in the fall of that year, a parliamentary delegation visited the USSR for discussions on regional and bilateral issues. Similarly, Bangladesh which had been receiving a lot of criticism in the Soviet press for its treatment of political opposition, particularly the Bangladeshi Communist Party, signed an agreement to acquire 40,000 tons of high speed diesel fuel from the USSR.[130] Indeed, the 1980s witnessed a substantial increase in Soviet trade with Bangladesh, rising from 53.7 million rubles worth in 1980 to 76.4 million rubles in 1985.[131]

But Soviet–Bangladeshi relations would suffer a setback in 1981. Ziaur Rahman was killed in May, leaving a confused situation in Dacca. In June, Bangladesh charged that it had discovered Soviet embassy personnel smuggling boxes of sophisticated electronic radio equipment into Bangladesh.[132] The situation prompted the unstable regime in Dacca, already fearful of Soviet motives after Afghanistan, to reevaluate Soviet embassy activities in Bangladesh. The USSR's aid offer to construct a thermal power station at Ghorasal and Soviet drilling for natural gas at Kamtha, however, helped maintain the continuity of Soviet–Bangladeshi relations as did the consolidation of power by General Ershad. But Ershad did not prove to be any more sympathetic to the Bangladeshi left than Rahman had, and his regime continued to build a foreign policy oriented more towards China and the West than toward Moscow. Another setback came in April, 1982, when the Ershad regime expelled two members of the Soviet embassy staff.

Suspicions about the role of the Soviet embassy in Dacca continued to grow. Bangladesh then ordered the expulsion of a number of Soviet diplomats under charges of espionage. While the USSR denied the charges and protested the expulsion, the Soviet press was uncharacteristically quiet about the entire matter. Indeed, the rift lasted through 1984, with 1985 bringing a warming of Soviet–Bangladeshi relations. Deputy Chief Marshal Law Administrator Sultan Ahmad went to Moscow for the funeral of Konstantin Chernenko and was told that the USSR was interested in improving relations with Bangladesh. In April of 1985, the USSR extended a credit of $82 million for electric power development and a barter agreement providing for the Soviet acquisition of Bangladeshi jute and other commodities for Soviet machinery and equipment was signed.[133]

If the USSR's relations with Bangladesh were particularly difficult to manage in the early 1980s, the Soviet Union's Sri Lanka policy appeared more successful. Sri Lanka had continued to oppose the Soviet intervention in Afghanistan, but like other countries of the region, it would not allow Afghanistan alone to alter substantially its ties with a superpower. Trade between the two countries showed a small increase, from 30.3 million rubles worth in 1980 to 38.1 million rubles in 1985.[134] Soviet trade accounted for only 0.3% of Sri Lanka's imports by 1984 but for 4.4% of her exports.[135] In February of 1982, Sri Lanka and the USSR signed a shipping agreement granting one another most favored nation status. Even though the two countries did not have extensive trade ties, economic relations were solid.

In the political/diplomatic arena, relations at first appeared smooth. In addition to the parliamentary delegation that visited Moscow in 1980, Foreign Minister Shahul Hameed went to Moscow in April, 1982, for meetings with Tikhonov and Gromyko. Despite the fact that Sri Lanka was no longer ruled by Mrs. Bandaranaike and a left coalition, the USSR had no government-imposed difficulties in maintaining ties with the Communist Party in Sri Lanka (at least prior to the 1983 communal riots when they were banned). Except for some Soviet criticism over the fact that Colombo considered allowing Deutsche Welle and Voice of America to set up stations in Sri Lanka;[136]

diplomatic/political relations, in short, were normal. It was not until 1983, with the outbreak of rioting by Sinhalese and Tamils, that Soviet–Sri Lankan relations took a real downturn. In September of that year, the government banned a number of left-wing parties, charging that they had incited the rioting. The Soviet Union quickly noted that the banning was unjustified since the Sri Lanka Communist Party had consistently opposed Tamil demands for a separate homeland.[137] Bilateral relations deteriorated as Jayewardene's government hinted that it thought the USSR (and the force of international socialism) partly responsible for the situation.

But the USSR was not Sri Lanka's concern in the mid-1980s. The Liberation Tigers of Tamil Eelam (LTTE) were becoming stronger and were waging a successful battle against the poorly trained and armed government troops. Secondly, the continuing violence, which bred retribution in the form of communal riots, took its toll on the support of the civilian population for the Jayewardene government. Many Sinhalese believed the government was too soft on the Tamil terrorists and too willing to listen to the political demands of Tamil malcontents. The Tamil civilian population, on the other hand, became ever more aware that the government was either unwilling or unable to protect them from the wrath of Sinhalese militants. In short, Sri Lanka was becoming increasingly polarized by the Tamil–Sinhalese rift.

Against this domestic turmoil was the growing tension between Colombo and Delhi. The Tamil Tigers were known to be based in Tamil Nadu, a Tamil state in South India that gave them protection from Sri Lankan forces but relatively easy access to northern Tamil areas of Sri Lanka. Colombo wanted Delhi to assist them in halting the LTTE's activities by prohibiting the shipment of arms and supplies between Tamil Nadu and northern Sri Lanka. Delhi, on the other hand, felt constrained to do this since there was support in Tamil Nadu for the plight of their Tamil brethren in Sri Lanka. The USSR, like the US and China, really had no role to play in the conflict. The Soviet press covered the state of affairs in Sri Lanka from time to time, but commentary was relatively rare since India's position was publicly against the separatist movement but its policies did little to assist Colombo in stopping it. Furthermore, the splintered Sri Lankan left held that, although the government's actions were not helpful in the crisis, a separate Tamil state (Tamil Eelam) could not be tolerated. It was not until Rajiv Gandhi took office that Indian policy and public pronouncements became more unified, with Rajiv expressing his willingness to aid Colombo in getting rid of the Tamil terrorist movement's threat. The Indian position, which would eventually lead to the introduction of Indian troops to Sri Lanka in 1987, was basically accepted by the USSR (and the United States) as the best hope for an end to the violence in Sri Lanka.

In both the Sri Lankan and Bangladeshi cases, relations with the USSR cooled in the mid-1980s, although Bangladesh and the USSR were able to reinvigorate their relations in 1985. In the Bangladesh case, tensions arose partly because of Afghanistan and Bangladeshi concerns over Soviet intentions in South Asia at large, partly because of the internal Bangladeshi political turmoil in the 1980s, and partly because of Soviet actions in Bangladesh itself. With Sri Lanka, the deterioration could be attributed less to the Soviet intervention, rather it was a product of Sri Lanka's ethnic strife and the resulting political instability.

Unlike the other peripheral nations, Nepal suffered no comparable internal crisis, and as a result, Soviet–Nepalese relations were notable only because they were so uneventful. Other than an occasional official visit (such as that by a Soviet delegation led by Kuznetsov in December of 1981), which usually had no significant outcome, Soviet–Nepalese relations were marked only by the ordinary contacts of the Soviet embassy. Soviet trade with Nepal increased from 14.4 million rubles worth in 1980 to 20.9 million rubles in 1985.[138] Soviet trade accounted for less than one percent of Nepal's imports and 2.3% of her exports, about the same as with Pakistan. But in Nepal's case this was actually a substantial drop-off from 1980 when the USSR accounted for 6.9% of imports and 14.2% of exports.[139] This was probably not due to any conscious move on Nepal's part to punish the USSR for its Afghan invasion but to Nepal's developing economic relations with China, the USSR's reluctance to part with so much of its oil to South Asia, and the drop in prices of certain commodities exported by Nepal.

Nepal's foreign relations, to a greater degree than those of either Bangladesh or Sri Lanka, still very much depended on the Sino-Indian factor. Despite the establishment of the SAARC, which Nepal wholeheartedly supported, Nepal's primary interest was in protecting its security through balancing its ties with both Asian superpowers.[140] In an effort to ensure its security, Nepal's King Birendra in 1975 proposed that Nepal be declared a zone of peace. The idea was endorsed by seventy countries, including China and the US, but the most important endorsement, that of India, had yet to be obtained.[141] Mrs. Gandhi had consistently opposed the concept, questioning who was threatening Nepal's security that this zone would be necessary.[142]

The USSR, taking India's position on the zone, argued that converting a small country like Nepal into a zone of peace would have no tangible effect.[143] Rajiv Gandhi, who tried to cultivate India's relations in the region, was more conciliatory towards the idea, although he did not endorse it.

Conclusion: The aftermath of Afghanistan and the emergence of the SAARC

The period 1978–85 witnessed the expanded use of the military instrument to secure Soviet policy objectives in South Asia, most particularly in Afghanistan and India. Soviet relations with most of the countries of the region were hurt by the intervention. However, as W. Raymond Duncan and Carol McGiffert Ekedahl point out:

> the Soviet invasion of Afghanistan marked the end of Moscow's era of greatest expansion. On the one hand, the invasion seemed a benchmark of Moscow's dynamic forward movement, positioning it for further adventures in South Asia and a possible drive toward the Persian Gulf. On the other, by demonstrating the need to invade in order to maintain a Marxist–Leninist government in power, it revealed the frailty of the Communist model and set the tone for the 1980s – a decade in which Moscow struggled to maintain its established positions.[144]

During the 1980s, the USSR was less inclined to use the economic instrument to improve its position with the smaller countries of the region or to encourage the development of the state sector in those countries. Indeed, with the regime changes in Bangladesh, Pakistan, and Sri Lanka in the mid to late-1970s, there was less commitment on the part of those countries even to use the rhetoric of socialist development. In India, too, in the early 1980s the mood began to change, and there was greater interest in the development of the private sector. The USSR, while never rejecting the contributions of the state sector in India, began to accept some of the advantages of the mixed Indian economy's private sector. If Afghanistan pointed up the necessity of continued vigilance in maintaining a favorable correlation of forces, socioeconomic conditions in South Asia also mandated the adoption of a more flexible and realistic approach to Soviet policy.

The Soviet invasion was not a sufficiently significant event to any of the countries of South Asia to force a revolution in relations with the Soviet Union. But the Soviet invasion did point up the vulnerability of the region, and caused Bangladesh's Ziaur Rahman to propose the establishment of South Asian regional cooperation (SARC).[145] Rahman visited India, Pakistan, Sri Lanka, and Nepal to drum up support for the SARC. Sri Lanka and Nepal gave Rahman positive responses, but India and Pakistan balked at the idea at first. Pakistan was concerned that the SARC would simply become a tool for Indian hegemony, and India feared that the other countries would use the organization to gang up on it and try to limit its power. Bangladesh kept up the pressure on the two major powers, however, and in 1983, the seven member countries (India, Pakistan, Bangladesh, Sri Lanka, Nepal, Bhutan, and the Maldives) signed an agreement establishing the SARC. Two years later the organization was renamed the South Asian Association for Regional Cooperation (SAARC). It would encourage regional cooperation and problem-solving in economic, social, environmental, and technological matters. The SAARC purposefully excluded bilateral disputes and difficult political issues from its immediate tasks, although it is clear that Ziaur Rahman had this in mind when he first proposed regional cooperation. It is noteworthy that, having excluded political issues from SAARC's purview, the countries of the region (with the exceptions of India, Nepal, and Bhutan) have more trade with developed countries than with other South Asian countries. Therefore, unless the SAARC acted to increase South Asian trade or broadened its mission to include political problems, its usefulness would be limited.

Soviet response to the SAARC was nonetheless cautious. On the one hand, if SAARC were successful, it would limit the USSR's future influence in the region. On the other, the Soviet Union's close ally, India, was a member, and the organization could actually prove useful in mediating regional conflict, making (often expensive) Soviet involvement less likely. Furthermore, there were important and conflictual issues in South Asia that had little to do with the basic Indo-Pakistani tension and related superpower linkages. For example, the Soviet Union, with its paucity of specialists on Sri Lanka was ill-equipped to understand, let alone solve, the ethnic conflict there. Some Soviet scholars have stated that it was better to leave such disputes to the South Asian countries themselves.[146] In the Sri Lankan example, however, that approach underlay the concerns of many Sri Lankans – that regional dispute solving would invite Indian hegemony.

The SAARC pointed up some key issues for the USSR's future policy in South Asia. What was the role of India to be in South Asia? Should the USSR sacrifice future opportunities to influence events in these countries for the sake of its ties to India? Would the USSR prefer that an organization like SAARC be the leading actor in influencing regional relations in South Asia? Would the Soviet Union be able to use its ties to India to steer events in South Asia in a direction favorable to Moscow? How would Moscow deal with these non-socialist countries now that they had created a regional organization to promote economic, social, and political cooperation and integration?

6   Soviet policy towards South Asia in the Gorbachev era

Introduction

When Mikhail Sergeevich Gorbachev was elected General Secretary of the Communist Party of the Soviet Union in 1985, few observers expected the kind of far-reaching reform of Soviet foreign policy which would be manifested in the next five years. The introduction of perestroika, however, necessitated rethinking of Soviet international relations as well. Perestroika made it difficult, if not impossible, to de-link foreign policy from domestic politics: if there were to be reform of the Soviet economy, foreign affairs would have to be put at the service of domestic economic and political requirements. Improved international stature, renewed detente with the West and *rapprochement* with China were seen as essential for the success of domestic restructuring; without these, cutbacks in military spending would be inconceivable, and without changes in spending priorities, reform would be unworkable. Thus, the New Thinking in Soviet foreign policy promoted interdependence, deideologization of inter-state relations, global security, and negotiated ends to regional conflicts. One of the most devastating conflicts in the Third World was one the USSR had helped foster: Afghanistan. In order to improve relations particularly with China but also with the West, the USSR had to resolve the problem of their military intervention. Also importantly, if the theoretical underpinnings of the New Thinking were to be carried forward, Afghanistan would have to be dealt with.

Afghanistan, therefore, was at the forefront of the foreign policy program from the beginning of the Gorbachev era. In February 1986 Gorbachev addressed the 27th Party Congress. In many ways, the speech was a traditional restatement of Soviet foreign policy aims: there were ample criticisms of imperialism and the United States, and references made to the peaceful nature of Soviet foreign policy and the need for peaceful coexistence. However, the report gave indications of the New Thinking that was to come in phrases like "comprehensive system of international economic security," and "cooperation and interaction between all states," and "the just political settlement of regional conflicts," and in attention to global issues like environmental degradation.[1] Most significantly for Soviet policy in South Asia, Gorbachev referred to Afghanistan as a bleeding wound and then continued:

> We would like in the near future to bring the Soviet forces – situated in Afghanistan at the request of its government – back to their homeland. The time scale has been worked out with the Afghan side, as soon as a political settlement has been achieved which will provide for a real end to and reliably guarantee a non-renewal of the outside armed interference in the internal affairs of the DRA. Our vital national interest lies in unfailingly good and peaceful relations with all states bordering on the Soviet Union.[2]

These sentiments were reiterated and expanded in Vladivostok in July, 1986. There, Gorbachev asserted "The Soviet Union is also an Asian and Pacific country."[3] The consequence of this assertion was that the USSR would have to be an integral part of establishing a security system in Asia, and of negotiations aimed at reducing nuclear and conventional forces in the region. Military-security relations, however, were only one component of the approach: Gorbachev expressed the interest of the USSR in expanding contacts with other countries to integrate the USSR into the region, and to develop further the Soviet Far East. He clearly communicated his intention to improve relations with China by addressing some of the concerns China had about restoring friendly relations: flexibility on the border dispute; troop reductions along the border; and Afghanistan. In particular, Gorbachev announced the withdrawal of six regiments from Afghanistan and the willingness to support a new government of national reconciliation that included non-PDPA members.[4]

These were reiterated in Mikhail Gorbachev's speech at the United Nations in December, 1988.[5] In that speech, Gorbachev announced some major, unilateral troop cuts which received much attention; however, he also emphasized the integral nature of the world economy, universal human problems, negotiated ends to regional conflicts, and other themes of New Thinking, and he recommended that the United Nations introduce a peace-keeping force to Afghanistan to assist with the establishment of a broad-based government.[6]

The New Thinking also brought about reforms of the foreign policy establishment.[7] Gromyko's election to Chairman of the Presidium of the Supreme Soviet in 1985 paved the way for the appointment of Edvard Shevardnadze as Foreign Minister. Shevardnadze oversaw the reform of the Foreign Ministry, including the professionalization of the ministry through the appointment of highly competent area and other specialists, and the establishment of new departments, including one for South Asia and one for international economics. In the CPSU, Boris Ponomarev was removed from his Politburo position and his position as head of the International Department. His replacement would be Anatolii Dobrynin. These top-level changes suggested that other personnel shifts would be occurring in the International Department, which was subsequently reorganized. However, as Karen Dawisha points out, as the status of the party diminished, the International Department had difficulty recruiting top-calibre experts, and so, many positions left vacant by the removal of conservatives remained vacant.[8]

There would be another important change in the Soviet foreign policy establishment in the Gorbachev era. As perestroika progressed, the resulting decentralization of domestic policymaking accentuated the likelihood of widened participation in policy formulation (via the Congress of People's Deputies) and decentralized foreign policy-making (via the republics). Republics began the complicated process of developing their own foreign ministries,[9] and generating foreign policy goals and strategies. The prospects of reconciling possibly competing national interests, particularly in late 1991, seemed daunting. Obviously, Soviet foreign policy would be little affected by these considerations in the early part of the Gorbachev era, but they became more critical in the 1990s.

The consequences of these changes, taken together, for Soviet policy in South Asia were far-reaching. The USSR would practice a more realistic, less ideological policy in Asia and South Asia, one that recognized the differences in the socioeconomic and political systems of the various countries and more importantly, accepted their potential benefits for the Soviet Union. It was the kind of approach that many of the scholars in the Institute of Oriental Studies, and other institutes, had been advocating for some time. But, it was also an approach that contained uncertainties. How would Soviet foreign policy fare with decreased reliance on the military instrument? Could expanded economic relations be developed with Third World countries with different economic systems? How would China and the United States respond? What would become of the Soviet relationship with India?

And most immediately, how could the USSR extricate itself from Afghanistan in a way that did not lead to further destabilization on its southern border?

Prior to the withdrawal

Against these uncertainties, Gorbachev made his first venture into Asia, a well-publicized trip to India in late November of 1986.[10] His large delegation[11] was warmly welcomed by India's Prime Minister, Rajiv Gandhi, with whom he had met three times previously.[12] Despite initial uneasiness about Gandhi and the kinds of policies he might pursue, the Soviet regime came to New Delhi with the intention of demonstrating the depths of the Indo-Soviet relationship and their commitment to its continued development. There were two main outcomes of the visit: the first had to do with bilateral relations; and the second, with regional and international issues. In the area of bilateral relations, Moscow offered New Delhi substantial new credits of 1.5 billion rubles, this in addition to the 1 billion ruble credit line extended during Gandhi's visit to Moscow in May, 1985. As Dilip Mukerjee points out, "The combined sum easily eclipsed the 900 million rubles of credits pledged by the USSR over the previous 30 years."[13] There were also commitments made to the further expansion of Indo-Soviet trade. Furthermore, the visit resulted in the two sides' agreeing to accelerate deliveries of the MiG-29, and it was revealed that the USSR had agreed to provide India with six Kilo-class submarines and Kresta II cruisers.[14] On this level then, the visit was a reaffirmation of long-standing geopolitical interests on the part of both the USSR and India.

In the realm of regional and international affairs, the visit was important for the prominence given to security and nuclear issues. The Delhi Declaration, which Gorbachev and Gandhi signed during the visit, stated that,

> The world we have inherited belongs to present and future generations, and this demands that priority be given to universally accepted human values ... The "balance of terror" must give way to comprehensive international security: the world is one and its security is indivisible. East and West, North and South, regardless of social systems, ideologies, religion or race, must join together in a common commitment to disarmament and development.[15]

The declaration urged that actions be taken to rid the world of nuclear weapons. At this level, the visit signified the on-going evolution of the new approach to foreign policy of the USSR, and (reinforced)

Gorbachev's interest in global security, human problems, and reduction in international tensions.

However, the most pressing concern for the USSR in South Asia remained its "bleeding wound." If the New Thinking were to have much meaning, the Soviet Union had to end its eight year involvement in Afghanistan. Militarily, the situation in Afghanistan in 1985–87 was one of stalemate. There had been a qualitative change in the Soviet conduct of the Afghan war in 1984 and 1985. As Mark Urban states, the Soviet and Afghan forces engaged in "more aggressive campaigns aimed at evicting the enemy from previously safe areas."[16] There were some highly successful campaigns, such as at Zhawar near the Pakistani border in Paktia.[17] The United States, however, had increased its assistance to the mujaheddin, channeling funds and weapons through Pakistan.[18] Afghan government attempts to close the border and seal off the mujaheddin failed. By 1986, Stinger and Blowpipe missiles had also been introduced, although there has been some debate about their effectiveness.[19] And there were reports that the mujaheddin had made incursions and attempted attacks into Tajikistan in 1987.[20] Thus, by 1988, as a Soviet withdrawal seemed imminent, the Afghan army was able to control the major cities, but much of the countryside still belonged to the mujaheddin.

The internal political situation in Afghanistan was also fragile. Despite attempts to disassociate the post-invasion regime from the Amin government, Karmal had not been effective in facilitating any kind of national reconciliation, and furthermore, had not been able to stop the squabbling within the PDPA. The USSR faced a situation whereby they might be leaving Afghanistan in the hands of a leadership that had failed for five years to improve its political (let alone military) viability. Thus, in May 1986, after a "period of illnesses," Karmal was replaced by Dr. Najib, another member of the Parcham faction and head of the notorious KHAD, as the General Secretary of the party. Najib's star had been rising because of his successful tenure in the KHAD, and additionally, unlike most members of the Parcham, Najib was a Pushtun. Supplementing his position on the Politburo, he had been named to the PDPA Secretariat in November of 1985, and in January of 1986, his agency, the KHAD, became the Ministry of State Security.[21]

A collective leadership of Najib, President Karmal, and Prime Minister Soltan Ali Keshtmand was announced, although this proved to be a temporary arrangement as Najib attempted to consolidate his position. In mid-December, 1986, Najib, who had begun calling himself by his full Muslim name, Najibullah, in an effort to improve his public image, visited Moscow for talks.[22] By the end of the month, he had announced a ceasefire and a program for national reconciliation, including the establishment of a government of national unity.[23] The new policies generated considerable debate within the PDPA, and in January, 1987, there were reports of a Parchami-led coup attempt. Furthermore, the new initiatives which were designed to broaden the regime's appeal and pave the way for negotiated settlement did not precipitate an end to the fighting. Without a significantly increased commitment to a military solution in Afghanistan, the Gorbachev regime could not hope to defeat the mujaheddin. Furthermore, it was not clear that even with a substantial effort the USSR would be able to stop the (sometimes deadly) bickering between the Khalq and Parcham. Remaining in Afghanistan would have cost the USSR dearly in its broader foreign policy objectives: withdrawal was necessary, as was a negotiated settlement.

The Soviet withdrawal

The negotiation process, of course, did not begin under Gorbachev's direction. As early as 1980, the regime in Kabul had announced its desire for a negotiated settlement.[24] However, Pakistan would not negotiate with a regime they refused to recognize. In 1982, Diego Cordovez, the Personal Representative of the UN Secretary-General, began the so-called proximity talks: Pakistan and Afghanistan would send representatives to Geneva, but they would not meet face-to-face. The negotiations were a painful, drawn-out process. As Selig Harrison points out:

> the U.N. settlement had slowly been taking shape behind the scenes since 1982. Each step forward in the Geneva negotiations strength-ened the forces in Moscow favoring disengagement ... By fashioning an agreement tolerable to Soviet hawks, the U.N. mediator, Diego Cordovez, deliberately nurtured the process of reappraisal that came to its climax after the advent of Gorbachev.[25]

With Gorbachev's ascent to power the negotiations finally began to make some headway. Moscow agreed that it would be willing to withdraw its troops if the United States, along with the Soviet Union, would act as guarantor of the agreement. After some months, the United States agreed to this provision.[26]

By 1986, Gorbachev had made his famous "bleeding wound"

statement and had indicated his willingness to withdraw Soviet troops. Much of the discussion in 1986 and 1987 then centered around a timetable for withdrawal and means of assuring the withdrawal. There was considerable disagreement about the composition of the Afghan government: the PDPA understandably wanted to retain control of a coalition government; the United States and Pakistan were opposed to this option. The Gorbachev regime had decided, however, that the USSR was leaving regardless of the composition of the government in Kabul. Edvard Shevardnadze, speaking in January 1988, said that,

> the essence of the policy of national reconciliation is to allow the opposing forces to shape the future of their country, not by armed struggle but by participation in an all-Afghan political dialogue, by participation in decisionmaking and in governing the country ... In our view, a constructive political dialogue in which no one claims a monopoly on power is an indispensable condition for an internal political settlement in Afghanistan.[27]

Finally, on February 8, 1988, Gorbachev announced that the Soviet Union would begin to withdraw troops on May 15. However, the dispute about an interim Afghan government continued. It seemed that even though the Soviet Union planned to leave the Afghans to fend for themselves, they would not negotiate over the composition of the Afghan government. Criticizing Pakistan's insistence, it was noted that Pakistan was still trying to link the accords to a suitable political situation, and that these attempts were simply interference in Afghanistan's internal affairs.[28]

A second disagreement also became important at this point – the issue of "symmetry." The United States argued that it would stop supplying the mujaheddin if the USSR stopped supplying Kabul. As Soviet negotiators saw it, attempting to stop Soviet arms assistance to Afghanistan infringed upon the right of the Kabul regime to defend itself. Similarly, the Soviet position was that in supplying the mujaheddin, the United States would be enjoining Pakistan to violate commitments under the accords; therefore, American status as good-faith guarantor was thrown into question.[29] This dispute too was never resolved, but the Geneva Accords were signed nonetheless in April, 1988, and Soviet troops began withdrawing as scheduled on May 15, 1988.

The Accords that were signed in Geneva on April 14, by Afghanistan, Pakistan, the Soviet Union, and the United States were actually four separate agreements. In signing the first, Afghanistan and Pakistan undertook to refrain from interfering and intervening in each others' internal affairs. The agreement specified that this included ensuring that each state's territory would not be used for terrorist, military, or other activities that could disturb the political order of the other party, and most particularly, the states undertook to prevent political, ethnic or other groups from trying to create disturbances in the other state. These articles of the Accords were obviously aimed at halting Pakistan's assistance to the mujaheddin.

Another of the agreements, the third, was also signed by Afghanistan and Pakistan and provided for the voluntary return of refugees. The second accord, a declaration, was signed by the United States and the Soviet Union and it was to provide the international guarantees for the other Accords. Specifically, the US and the USSR agreed to refrain from engaging in activities that would interfere with the internal affairs of Afghanistan and Pakistan. The final accord, an agreement between Afghanistan and Pakistan that was witnessed by the US, and the USSR, went to the question of the troop withdrawal. It is interesting that nowhere in the Accords is there any mention of the *Soviet* military intervention that brought the four parties together for the Accords. As Rosanne Klass notes:

> The documents do not, however, deal directly with the Soviet presence in Afghanistan per se. This is consistent with the insistence of both the Soviet Union and its Kabul client that the Soviet-installed regime is the lawful government of Afghanistan, and that any Soviet involvement in Afghanistan is a purely internal matter to be determined by that government on the basis of bilateral arrangements between two sovereign states.[30]

Thus, the fourth accord noted that the timetable was agreed upon by the Soviet Union and Afghanistan and specified only that foreign troops would be removed within the timetable set out in the agreement.

Several of the key disputes between the signatories were never fully resolved and so, the Accords were noticeably vague in many respects. For example, as William Maley points out, there is no definition of what constitutes "foreign forces."[31] As importantly, differences in understanding of what had been agreed upon persisted. As it signed the Accords, the United States was notifying the Secretary-General of the United Nations that symmetry would be required if the US were to honor its commitments under the agreement.[32]

Despite these problems, the USSR commenced its withdrawal on schedule on May 15, 1988; the USSR had withdrawn half its troops prior to August 15, the deadline set in the Accords. Some mujaheddin groups, like that of Gulbeddin Hekmatyar, tried to confound the

Soviet withdrawal; others, like Ahmad Shah Massud's, made no attempt to slow the withdrawal.[33] Alexander Bessmertnykh, then Deputy Foreign Minister, reported that the mujaheddin had continued to attack Soviet personnel after the Accords were signed.[34] Nonetheless, the withdrawal proceeded relatively smoothly, with Soviet troops leaving Afghanistan by February 15, 1989, as required under the Accords. The Accords allowed the USSR to implement a decision that it had taken years earlier: to get its troops out of Afghanistan in a way that attempted to maximize constraints of Pakistan and the United States. Furthermore, as William Maley puts it, "the Accords provided an indispensable veil for ignominious retreat by a major power."[35]

The Accords' main purpose then, securing a timely withdrawal of Soviet troops, was achieved; however, for those who looked to the Accords to bring peace to Afghanistan, the withdrawal would soon be a bitter disappointment. UN Representative Cordovez and Soviet diplomats had insisted that the Accords were only a first step in the process of a settlement. As an article in *International Affairs* tactfully put it, the Accords "opened the way for a comprehensive Afghan settlement," and they served to impress "upon Afghans the unconditional conclusion that a constructive search for ways to overcome strife by peace negotiations and political compromise is an absolute necessity."[36] The failure of the Accords to address the issues of governance and the right of the Afghan people to choose their government meant that although the Soviet troops had gone, the war continued.

The aftermath of the withdrawal: bilateral relations and regional developments

In some ways the Soviet withdrawal dramatically changed the South Asian geopolitical situation, but in other ways, the regional balance of power looked very familiar. Most obviously, the USSR had given up its role as a South Asian power. The troop pull-out might have left a glaring power vacuum in Afghanistan; however, the withdrawal also refocused attention on the fact of continued Indian predominance in the region.[37] Virtually every country of the region was pleased with the Soviet decision, every country including Pakistan. However, despite the dangers and instabilities that the Soviet intervention entailed, an end to the superpower conflict in Afghanistan brought Pakistan face-to-face with the threat of Indian hegemony and the prospect of reduced assistance from the United States. The withdrawal then would force various readjustments in South Asia, but particularly acute ones in the case of Afghanistan.

Afghanistan. The years after the Soviet withdrawal were both trying and rewarding years for the People's Democratic Party of Afghanistan (PDPA): the government had lost the military backing of the USSR, but contrary to most predictions, did not immediately fall. Like communist parties elsewhere in the world, the PDPA leadership had to learn to cope with the changing realities in the Soviet Union and Eastern Europe, but the Afghan government felt the impact of those changes in a much more direct way, with the Soviet troop withdrawal and the continuing civil war. The General Secretary of the PDPA and President of the Republic of Afghanistan, Najibullah, responded to these challenges by trying, once again, to promote what for many was an already bankrupt policy of national reconciliation while maintaining the tenuous political position of himself and his party. In short, while conditions on the ground in Afghanistan remained the first order of business and affected the approach of the PDPA government in its attempts to reform "socialism," changes in the Soviet Union and Eastern Europe were important for Afghan communism, and Najibullah's response was to escalate the rhetoric of perestroika in Afghanistan.

These actions were welcomed by the Soviet leadership which continued to support the Afghan regime financially and with arms. In October, 1988, the USSR pledged $600 million of the estimated $2 billion aid program proposed by the United Nations to reconstruct Afghanistan. Then in January, 1989, Foreign Minister Shevardnadze and Defense Minister Iazov visited Kabul where a continued flow of arms to the regime was promised. Furthermore, the USSR was also assisting Afghanistan through foreign trade: in 1988 and 1989, Soviet exports comprised 72 per cent and 87 per cent, respectively, of an annually decreasing total trade turnover.[38] If the USSR were to reduce its commitments in Afghanistan, a political settlement was needed.

Thus, a two-pronged attack was undertaken after the withdrawal. First, the USSR would attempt to act as a good-faith intermediary in a negotiated settlement. Second, continuing with a policy begun when Babrak Karmal was first installed, the Afghan regime would do what it could to improve its image and effectiveness under the rhetoric of national reconciliation.

The main individual responsible for the first task was Iuli Vorontsov, Deputy Foreign Minister and Soviet ambassador to Afghanistan. Throughout the end of 1988 and into 1989, Vorontsov was engaged in shuttle diplomacy with all parties to the dispute. In early December, Vorontsov met with the leader of the Group of Seven, Burhanuddin Rabbani, in Taif, Saudi Arabia, to try to persuade him of the need for a negotiated settlement.[39] Later that month, Vorontsov met with King Zahir Shah to discuss the situation in Afghanistan and to try to convince him to head up an interim coalition government.[40] There were also reports of meetings between Vorontsov and mujaheddin leaders in Iran. And in January, 1989, Vorontsov flew to Islamabad for more talks with Pakistani leaders. It was reported that in these discuss-ions the USSR continued to support the position that the PDPA should be included in any government of national reconciliation.[41] Mean-while, a Najibullah proposal for an international conference, possibly under UN auspices, was announced.[42] Several days later, Gorbachev promoted the idea in his speech to the General Assembly of the United Nations. Although Vorontsov was not able to engineer any accommo-dation between the feuding parties and the international conference never occurred, the USSR continued to pursue the diplomatic track in an effort to settle the Afghan problem. Indeed, there were reports that a secret Soviet visit was made to Pakistan in early 1991, offering to remove Najib in the hope that an acceptable coalition could be con-structed.[43]

The second strategy was to promote national reconciliation. The backdrop for the program of domestic reform and the campaign to overcome the illegitimacy of the regime, however, remained the faction-ridden PDPA. A PDPA-led government was problematic not only because of the mujaheddin, but also because of the extreme tensions within the PDPA organization itself. The existence of factions within the PDPA meant that Najibullah had to navigate a perilous course not only with the mujaheddin and domestic political oppo-sition but also with Khalqis and pro-Karmal Parchamis of questionable loyalties.

Factionalism writ large. Afghanistan was certainly not unique in having a ruling party beset by factions. In some respects the two PDPA factions functioned in much the same way as for example, factions in Japanese or other political parties did (e.g. loyalties are primarily to the faction rather than the party, political positions and votes tend to reflect individuals' factional affiliation, etc.). As Chapter 5 demon-strated, the existence of the Khalq and Parcham meant that the PDPA leadership carefully constructed membership in ruling institutions (i.e., the Politburo and the cabinet) to include or exclude Khalq or Parcham members. For example, after the Saur Revolution, the new

regime (led by the Khalqi Taraki) was organized to share power
between the factions, but as Hafizullah Amin's influence increased,
many Parchamis were relieved of their duties. When Karmal was
brought to power after the Soviet invasion, Parchamis gained positions in the government. After a Khalqi coup attempt in March 1990,
Najibullah was careful to note that the newly appointed defense
minister was also a Khalqi. Najibullah, however, worked quietly to
replace Khalqi defense offficials with loyal Parchamis, despite the
objections of Watanjar.

Najibullah's attempts to cement a working coalition of Khalq and
Parcham, however, did not obscure the depth of the differences
between the groups. There were policy as well as political controver-
sies, the most important of which was probably the issue of ending the
civil war. Najibullah and other Parchamis pressed for a negotiated
settlement, while many Khalqis believed the government ought to
pursue a military solution – not surprising considering Khalqi ties to
the army, ties which the Khalq was not averse to using for attempted
coups against Karmal and then Najibullah. Furthermore, after Karmal
was removed from office, Najibullah was faced with yet another
manifestation of factionalism: Parchamis loyal to Karmal.[44]

The proliferation of violence and coups within the PDPA meant that
it in many respects operated like two distinct parties in a dysfunc-
tional political system.[45] Repeated coup attempts revealed divisions
within the party remained strong. As many countries in Eastern
Europe were beginning a peaceful transition from communist party
rule, in Kabul in December 1989, there were rumors of no less than two
coup attempts, at least one of which was supposed to have been
planned and executed by Khalqis within the armed forces. Najibullah
arrested over 100 Khalqis believed to be responsible for the attempt.
But the Khalqi Defense Minister, Shahnawaz Tanay, went on strike to
secure the release of the defendants.

Some of the defendants were freed, but the trial for 124 others was
held on March 5. Evidence from that trial apparently implicated Tanay
and other high-ranking PDPA officials. On March 6, Tanay himself led
an insurgency against the presidential palace. Tanay was to have
orchestrated the attack from his stronghold in the defense ministry,
ordering planes to take off from Bagram Air Base (about 70km north of
Kabul). Najibullah retaliated with troops loyal to the regime by staging
an attack on Tanay and the defense ministry. Fighting in Kabul lasted
through March 8, when Najibullah's forces were able to cut defense
ministry command and control. More than 100 people died in the

fighting, some of them civilians. Tanay, his family, and key accomplices were apparently able to escape to Pakistan on a helicopter.[46]

The lust for power can make for strange bedfellows but none stranger than the communist Defense Minister and an Islamic fundamentalist who had been fighting the regime since its inception. The link between army malcontents and Gulbeddin Hekmatyar, leader of Hezb-i-Islami, was denounced by the Najibullah government in December with the arrests of those charged in the coup attempts; Hekmatyar promptly denied any connection. Similarly, after the March coup attempt, the government repeated the charge naming Tanay as Hekmatyar's contact. Many found the charge too bizarre to be believed until the mujaheddin, led by Rabbani, also implicated Hekmatyar.[47] There were also rumors that Pakistan's Inter-Service Intelligence (ISI), which had maintained excellent connections to Hekmatyar's Hezb-e-Islami, served as intermediary for Tanay and Hekmatyar, and insinuations by the mujaheddin that the Soviet Union was responsible for the abortive coup.

In the aftermath of the coup attempt, Najibullah tried once again to glue the party together and forge an alliance between Parcham and Khalq. The official Politburo statement on the coup attempt stated:

> Do not allow anyone to paint this conspiracy as factionalism, and thus by utilizing the present event damage party unity. The treacherous Shahnawaz and his collaborators do not belong to any of the previous factions of the party. They are only the agents of fundamentalist extremists who penetrated the party.[48]

Najibullah then replaced Tanay with another Khalqi, the former interior minister Watanjar, and filled the interior position with the Khalqi Paktin (former minister of water and electricity), leaving two critical organizations in at least nominal control of the factional opposition. But the persistent fighting within the PDPA suggested that factionalism might succeed in doing what the mujaheddin had not yet been able to do – bringing down the Parchami-led government. Indeed, there were rumors (denied by the government) in November and December, 1990, of other coup attempts.

Reviving the party. The PDPA in 1990 attempted to develop a strategy to preserve its political power and to cope with the post-Cold War world. The first step for the PDPA in March 1990, was to rid itself of the enemy within. Immediately after the coup attempt, Najibullah marked those members involved in the coup as traitors and expelled seventeen high-ranking military officers and other officials from the party including Tanay, Niaz Mohammed Mohmand (Central Committee Secretary

and Politburo member), and three other members of the Supreme
Council for the Defense of the Homeland.[49] The expulsions were
necessary not only for security reasons but also as part of the party's
self-cleansing. As Najibullah put it, "with the expulsion of anti-party
elements and those who opposed the national reconciliation policy,
the party has been strengthened even further."[50]

After the expulsions, the party turned to reevaluating its policies
and goals and rededicating itself to the process of perestroika in
Afghanistan. But divisions within the party remained along factional
lines and on issues of policy. It is not surprising then that not all party
members were pleased with Najibullah's decisions to forge ahead on
issues of democratization within the party and in the country. Just two
weeks after the Tanay débâcle, on March 18, Najibullah proposed to
end the PDPA monopoly on power and raised the possibility of free
elections.[51] He also issued a decree on ownership of private property.
(Interestingly, on Shevardnadze's January trip to Kabul, he met with
representatives of Afghanistan's business class.) Thus, apparently, the
coup attempt would not halt Afghan perestroika; indeed, perhaps the
coup attempt helped to push it forward as the leadership realized that
in order to retain power, national reconciliation had to succeed.

The culmination of party attempts to renew itself came in the
summer of 1990 with the Second Congress of the PDPA, a Congress
which would oversee the renaming of the party, now the Homeland
Party. The Congress opened with Najibullah acknowledging the
importance of international events to the situation of the PDPA:

> Internationally, fundamental changes have taken place to cease con-
> frontation, to revive and strengthen detente, to put an end to the
> arms race and secure disarmament, to de-ideologize international
> relations, and to encourage mutually useful cooperation for the
> advance of democracy and the observance of human rights ... It has
> left a positive impact on the settlement of various world problems,
> among them regional disputes, and has increased the inclination
> towards the political solution of regional disputes.[52]

In other words, without a Cold War, Afghanistan had no key supporter; it had to pursue a negotiated settlement. Najibullah then
proceeded to criticize the decision to use Soviet troops in Afghanistan,
charging that this policy was against Afghanistan's national interest.
Throughout the Congress there was a blatant attempt to divorce the
"new" Homeland Party from the mistakes of the PDPA: "These mistakes emanated mainly from factional conflicts and party divisions,
from unrealistic assessment of the country's objective realities, and

from the role of the party and other forces in society's political life."[53] This revitalization was applauded by the Soviet Union, but more importantly, the admissions of guilt were necessary if the PDPA was to gain any legitimacy among the Afghan people,[54] and they were also important in order for the party to push forward with political and economic reform and most importantly, to face the difficult task of competing in open elections. In criticizing the policies of the past, the Homeland Party hoped to draw members together on a platform that rejected a military solution to the civil war, strengthened their commitment to national reconciliation and a negotiated settlement (recognizing the possibility that the PDPA might lose control), promoted national interest over class interests, deideologized party politics and policies, and resolved to develop a market economy. Feeling bolstered by the Congress and holding the mandate for reform, Najibullah set off to pursue a negotiated settlement to the war, which was exactly what the Soviet leadership had been urging.

Reforming the political system and ending the civil war. When the USSR completed its troop pull-out in February 1989, the Kabul government established a national reconciliation committee to assist in the process of settling by negotiated means what had not been settled by military means. Most observers were predicting that Najibullah's regime would fall by summer, victim to its own factional politics and the attacks of the mujaheddin. Following the Soviet troop withdrawal, the Kabul regime instituted a state of emergency that would last until May of 1990.[55] The regime did nearly fall because of internal divisions, but the successes many predicted for the mujaheddin did not materialize. In October 1989, fearing a halt to arms supplies from the West in the post-Cold War environment and enjoying the departure of the Bhutto regime from power, the mujaheddin began a major offensive. Kabul, Jalalabad, Kandahar, Khost and other cities were bombarded. The attacks intensified, but the mujaheddin were unable to turn their onslaught into a victory. As 1990 progressed, it became apparent that the still deeply divided mujaheddin forces would not be able to vanquish the regime militarily, and moreover, political tensions within the mujaheddin ranks created legitimacy problems for the Islamic Interim Afghan Government (IIAG). In 1991, the mujaheddin fared better, capturing Khost in March. Despite this important victory (important for morale as much as military reasons), it was not until 1992, after the demise of the Soviet Union itself, that the mujaheddin were able to overthrow the Najibullah regime. Thus, contrary to the opinion of many experts and despite continued assistance to the mujaheddin by the Pakistani ISI,[56] the military stalemate remained after the Soviet troops had gone.

Najibullah began to distance himself from Marxist–Leninist ideology long before the Soviet troop withdrawal. Indeed even his speeches to the party faithful by 1990 were lacking in Marxist–Leninist rhetoric. Instead, Najibullah and the regime intensified efforts to portray the Homeland Party as the defender of the faith and Afghan culture. Moreover, the regime continued its strategy of using traditional Afghan political institutions to achieve political integration in the country. As the democratization theme was expanded in 1990, there was a major cabinet reshuffle in which more than twenty members of the new cabinet were not party members and the number of PDPA members was reduced from twenty-five to six. The PDPA, however, continued to hold the critical ministries of defense, police, foreign affairs, and transport, and no members of the opposition parties were included. The government held a *Loyah Jirgah* (traditional, national meeting of tribal leaders) in Kabul on May 28 and 29. The *Loyah Jirgah* retracted the PDPA's monopoly on power, approved a multi-party system, and encouraged the development of the private sector. One month later, the Homeland Party would affirm these positions at its Congress.

Talk of national elections became a focal point of Kabul political life in the second half of 1990. Having suggested the possibility of free elections in March, Najibullah and other PDPA leaders continued to use the promise of the ballot box to encourage an end to the war. Foreign Affairs Minister Wakil suggested in early May that internationally monitored elections might be held later in the year. But in order to have multi-party elections, groups and parties other than the PDPA would have to agree to the format. The mujaheddin, as might be expected, demanded the removal of the Najibullah regime as a precondition for elections, a precondition completely unacceptable to Najibullah. The Soviet Union wanted Najib to remain in power, at least in an interim arrangement, during elections while the United States initially argued for Najibullah's removal. In considering the consequences of the fall of the PDPA government, one observer bluntly stated,

> a new government would come to power in the capital, one that would hardly intend to forgive us for all the destruction and death Afghanistan suffered during the nine years of our military intervention. The mujaheddin "provisional government," based in Pakistan, has already demanded reparations ... we are talking about a sum of $50 billion or more.

> Moreover, who can guarantee that Islamic fundamentalists, who play a considerable role in the opposition's military formations, might not try to back up their demands by mounting incursions into our territory?[57]

The positions of the US and the USSR softened somewhat in 1990, with the US suggesting an interim government supervised by the United Nations, and the USSR indicating that it was not their intransigence on the Najib issue that was holding things up, but Najib's own insistence. The diminished influence of both the US and the USSR probably reduced the possibilities for settlement of the elections issue since the Afghans themselves were so far apart on the issue.

The failure of the Geneva Accords to address the political dimensions of the conflict meant that PDPA policy remained centered on the notion of national reconciliation and the prospects for a negotiated settlement. Najibullah repeatedly stated that all Afghans had a role to play in that reconciliation process.[58] Since most politically important Afghans could not or would not come to Kabul to talk with the leader, he traveled to them, meeting with opposition representatives in Delhi in August and in Paris in September. His most ambitious trip took place in November of 1990, when he set off on a well-publicized "secret" peace trip to Switzerland for meetings with the opposition and representatives of King Zahir Shah. Najibullah's peace offensive did not result in national reconciliation, but given his alternatives, he could ill afford to be impatient. With rumors in 1991 that the party might try to remove him in order to effect a negotiated settlement, Najibullah's patience may have been wearing thin.

Economic restructuring. Another aspect of the Afghan government's reform program centered on reform of the Afghan economy which was ravaged by the war. Afghanistan was so economically dependent on the USSR, it had no choice but to pursue its own perestroika. Not to be out-done by other communist reformers, Najibullah began to promulgate a series of economic policies designed to move the Afghan economy towards a market economy. Were it not for the war, this task would be much easier in Afghanistan, where there had been little communist institution-building possible, than in the USSR or Eastern Europe. Najib's reforms seem to have had little effect given the disarray, but the fact that the reform efforts continued to include close contacts with the Soviet economy, whose own reform efforts were floundering, was not an auspicious sign.

The general thrust of the economic reforms was to open up the Afghan economy to the world economy, to encourage foreign investment and assistance, and to revitalize the private sector. Although early in the year, the government tightened foreign exchange controls in an effort to conserve dollars and check inflation, later controls on the afghani were relaxed and the exchange rate settled at about 500 afs to the US dollar. Finance Minister Hakim stated that the economy was in desperate need of foreign investment, that aid and investment were some of the early casualties of the Soviet intervention, and that Afghanistan required an end to the violence and the return of the refugees in order to build its economy. To assure those refugees and potential foreign investors of its sincerity, the government passed a decree on property in March 1990 which provided for the return by the state trustee of all private properties to their owner or legal representative.[59]

Even in some of their dealings with the USSR, which would remain Afghanistan's most significant aid and trade partner, the private sector was not ignored. An agreement signed in April, 1990, provided for investment in the domestic and foreign private sector. That agreement, however, was more the exception than the rule. Close coordination and planning of trade between the two countries continued, and after a two-year hiatus, the shipment of natural gas from Afghanistan to the USSR resumed in January.[60] Despite the fact that economic relations still primarily centered on Moscow and Kabul, there were signs that the republics, particularly Uzbekistan and Tajikistan, were beginning to develop economic ties with Afghanistan.[61] The ability of the government to reform the Afghan economy, however, had less to do with its skill in exploiting the changes in the USSR or in attracting international investors, and more to do with the political and military instability in Afghanistan itself.

Although the Soviet scholarly literature of the 1970s and early 1980s had clear implications for Afghanistan and its prospects for political consolidation and economic development, direct criticism of Afghan government policy or Soviet policy in Afghanistan was not to be found until the late 1980s.[62] Most common was the complaint that the Brezhnev regime simply did not understand or consider conditions in Afghanistan. As Alexander Prokhanov wrote:

> When it looked as if socialism could win in Afghanistan one would wish to do all in one's power, even using military, political, and economic means, to bring about socialism in Afghanistan. This was an understandable aspiration. On the other hand, it now seems strange, of course, why all that is obvious today was not properly weighed in at that time ... There were prominent scholars and noteworthy

schools, and major treatises were written. Why were these traditions and valuable works ignored in the 1980s? Why were all decisions made behind closed doors?[63]

And what of the fate of socialism in Afghanistan? Soviet scholars and commentators in the late 1980s were nearly unanimous on this question: Afghanistan was a largely feudal or semi-feudal society; the PDPA regime had not developed broad-based support from the people; in short, Afghanistan lacked virtually every necessary precondition for a transition to socialism.[64] Najibullah himself stated in response to a question about the PDPA's plan to build socialism in Afghanistan, "These were flashy words used earlier just for fashion. Even earlier, it did not conform with the social characteristics of Afghan society."[65]

India. Gorbachev's 1986 visit to New Delhi was meant to set the tone for the future of Indo-Soviet relations under the New Thinking. That the Soviet delegation was exceedingly well received and that they were generous in bestowing economic assistance on India is obvious. In many ways, the international forces which supported this long-standing relationship continued to plague the region: China and India had not solved their border dispute; India's chief security worry, Pakistan, was being armed to the teeth by the United States; and Indo-American relations were still uneven. Indeed, one month before border talks resumed in July, 1986, a major Chinese border incursion into Arunachal Pradesh was reported. The inability of the US and India to improve relations, of course, was largely due to US policy on Pakistan, which of course was related to the situation in Afghanistan; the US had approved an economic and military assistance package for Pakistan worth over $4 billion.[66] (India unabashedly ignored the entire issue of Afghanistan during Gorbachev's visit.)[67] Thus, from the Indian perspective, the visit of the Soviet leader came at a most welcome time: the visit allowed the two countries to reaffirm their long-term commitment and sent the message to India's foes that the New Thinking and perestroika would not weaken the Indo-Soviet relationship. For the Soviet Union, the meeting was necessary to build Indo-Soviet relations and it served as an important venue for further emphasizing the new Soviet approach to international relations.[68] As Leonid Sedov put it, the visit "by far exceeded the limits of bilateral Soviet–Indian relations."[69]

It seemed that the same geopolitical forces and interests that had brought these two countries together would hold them together during the Gorbachev era. If the relationship at root seemed motivated by geostrategic interests, it had engendered a broad set of military linkages that also continued into the late 1980s. The 1980s witnessed the rapid expansion of Indian defense, in which the USSR was a ready supplier, and as discussed in Chapter 3, the USSR maintained its position as India's main arms supplier throughout the 1980s. Under Gorbachev, India, in addition to the MiG-29, received the MiG-35 helicopter, AN-124 Condor transport plane, the KA-27 Helix and Mi-26 Halo helicopters, SA-N-5 as well as SNN-2 Styx launchers, the SA-N-5 and Styx missiles, Kilo and Charlie class submarines, Kashin class destroyers, and Pauk and Tarantul class corvettes, among others.[70] In addition, India was given licenses to a number of Soviet weapons systems such as the MiG-27 fighter plane, the T-72 battle tank, and the BMP-2 personnel carrier. The USSR was at the ready with weapons as India escalated her defense requirements in the 1980s. That Soviet arms continued to be important to India is clear; however, their value was increased by the fact that India was able to pay for these arms through the clearing system of trade that the two countries had.

That system of trade also worked to make the USSR India's major aid and trade partner. Economic assistance had often come in the form of project aid for large, industrial projects (the earliest example is the Bhilai steelworks). As Indian priorities shifted into the energy sector, Soviet aid followed so that some of the major projects decided on in 1986 were Tehri hydroelectric power plant, the Jharia coal mines, and oil exploration in West Bengal.[71] Soviet credits to India made India the USSR's largest debtor, with a debt of 907.5 million rupees in March, 1990.[72] Furthermore, in addition to the economic ties discussed in Chapter 3, the USSR under Gorbachev encouraged joint ventures. As Peter Duncan points out, "At the start of 1988, some thirty Indian state and private companies had submitted schemes for joint ventures with the Soviet Union. Ten projects for hotels and other construction schemes to be built by Indian firms, and 125 co-production projects, were under consideration."[73] Given the extensiveness of the Indo-Soviet economic relationship, India might have enjoyed some advantage in establishing joint ventures, especially when compared with other Third World countries. That both countries valued these contacts was reemphasized by their decision to continue the 1971 Treaty of Peace and Friendship which was scheduled to terminate in 1991.

However, the relationship between the USSR and India was not without its difficulties. First, as the Vladivostok speech pointed up, Soviet and Indian security interests would be less complementary under the New Thinking. At Vladivostok, Gorbachev expressed his interest in promoting Asian-Pacific security, an arrangement that was clearly intended to include China, and not simply contain it, as Brezhnev's Asian security plan proposed. When Gorbachev raised this issue during the Delhi visit, Mr. Gandhi politely listened but gave no commitment to the plan.[74] Second, despite the commitment in the Delhi Declaration by both sides to removing the global nuclear threat, India had its own interests in preserving its nuclear program, and without a radically changed regional environment, those interests were unlikely to accord with the USSR's under the New Thinking. Third, the regional balance of power in South Asia had been and remained in India's favor, and domestic Indian politics in the 1980s acted to maintain and build on that situation. Indian governments, therefore, were unwilling to adjust their perceived security interests to accommodate Moscow's plans for Asian security and an end to regional conflicts. While there had always been differences in interests then, there seemed to be less in the late 1980s and early 1990s that would hold the two countries together.

In the economic sphere, there appeared to be some real problems on the horizon. As James Clad states, "As both countries move into the world marketplace and as individual enterprises become more important, they may have to find some new way to conduct business."[75] Neither the Indian nor the Soviet economy performed well in the second half of the 1980s: both became more indebted, and hard currency poor. With little hard currency to spare, the Indo-Soviet economic arrangement might have helped ensure the expansion of trade. Indeed, at the time of the Gorbachev visit and for several years thereafter, it was assumed that their mutually dire economic conditions would keep them together. The USSR would be able to acquire high technology goods without paying hard currency and could then resell some of those goods on the international market for hard currency: the USSR would acquire badly needed consumer goods for its own population and would have the possibility to increase its hard currency holdings. India would continue to have a market for some of the goods that might not fare well on the international market (e.g., some knitwear manufactures of low quality) and for unstable commodities, and it would receive oil and arms without putting out hard currency.

Under these conditions, the prospects for the kind of extensive, long-term trade expansion that the New Delhi meeting promised seemed likely. However, with the USSR moving in 1991 towards ruble convertibility and towards conducting all trade on a hard currency basis, the question became: what would the effects be on Indo-Soviet trade?[76] The USSR and India clearly had to rethink their relationship and struggle to find ways to maintain their close economic relations – looking for answers, however, did not require much ingenuity. As one Soviet economist, evaluating the prospects for expanded trade with the Third World, stated, "At the very least, these patterns must conform to the accepted business practices which have developed between the industrial capitalist states and Third World countries since the end of the Second World War."[77] Implementation of "accepted business practices" by the USSR, particularly an end to the clearing system, however, presaged a reduction in Indo-Soviet trade.

Economic liberalization and rationalization would likely have affected the arms trade too. Moscow announced that India, like other buyers, would have to pay for its arms in hard currency. Would India be likely to purchase Soviet weapons for cash? India had already recognized that in order to keep up with its own defense needs, it would have to export the arms it produces.[78] India simply would not have large quantities of hard currency to purchase weapons at the rate it had been procuring them in the 1980s. On the one hand, this situation complemented the goals of the USSR to convert its own military industry to civilian use, to quiet regional tensions, and to reduce conventional arms. On the other hand, India's inability to pay came at a time when the USSR (and later, Russia) badly needed hard currency and its arms exports remained one way to supply it. As Peter Duncan notes, "Pressure from within the Indian armed forces favors diversification of arms imports, but the country's shortage of hard currency continues to place limits on this."[79] Thus, there were pressures that might have lead to a continuation of the relationship; however, if the USSR were to continue to be India's major arms supplier, concessionary deals would likely remain.

The difficulties in the relationship were compounded by the problems of domestic political instability and separatist movements in both countries. Although the Gorbachev era did not begin this way, for the first time in the history of their relations, India was dealing with a Soviet Union with a weakened center and separatist claims. The devolution of power in the USSR and its eventual demise made it unlikely that any individual former republic, even Russia, would be able to court India the way the Brezhnev and Gorbachev regimes had. India, too, had long been plagued with secessionist and other movements that threatened to tear the state apart, and the USSR had been concerned about these. In *International Affairs* in 1986, one writer commented, "Notwithstanding the progress made in consolidating national unity, the struggle against ethnic and communal discord and separatism is still one of the main tasks facing the ruling party and the leadership of the country."[80] Just a few years later the demise of the Congress Party's relative monopoly on the prime ministership and the government would, in a small way, echo that of the CPSU:

> the Soviet Union and India are at a turning point in their internal development to a certain extent at the present time. Our country is in the process of reshaping society in the sense of promoting democracy and glasnost and recreating the humane image of socialism. India, which has made notable headway in her economic, scientific and technological development in the years since independence, is also striving to make these advances benefit the human being.[81]

Moscow's assessments of conditions in India and of the state of Indo-Soviet friendship in the Gorbachev era continued to reflect the nuanced and dynamic approaches generated by some scholars in the Institute of Oriental Studies in the 1970s. Attention to multistructuralism and the mixed economy formed the foundation of Soviet scholarly approaches to socioeconomic development in India (and the rest of South Asia), and consideration of extra-class factors, such as ethnicity and religion, continued to evolve in the literature.

The scholars, who had first questioned, albeit sometimes in an oblique way, the inevitability of the transition to socialism and the primacy of class in the Soviet analysis of South Asian countries and international relations, had helped to dislodge correlation of forces as the central image guiding Soviet policy. Many pushed further to deideologize international affairs. As the 1980s progressed, the writings of Soviet scholars even more directly attacked the problems of economic development, ethnicity, communalism, and politics in South Asia. For example, in the area of economic development, scholars like Elianov could argue openly that it was not capitalism, *per se*, that caused India's underdevelopment but a panoply of socioeconomic problems such as population growth.[82] Economic development issues then were more related to complex, internal conditions than to the ravages of external imperialism. Political science or politology, related to the Soviet Union naturally and also to South Asia and the Third World, began to develop since scholars finally could directly examine questions of politics and policy. Thus, caste in India began to be openly addressed as a phenomenon having political effects, a phenomenon that would persist for many years.[83] Separatist movements were not simply seen as problems incited by nefarious, external actors: two scholars at the Institute of Oriental Studies, for example, argued that Sikh nationalism was related to the issue of secularization in modern India.[84] The roots of the New Thinking that had been laid down by scholars were flourishing under glasnost and perestroika.

One of the consequences of the deideologization of foreign policy under the New Thinking was the relative neglect by the USSR of Pakistan and the smaller countries of South Asia. If the struggle between capitalism and socialism was no longer to be central to the conduct of Soviet foreign policy, there was simply very little to attract the USSR into many parts of the Third World. *Rapprochement* with China in Asia also reduced Soviet worries about Chinese collusion. Thus, the Gorbachev period can be seen as one of retraction from the periphery of South Asia.

Pakistan. Soviet relations with Pakistan, which had always been difficult, were ravaged by the invasion of Afghanistan. As noted in Chapter 5, Pakistan was deeply affected by the Afghan crisis. The millions of Afghans who had poured across the border seeking refuge from the war brought with them an arms and drug trade which crept into virtually every major city in Pakistan.[85] Communal violence involving Afghans had erupted in Karachi, Peshawar, and other major cities. The war also brought large quantities of arms and economic assistance from the United States, all of which aided Pakistan in the regional balance of power.

The position of Pakistan *vis-à-vis* India was always a concern to the Zia ul-Haq regime. As Marvin Weinbaum observes:

> Pakistan's strategic aims have in great measure revolved around trying to assure that India will not be able to sustain good relations with the Kabul government, ties that are seen to involve mutual opposition to Pakistan ... To deal with this threat, Zia and others had conceived of a fundamentalist Muslim regime in Kabul as the best way to safeguard against such an eventuality.[86]

Thus, Zia not only protected and gave humanitarian aid to the refugees, he also promoted, supplied and trained the mujaheddin. The Islamabad regime under Zia especially favored Hekmatyar's Hezb-i-Islami.[87] Through its Inter-Services Intelligence (ISI), Pakistan attempted to coordinate and control the mujaheddin. The ISI, however, had its favorites: thus, Hekmatyar fighters were provided with arms and training, and they were the first to receive US-supplied Stingers in 1986.[88] The ISI was also implicated in inter-mujaheddin fighting,[89] and it was the ISI that urged the mujaheddin to attempt a rapid overthrow of the Kabul regime after the Soviet withdrawal.

These actions prompted strong reaction from Moscow. The Soviet press routinely denounced Pakistan's leadership as a stooge for the United States:

> The military regime of Zia ul-Haq ... is becoming ever more dependent on the United States. This is well in accord with the plans of U.S. imperialism, which is striving to make Pakistan an instrument of its policy and to use its territory as a U.S. strategic bridgehead in South and Southwest Asia.[90]

With the signing of the Accords, and particularly with the accelerated attacks by the mujaheddin with the aid of the ISI, the USSR voiced the concern that the Islamabad regime, assisted by the United States, was reneging on its commitments and that their actions would cause the Accords to fail.

Pakistan, therefore, became a target of press criticism on the one hand and one of the objects of Vorontsov's diplomatic initiatives, on the other. Islamabad, restrained by the presence of more than 3 million Afghans within its borders, continued to support the mujaheddin position that they would not accept an interim government with Najibullah, and apparently from the Pakistani perspective, Soviet negotiators were able to offer nothing to move them.[91] In addition to the Afghanistan problem, there was also the question of Pakistan's nuclear development program. As noted in Chapter 5, Western experts had charged that Pakistan was about to join the nuclear club, and yet, knowing this, the United States had continued to pour in economic and military assistance. India, as the country most likely to suffer in the event of a Pakistani decision to deploy and use nuclear weapons, had particular fears of a Pakistani bomb and believed the United States ought to be doing more to stop its development; the USSR apparently concurred with this assessment.[92]

Afghanistan then had brought Pakistan–Soviet relations to a low point. With the death of General Zia and the election of Benazir Bhutto, Moscow seemed hopeful that there would be an improvement in regional relations in South Asia. Although Prime Minister Bhutto did not really alter the policies of the Zia regime on Afghanistan substantially (indeed, she retained Foreign Minister Yaqub Khan to maintain continuity),[93] there was a perception in Moscow that she was doing her best to create conditions for peace on the subcontinent and struggling against fundamentalists.[94] Furthermore, the new leadership was seen as having a positive effect on the course of Pakistan's internal development, which was viewed as having taken a conservative course under Zia's program of Islamicization.[95] The USSR, however, understood Bhutto's difficult position, and therefore, was not surprised when her government fell.

The periphery and SAARC. If Soviet policymakers seemed comparatively disinterested in the peripheral countries of South Asia in the 1970s and early 1980s, that situation only continued in the late 1980s. Given political and economic conditions in the Soviet Union and those Bangladesh, Nepal, and Sri Lanka faced, it was not surprising. The press gave very little attention to these countries, and few articles appeared even in academic journals. While each of these countries faced a myriad of problems, there were three main issues which constrained foreign relations with the USSR: ethnic and communal violence (mainly in Sri Lanka, but also in Bangladesh); political instability (in Bangladesh and Nepal); and economic difficulties (all three countries).

Coming off a period of relatively good growth in the mid-1980s, the Bangladeshi economy experienced some difficulties from natural disasters (e.g., the 1988 floods and cyclone) and man-made calamities (e.g., political instability). Food and agricultural production stagnated or declined, but the industrial sector fared better as government programs to encourage private sector development continued. Sri Lanka's agricultural productivity also declined; in particular, production of its major export-earner, tea, was down because of the civil war. The United National Party government of Mr. Premadasa pursued further liberalization of the Sri Lankan economy, although he tempered this strategy with *janasaviya* (a poverty alleviation program).[96] The export-earning problem was compounded the following year with the Gulf War since Iraq was Sri Lanka's main importer of tea.[97] Both countries found themselves highly reliant on external assistance and increasingly taxed to secure and effectively use the aid. Nepal faced economic hardship of another kind. In March of 1988, Nepal's trade and transit treaties with India expired, and India closed all but two border transit points. India wanted to renegotiate and unify the two treaties, a move which Nepal had opposed in 1978 when the agreements were first made. The effect of the border closings on the Nepali economy was devastating: there were shortages of basic goods in Kathmandu and rising prices. The government signed a new treaty in 1990, but by then, political pressures had begun to build against the monarchical regime.

The USSR was facing its own economic crisis in the 1980s. From the

Soviet perspective, there was little in the economic sphere to entice them into increasing relations with Bangladesh, Nepal, and Sri Lanka. Bangladesh received a small amount of assistance from the USSR, but Nepal and Sri Lanka received none. Furthermore, by 1989, trade with Bangladesh was at approximately the same level as it was in 1985; trade with Sri Lanka had declined by approximately 70 percent between 1985 and 1989; and there was no trade at all with Nepal.[98] The types of goods that these countries could offer were either not wanted or largely available from India under a barter arrangement.

Furthermore, each of the countries of the periphery faced acute political crises which absorbed much of their governments' time and attention. In Bangladesh, the second half of the decade witnessed almost constant political turbulence as Ershad attempted to hold onto power. In addition to constant pressure from his political opposition, repeated general strikes and demonstrations, and demands for his resignation, and communal violence in western Bangladesh, he faced troubles with India including several border incursions. Ershad's policies of the early 1980s concerning denationalization did little to endear him to the Brezhnev regime, and his 1988 call for Islamicization did not meet with a warm welcome in a Soviet Union that was trying to extract itself from a war with Muslim *dushmany* (bandits) in Afghanistan. Relations then have continued to be friendly, but there has been no dramatic increase in the tangible effects of improving relations.

Nepal had a relatively high diplomatic profile in the late 1980s, receiving visits from Queen Elizabeth in 1986, Helmut Kohl and Nicolai Ceausescu in 1987, but it was still its relationship with China that most concerned New Delhi and may have precipitated the 1989 trade blockade.[99] The trade blockade, however, helped bring about increased dissatisfaction with the monarchy of King Birendra. Nepal's government then spent much of 1989 and 1990 trying to stop, or at least slow, the onslaught of demands from its opposition. The efforts were in vain. In June, 1990, the king installed a new Nepali Congress Prime Minister, promulgated a new constitution that did away with the old (partyless) *panchayat* system, and held free elections in 1991. The reforms were duly noted in Moscow, but brought no escalation of relations.[100]

Of the three peripheral countries, Sri Lanka received the most attention in the Soviet media. This was in part due to the duration and severity of the conflict there, and in part due to India's involvement. The Tamil–Sinhalese struggle continued, almost unabated, since 1983. The Tamil forces insisted that they must have an independent state in the northern and eastern sections of the island; the Sinhalese majority had insisted that the state remain unified. The dilemma seemed intractable and was complicated by the fact that the minority Tamils had secured support and protection from fellow Tamils in the southern Indian state of Tamil-Nadu. The Indian government was therefore especially anxious to contain the Tamil problem and find a solution to the Sinhalese–Tamil rift. Finding a solution to the Sri Lankan tragedy then required attention by Colombo to the Tamil–Nadu connection. J. R. Jayewardene, the President of Sri Lanka, turned to Rajiv Gandhi for assistance in settling the Tamil question.

They signed an agreement in 1987 which was to settle the Tamil question, provide for the creation of a northeast province, and allow Indian troops to enter Sri Lanka. Indian troops remained in the northern part of the country to control the situation. With Indian pressure, the leader of the Liberation Tigers of Tamil Eelam (LTTE) finally agreed to turn over their arms to the Indian Peace Keeping Force (IPKF) in 1988, but many Tamils kept their arms. In the meantime, the opposition supported by the majority of the Sinhalese population objected to the insertion of their powerful northern neighbor into their affairs. The IPKF was unable to fulfill its mission, and the new Sri Lankan President requested India to remove its troops in late 1988.

More than any other country of the region, with the exception of Afghanistan, Sri Lanka was completely engrossed in its domestic troubles. Receiving no arms or economic aid from the USSR, and having very little trade, there was no expansion of relations between the two countries. However, Sri Lanka was interesting to the Soviet Union for two main reasons. First, except in the case of Bangladesh (and as Chapter 4 showed, then only reluctantly) the USSR had never been supportive of separatist movements. The USSR was eager to prevent a wave of secessionism in South Asia. One article in *International Affairs* stated frankly: "The main thing is that the leaders of India and Sri Lanka are working hard to the implementation of the Colombo Agreement, seeking the preservation of Sri Lanka as a territorially integral state."[101] Second, the New Thinking had argued that superpowers should not become involved in regional conflicts; instead regional solutions should be found. It was therefore not surprising, although politically naive given the political situation in Sri Lanka, that the Soviet Union approved of the Indian action in Sri Lanka.[102]

Indeed, the Soviet Union under Gorbachev saw the South Asian Association for Regional Cooperation (SAARC) as affording the countries of the region a genuine chance for regional peace and political stability: "The fact that SAARC unconditionally supports peace and security, and comes out against the threat of a thermonuclear catastrophe, testifies to its desire to contribute to lessening world tensions."[103] Even though the organization's charter limits its mission to economic, social, and cultural issues, the SAARC was viewed as helpful in bringing leaders together on a regular basis on issues of mutual concern.[104]

Conclusions

When Gorbachev assumed the position of General Secretary of the CPSU in 1985, the Soviet position in South Asia was an ambivalent one. On the one hand, the USSR had been mired in the Afghanistan crisis for over half a decade, the USSR's relations with many of the countries of the region had chilled in reaction to the invasion, and no country of South Asia, with the possible exception of Afghanistan, was any closer to making a transition to socialism than they had been in the early 1970s. Indeed, in several countries, even the rhetoric of dedication to socialism had diminished or disappeared (e.g., Bangladesh, India, Pakistan, Sri Lanka). On the other hand, the regime in Kabul, which looked like it would fall in 1979 without Soviet assistance, had been maintained in power; the USSR did not have another Islamic republic on its southern border; and relations with India were salubrious, even if they lacked the warmth of the Brezhnev–Gandhi period. The USSR still relied heavily on the military instrument in its South Asian foreign policy, although it did selectively target countries (i.e., Afghanistan and India) for economic aid and expanded trade as well.

The most dramatic effect of the New Thinking, obviously, was the decision to withdraw from Afghanistan. The decision to withdraw was clearly an admission of the incorrectness of the earlier assessment of Afghanistan's readiness for socialism. From a geostrategic perspective, the decision was a critical one for the USSR – by withdrawing from Afghanistan the USSR not only lost enhanced power projection capabilities but also greatly reduced its ability to determine the political order (or disorder) in a country on its sensitive southern border. The withdrawal had the possible effect of reducing tensions between India and Pakistan. To the extent that military assistance from the United States decreased, India might feel less nervous about Pakistani capabilities. The decision to withdraw, seen in the context of the

New Thinking, affirmed the new regime's interests in reducing the potential for conflict between the superpowers and finding negotiated ends to regional disputes. It also signaled a possible reduction in the use of the military instrument in favor of political, and to a lesser extent, economic means.

7   Conclusion

In some ways, Soviet policy in South Asia in the early 1990s appeared remarkably similar to its policy in the early 1970s. The USSR continued to have close ties to India and Afghanistan; relations with Pakistan were very tense; and there were cordial but limited relations with the peripheral countries of Bangladesh, Nepal, Sri Lanka. Furthermore, with the Soviet withdrawal from Afghanistan, the regional balance of power looked very much as it did in 1971, with India as the regional power. Yet, there were enormous changes, in the countries of the region, and most significantly, in the Soviet Union itself and its conduct of foreign policy. Soviet views of the regional environment and its capabilities in that environment changed. This study has attempted to explain the consistency and change in Soviet policy in South Asia through an examination of the evolving Soviet views, policy objectives, and behavior in South Asia.

Perceptions

This study has suggested that there was a fundamental shift in the perceptual framework not only of academics but also of Soviet policymakers in the mid to late-1980s (coincident with Gorbachev's coming to power) and that some of the roots of that shift can be seen in analyses of the Third World (and South Asia) in the 1970s and early 1980s. In the 1970–85 period several factors influenced the Soviet view of South Asia and the Third World. The first was the Soviet view of the relationship between the forces of world socialism and world capitalism, that is the global correlation of forces, and how the Third World fitted into that relationship. While many Soviet analysts saw an international environment that was interdependent, the struggle between socialism and capitalism persisted.[1] Third World national liberation movements were seen as an important part of the struggle against

178

capitalism. In shifting from a phase of fighting for political independence to economic independence, national liberation movements' successes in countering imperialism slowed as imperialism retrenched and mustered its considerable economic resources to maintain control.[2] States like Pakistan which maintained close political and military alliances with the West after independence were seen as having betrayed the national liberation movement.[3] "Newly independent states" like India which practiced neutralism in foreign policy or, preferably, developed close ties with Moscow were considered to be striking a blow against imperialism despite the continued development of capitalism within their own borders.[4]

It is not difficult to see how these views reinforced the geopolitical aspects of Soviet policy in South Asia: regional politics reflected the alignments between the Soviet Union, the United States, China, and India and Pakistan. At first glance, it would seem that an evaluation of the correlation of forces in South Asia would have been favorable to the USSR, since India had been the regional hegemon since the early 1970s. However, Soviet analysts and policymakers were cognizant of the potential strength of reactionary forces (aided by imperialism), as witnessed in Afghanistan, and could not treat them glibly. Evaluation of the complex environment of South Asia was an on-going process. It was not merely a matter of perception rationalizing *realpolitik*, but also of perception making certain assessments of the environment more likely.

Although the evaluation of the global correlation of forces was certainly a key factor in understanding the Soviet view of the Third World and South Asia, the local situation was not completely neglected. Marxist–Leninist doctrine advocated analysis of class forces in society. Indeed, changes in individual countries had often been the catalyst for Soviet reinterpretation of the general condition in the Third World (e.g., Egypt, Indonesia, and most recently, Afghanistan). As the academic literature evolved, most Soviet scholars no longer saw the West's evil hand in all facets of Third World underdevelopment. Imperialism was still portrayed by scholar and policymaker alike as a pervasive evil,[5] but analyses of individual Third World countries took into account domestic political, economic, military, and ethnic forces (and their relationship to the external environment).[6] Through the examination of India and other developing societies, there was a recognition of the great diversity of the Third World, its problems, and their solution. Indeed, Soviet assessments of South Asia, particularly of India, were, to some extent, to serve as the basis for subsequent Soviet reevaluations of other Asian and African societies. The theoretical basis for the work done on multistructuralism and the complexity of class and production structures in multiethnic societies like India was later applied elsewhere in the Third World.[7]

The increased attention to various paths of development in the Third World, to its diversity, and to factors such as ethnicity, religion, population, and other sociopolitical forces forced a questioning among analysts of the validity and utility of class analysis and the role of imperialism in the Third World. Thus, there was greater recognition under Gorbachev that correlation of forces was a relatively blunt instrument and that in order to avoid assessment failures (like Afghanistan), there was a need for a more sophisticated, multifactoral approach to Third World underdevelopment, political instability, and the role of imperialism. This reexamination of the role of imperialism became a central concern of proponents of the New Thinking. As Allen Lynch notes:

> By raising the possibility that imperialism may not require militarism, neocolonialism, and war, Gorbachev is implying (as had Varga in the 1940s and 1950s and Burlatsky in the 1970s) that the fundamental *nature* (as opposed to its conduct) of imperialism may be changing. If imperialism can be restrained not merely by the incessant application of Soviet power but by processes internal to imperialism ... then the requirements for Soviet foreign and defense policy will have been significantly diminished.[8]

By asserting that factors other than class may be critical in understanding and formulating policies for South Asia and the Third World, the proponents of New Thinking cut the ideological lifeline of correlation of forces and opened the way to deideologization of Soviet policy.[9]

Thus, a more pragmatic, less conflictual approach to the conduct of Soviet policy in South Asia and elsewhere emerged. In South Asia, that meant, first and foremost, a reassessment of Soviet policy in Afghanistan and the internal situation there. However, the theoretical groundwork for that reassessment had occurred some years earlier, through the work of scholars such as Georgi Kim, Nodari Simoniia, and others (see Chapter 2). As the New Third World Thinking developed in the late 1980s, analysts became more direct and bolder. Andrei Kozyrev and Andrei Shumikhin sum up the old approach to the Third World:

> Instead of realistic and dialectical analysis of economic, social, and national processes in the Third World, Soviet concepts and criteria of social order were mechanically applied to conditions in the Third

World which were often vastly different from our own ... Only ultra
Leftism and wishful thinking in assessing social evolution can
account for the conception which arose and was taken up ...
whereby these countries would almost automatically be able to
embark on the "non-capitalist" and even socialist road if they copied
the administrative-command methods of rigidly centralized leadership.[10]

This kind of pointed (but theoretically based) criticism found its way
into the literature on South Asia as well. In discussing the failure of the
Saur Revolution in Afghanistan, Alexander Bovin, for example, asserts
that the policies of the PDPA regime and its destructive factions were
the principle cause of the rebellion. Bovin says, "I am deliberately
downplaying the role of foreign counterrevolutionary forces ... [T]he
main reasons why the peasants took up arms and followed the
counterrevolutionaries were of an internal, not external nature."[11]
There developed a widespread acceptance among analysts and policymakers alike that Afghanistan was in no way prepared for a socialist
revolution and that the Kabul regime, aided by Moscow, pursued
policies that were destined to alienate the masses.

More broadly, analysts had begun to explore what the experiences
of the Asian countries could teach the USSR. The articles in *Narody Azii
i Afriki* by Valentin Uliakhin in 1989 suggested that the USSR ought to
look carefully at the Asian small business experience.[12] In the area of
foreign trade relations, one economist at the USA and Canada Institute
argued that Soviet–Third World trade "must conform to the accepted
business practices which have developed between the industrialized
capitalist states and Third World countries." The author goes on to
argue that capitalism is not inherently exploitative and states that
"Western experience in directing investment flow into Third World
economies is a sound proposition, and I know of no compelling
reasons why it should be dismissed offhand in formulating our own
investment policies in developing countries."[13]

Such explicit references to the benign, even beneficial, effects of
capitalism would have been impossible just a few years earlier, but
became indicative of the distance Soviet perceptions of the international environment had gone. Soviet analysts in the late 1980s and
early 1990s were pushing the logic of the New Thinking even further.

Finally, the shifts in the USSR's South Asia and Third World policies
must also be seen in light of Soviet perceptions of their own economic
capabilities.[14] In the 1970s, increasing domestic military expenditures
without a corresponding increase in the standard of living of the

average Soviet meant that the USSR could no longer afford to compete with the West on all fronts in the Third World. Thus, the policy of targeting specific countries, those with whom the USSR already had close ties (like India) or those which appeared likely to set off on a socialist development path (like South Yemen, Angola or Afghanistan), became preferable under Brezhnev to trying to spread a small amount of benefits to the many.

Economic considerations became more significant, of course, under Gorbachev. By linking domestic and foreign policy restructuring, the Gorbachev regime was slowly moving towards the requirement that economic activities benefit the domestic economy (a trend begun in a more limited way under Brezhnev). Under Gorbachev, economic objectives became increasingly important and were intimately tied to the conditions of the domestic Soviet economy. The debate over the domestic economy's reform, the notion that ruble convertibility would be implemented in the near-term, and the recognition of the need to trade in convertible currency all would affect Soviet economic objectives.

Furthermore, domestic economic considerations placed even stricter constraints on the Soviet choice of foreign policy instruments. In the interest of improving East–West relations and reducing regional tensions, the Gorbachev regime had to diminish its use of the military instrument in foreign policy; however, it was in the military field that the USSR could compete with the West. By relying more heavily on political and economic means instead of military, the regime was ultimately laying the groundwork for a retraction of Soviet aid commitments in the Third World.

Objectives and instruments

Objectives. There is evidence of both continuity and change in Soviet objectives in South Asia since 1970. The Soviet Union witnessed dramatic changes in the domestic politics of particular countries which could have upset bilateral relations and foiled their objectives not only for that country but for the entire region. Part of the problem for the USSR was a need to recognize the instability in the area and to respond to it by modifying objectives and instruments, but the dilemma also had to do with Soviet inability to manipulate political circumstances in South Asia, at least in a cost-effective way. Although Soviet objectives and policies varied widely in each of the countries of the region, and the internal dynamics of each case differed, all five

South Asian cases point up the difficulties the USSR faced in trying to create viable policies and long-lasting influence.

For example Soviet relations with Sri Lanka were severely constrained by the anti-communist attitude of the United National Party (UNP).[15] The UNP sharply turned the island's economic and political development to the right in 1978, increasing the distance between the two countries that had been closed under Mrs. Bandaranaike and the Sri Lanka Freedom Party (SLFP). Furthermore, the Sri Lankan left was dominated by Trotskyists who were, of course, not enamored of close alliance with the Soviet Union. Thus, even if the Soviets had been inclined to woo Colombo, the political environment there was not conducive to such a courtship. Objectives then had to take into account actual conditions in South Asia.

In the 1980s, Afghanistan presents the conundrum most graphically: clearly Soviet intentions did not include a drawn-out civil war and an Afghan communist party racked with internal dissention. The USSR sought to control events through the instrument of armed intervention, but even this proved to be inadequate. The assessment of the situation in Afghanistan led the Soviet leadership to believe that a quick military intervention would be sufficient to quash the opposition and reestablish a friendly, stable regime on the USSR's southern border. The failure to evaluate accurately the depth of animosity between the Khalq and Parcham factions of the PDPA, the willingness of the mujaheddin to fight the Soviet army, the general disrepute of the government of the Democratic Republic of Afghanistan among Afghans, and perhaps the effectiveness of its own armed forces, led the Soviet leadership to devise objectives and policies whose implementation would prove impossible. Those objectives would subsequently be revised to meet the demands of the domestic Soviet situation and the conditions on the ground in Afghanistan, and it is in this reassessment that the role of Soviet analysts (outside the Politburo) could be felt. By 1985, academics and journalists had raised the doubts of large sectors of the intellectual community that objectives formulated by the Brezhnev regime had no basis in modern Soviet development theory and certainly could not be implemented in a cost effective way. Objectives in South Asia then were modified as perceptions of the regional environment and Soviet capabilities in that environment changed.

Nonetheless, some long-range objectives of Soviet policy in South Asia remained fairly constant, reflecting the relatively stable yet increasingly realistic Soviet assessments of the regional and international environments *vis-à-vis* their own interests. During the 1970–85 period, these objectives included (1) countering US and Chinese influence in the region; (2) developing their relationship with India; (3) ensuring a stable, pro-Moscow regime in the neighboring country of Afghanistan; (4) maintaining cordial relations with other countries of the region; and (5) pursuing economic relations that would benefit Moscow, if not economically then politically. The relative importance of each of these objectives, however, shifted during the 1970s. While the Indo-Soviet relationship remained of paramount importance to Moscow's regional and Third World policy, Afghanistan raised the question of border security and socialist internationalism for the USSR and so, became a critical issue in the late 1970s and early 1980s. Similarly, the decline of American influence in the region in the early to mid-1970s meant that American activism in South Asia was less of a concern then than after the Soviet invasion of Afghanistan when the profile of US policy in the region was again raised. Thus, at the outset of the 1970s, the USSR's South Asia policy was clearly focused on India and the subcontinent proper; by the late 1970s, the Soviet Union's main concerns were in Southwest Asia.

Furthermore, the nature of the objectives pursued in the 1970s and early 1980s in the different countries of the region varied according to several factors; (1) the geographic location of the country, that is whether the country was contiguous to the USSR, like Afghanistan; (2) whether the state was anti-imperialist; (3) whether the state was a major international actor, like India; and (4) what US and later Chinese interests were in the country. Thus, a small and otherwise insignificant country like Afghanistan took on great importance in Soviet Third World policy because of its location and the fact that it could pose a security threat to the Soviet homeland. Soviet objectives there prior to 1978–79 revolved around keeping Afghanistan a friendly, nominally non-aligned state with a tilt in its foreign policy towards Moscow. At the other end of the spectrum were Nepal and Sri Lanka, small non-aligned countries, geographically isolated from the USSR. Objectives there were limited to the maintenance of normal, friendly diplomatic and political relations and discouragement of a major foreign policy realignment.[16]

Short-term, more limited objectives, however, experienced considerably more flux. In the economic sphere, one of the USSR's objectives was to increase Soviet exports of heavy industrial goods in exchange for primary South Asian commodities. Most South Asian economies had little more to offer the world market than items like tea, rubber, leather and skins, jute and cloth, while needing to import industrial equipment; thus, there were few difficulties for the USSR's trade strategy. However, India was the USSR's main South Asian trade partner and her share of the USSR's Soviet trade grew after the signing of the 1971 Indo-Soviet Friendship Treaty. India's own economy continued to develop so that India no longer desperately needed to import industrial equipment; it was exporting such goods itself. Furthermore, India's private sector, particularly in high-tech and service areas, expanded even more rapidly in the 1970s than its (largely industrial goods producing) state sector. The USSR found itself exporting its precious oil in exchange for both Indian machinery and consumer goods. While the USSR would have liked to have seen a return of the days when India imported Soviet machinery, it also needed the imports provided by India's cosmetics and other consumer goods industries. Thus, by 1985, economic objectives had become more complicated: the USSR continued to push for expanded industrial and reduced oil exports, but was inclined by the failures of its domestic economy to pursue agreements which allowed it access to free trade zone products (like cosmetics) and Indian high-tech goods.

At the same time, economic objectives were entwined with Soviet military objectives in India. Since the 1960s, the Soviet Union had been India's number one arms supplier. One of its main objectives was to increase Indian reliance on the USSR for hardware and expertise. Under Mrs. Gandhi in the 1970s, the USSR's percentage of India's total arms imports reached 80%. While India was clearly an important client to Moscow, it is also true that India received highly favorable terms on arms provided and had been offered licensing arrangements to some of the USSR's more advanced weaponry. India had not become self-sufficient in arms production by a long shot, but with a large and well-educated research establishment, access to Soviet and other Western European technology, and a developing industrial base, India was in a not altogether unattractive position. Thus, when India began efforts to diversify arms supplies in the late 1970s and early 1980s, negotiating with the French for Mirage aircraft and licensing agreements, Moscow saw its position in New Delhi threatened. The USSR offered India highly concessionary deals on their most advanced weaponry, including licensing agreements, even to the then unfinished MiG-29. Moreover, the USSR was compelled to increase exports of oil under barter arrangements. India eventually made deals with both the Soviets and others. The French licensing arrangement proved to be too technologically sophisticated for Indian production and was therefore dropped, proving two points: (1) Soviet licenses were valuable to India, but (2) the USSR could not be sure how long that situation would continue. What is interesting is that the Soviet desire for continued influence in Indian military matters was no longer for geopolitical reasons alone, but also served long-term Soviet economic objectives.

By 1986, some Soviet objectives had changed. On the one hand, the Soviet Union under Gorbachev strongly promoted its friendship with India, and was not able to rejuvenate its relationship with Pakistan. On the other hand, the USSR was interested in improving relations with the West, reducing its own military spending, and easing regional tensions. A core short-term military objective therefore became the need to end the conflict in Afghanistan and withdraw Soviet troops. The formulation of this objective resulted from domestic Soviet needs as well as from the recognition of the futility of supporting the PDPA regime and the failure of Soviet and Afghan troops to achieve a victory, at the levels of commitment the regime in Moscow had taken. The USSR was able to fulfill the aim of troop withdrawal, but Moscow did not have the ability to end the conflict in Afghanistan, particularly without use of its military might. Thus, if security concerns were a motivating factor in the Soviet decision to enter Afghanistan in 1979, it is ironic that its security needs would be no better met in 1989, after the troop withdrawal.

Afghanistan also pointed up some shifts in short-range political/diplomatic objectives in South Asia. The Soviet leadership had previously looked to the Third World, and particularly, to India for support in international fora on critical issues, but as far as Afghanistan was concerned, the USSR pursued a damage limitation strategy in South Asia: the objective was merely to discourage New Delhi's overt criticism rather than its open support.

Instruments. As the foregoing discussion suggests, Soviet leaders had to adjust the means by which they pursued both long and short-term objectives. In the 1950s and 1960s, personal diplomacy played a great role in Soviet policy, particularly in India; it continued to be important to the USSR, especially in times of crisis or tension (e.g., Vorontsov's attempts to mediate the Afghanistan crisis), but other instruments of policy were also very effective. Embassy and consular staffs were well developed and trained by the 1970s and 1980s, and they helped to support the work of joint commissions and organizations such as the Indo-Soviet joint planning commissions. Communist parties of the region, particularly the Communist Party of India and the PDPA, were of continued interest to Moscow, but not necessarily in terms of their ability to transform the countries into socialist regimes. The CPSU's International Department used them to acquire information about domestic politics in these countries, to temper government positions in domestic and foreign policy, and to gain support in international and regional fora on issues important to Moscow.

In addition to these political instruments of power were economic and military/security instruments, and the use of these changed significantly in the last twenty years. First, over the 1970s, economic aid was used in an increasingly more limited and cautious way in the region as a whole. Aid was less targeted for large projects and was usually tied to the purchase of specific Soviet goods, such as machinery. Although trade with the region increased in absolute terms, its significance to the USSR declined over the 1970–91 period. However, there were two important exceptions: India and Afghanistan. After the signing of the 1971 Friendship Treaty, India became the USSR's major non-communist trade partner. Afghanistan's trade with the USSR, not unexpectedly, also increased dramatically over the period, particularly after the Saur Revolution. Thus, although the economic instrument was used in a more circumspect way in the 1970s and 1980s than it was in the 1950s and 1960s (confirming trends in the Soviet use of the economic instrument elsewhere in the Third World), it continued to be a widely used policy means in Afghanistan and India. Afghanistan became increasingly dependent on the USSR for aid and trade after 1978. The significance of Soviet economic relations to India, on the other hand, did not increase; however, the USSR was willing to use oil exports in its dealings with New Delhi.

Perestroika in the Soviet Union and the linkages between domestic politics and foreign policy, however, raised some questions about the economic instrument. Although the USSR continued to pour large amounts of aid (economic and military) into Afghanistan and India well into 1991, it was clear that there were real limits to the use of this instrument. The USSR had effectively given no aid to any other country of South Asia and its ability to entice trade partners seemed limited. The continuing transformation of the command economy and requirements that even India pay for arms in hard currency suggested that even though much of the New Thinking was concerned with Soviet economic interdependence there would be an even more judicious use of the economic instrument.

Finally, the USSR's use of the military instrument had changed since 1970. In 1970, the USSR was an important supplier of arms to the region. Afghanistan was almost entirely dependent on the USSR for arms, and India had been purchasing large quantities of arms from the USSR for several years. By the 1980s, it was clear that India was too heavily reliant on the USSR for arms, despite attempts in the late 1970s to diversify arms suppliers. The new military dimension to Soviet policy in the region was the introduction of troops into Afghanistan in 1979. The 1989 withdrawal marked a dramatic change in use of the military instrument: Gorbachev had decided that Soviet interests were not being well served by the presence of troops in Afghanistan. Moreover, the September, 1991, decision to stop arming the PDPA regime marked another retraction of this instrument.

Regional politics and Soviet policy implementation

A worldview dominated by correlation of forces in the 1970s and early 1980s seems to have affected the policy options the Soviet leadership saw in South Asia and the ways in which it pursued those options. Correlation of forces recognized the significance of the regional political/military balance of power and accepted that states with different social systems could have similar interests (i.e., in combatting imperialism).

There was a mutuality of geopolitical interests that helped the Indo-Soviet relationship to develop as fully as it did. To the extent that both countries wanted to counter Pakistan, for immediate security reasons in India's case and because of its links to the imperialist US and China in the USSR's case, they could agree on many regional issues. The USSR's interest in forming a closer relationship with Pakistan was affected by broad patterns of superpower relations and Pakistan's relationship with India and more particularly by the Indo-Soviet Friendship Treaty. As detailed in Chapter 4, while the USSR did not abrogate its relationship with Pakistan entirely after 1971, its ability to influence Pakistan was clearly diminished by its growing commitment to India. Similarly, Moscow's ability to influence the peripheral countries of the region, other than Afghanistan, was affected by its ties to New Delhi. For example, the USSR backed India and did not endorse Nepal's proposals to establish a zone of peace in the Himalayas even though it might have reduced the potential for conflict between Beijing and New Delhi. More recently, for example, the USSR lauded India's role as regional peacemaker in the ethnic crisis in Sri Lanka and offered no alternatives to Rajiv's prescriptions for ending the conflict.

Obviously, India's perception of its role as regional peacekeeper, a perception which was dramatically reinforced and expanded after the 1971 war, constrained Moscow's behavior. Ashok Kapur has argued that New Delhi organized an Indocentric power system on the subcontinent as a response to hostile foreign policy alignments in the region. This new political structure consciously sought to exclude superpower influence in the area and enable India to establish principles for regional conduct.[17] To the extent that New Delhi wished to minimize superpower influence in the area, there was a potential for collision in Soviet–Indian interests, particularly when the USSR invaded Afghanistan. As Chapter 5 demonstrates, despite this potential conflict of interests, New Delhi and Moscow managed to contain the development of an overt rivalry. Had the Indocentric power system not emerged, however, the USSR would have faced fewer limitations in the formulation and implementation of its objectives in South Asia. On the other hand, the advantages of a close relationship with India far outweighed anything the USSR could have obtained from warmer ties with the peripheral countries of the region.

There are a number of other reasons that help explain the USSR's pursuit of the India relationship and its seeming restraint elsewhere in South Asia. There was the matter of the non-aligned movement: no other country in the region had the status in the movement that India had. Although in the 1970s and 1980s, suspicions over India's close contacts with Moscow may have reduced its significance in the Third World since the days of Nehru, it was also unique in the Third World. Its democratic political institutions, its technological and industrial capabilities, its military might, and its sheer size all contributed to its continued importance in the non-aligned movement.

Then too, the USSR was still concerned with the competition of capitalism and socialism in the region. Despite the collapse of SEATO and CENTO and tensions in the American–Pakistan friendship after the débâcle of 1971, the "imperialist" presence in Islamabad was certainly more prominent than the Soviet. Furthermore, even if the United States was criticized in South Asia for its foreign policy failures, its influence in the region was not insignificant: all countries of the region relied on US and other Western bilateral and multilateral assistance for economic development, and trade with the US and the West was important as well.

It was not just the United States and its Western allies that the USSR had to worry about. China had raised its profile in the region in the late 1960s, and in the 1970s, by Soviet reckoning, China was in collusion with the imperialist United States. Its presence in the region increased sharply after 1971 since it had been the only major country to support Pakistan in its claims for Bangladesh. The Islamabad–Beijing relationship then actually improved after the war. It would seem that Beijing's support of Pakistan would preclude the development of close relations between Beijing and Dacca, but Bangladeshi gripes with India helped push them toward China. Similar fears about Indian hegemony motivated Nepal to seek out a warmer relationship with Beijing in hopes that the "China card" would help in bilateral negotiations with New Delhi. By the early 1980s, goodwill towards China extended as far south as Sri Lanka which appreciated Chinese development assistance. Thus, one of the main rivals of both India and the USSR had managed to promote its interests in South Asia quite successfully since 1970.

The Soviet invasion of Afghanistan reinforced the various sets of triangular relations, pitting those who opposed the intervention (the states of South Asia, the United States, and China) against Afghanistan and the USSR, and leaving India to walk a tricky course between condemnation of Moscow and alienation from the international community. Tensions between the three superpowers then were played out in South Asia and fed into the regional power system and the India–Pakistan animosity.

Third, Soviet policy was influenced by their views of the domestic political and economic situation in each country. The struggle against British rule established South Asian countries as opponents of colonialism and imperialism. Nehru had championed the cause of neutralism and globalism and established India as one of the leaders of the non-aligned movement. After independence, every country of the region, except Pakistan, accepted non-alignment as a basic tenet of its foreign policy; however, Sri Lanka's ruling United National Party was decidedly anti-communist in both its domestic and foreign policy orientations.

Analysis of the domestic socioeconomic situation of each country further helped to reinforce Soviet policy. By Soviet reasoning during the Brezhnev era, India presented a more favorable composition in the correlation of forces. Through her constitution, India had made a commitment to establishing socialism, Nehru himself having paid lip-service to the merits of "scientific" socialism. Like many other newly independent countries, India developed certain industries in the state sector; this was seen as a positive step by the USSR. Furthermore, the existence of a legal, well-developed communist party that participated in elections indicated that India was the most progressive, albeit bourgeois nationalist, state in the region.

Other countries of South Asia either displayed a pro-imperialist foreign policy (i.e., Pakistan) or conservative sociopolitical situation (e.g., Nepal). In the case of Sri Lanka, for example, the government was passed between the conservative UNP and the more progressive SLFP: it did not have the consistent years of leadership by one party that was nominally committed to socialism that India had. On top of the island's anti-communist stance in the years immediately following its independence, the tiny Communist Party in Sri Lanka was Trotskyist. Relations between Moscow and Colombo did warm when Mrs. Bandaranaike and the SLFP took power in 1970 but cooled again with a UNP victory in the 1977 elections. Assessments of the internal political, economic, and social conditions in each country then helped to direct Soviet policy.

Finally, economic considerations played a role in Soviet policy in two ways. First, although it suffers from desperate poverty, India was also the area's most advanced economy. India could therefore offer the USSR, under its barter arrangements, various products such as computers and consumer goods which few other countries of the region could match. The downside to trade with India for the USSR was that India could obtain oil from the Soviet Union without having to pay out hard currency. This points up a constraint on Soviet policy in South Asia and elsewhere in the Third World. The USSR could not effectively compete with the West (or with some other developing countries, for that matter) in the economic sphere, be it in aid or trade. The limitations on its use of the economic instrument meant that the USSR had to be cautious in taking on new responsibilities. The USSR simply could not afford to support the economic modernization of some of the world's least developed countries, particularly when there might be few economic and political advantages to Moscow. Having long established, extensive economic, military, and political commitments to India (and Afghanistan) meant that the Soviet Union would curtail its activities in other countries of the region.

It is interesting that having rejected the class-based analysis inherent in correlation of forces thinking, many Soviet analysts took up a kind of neorealist approach to the study of regional politics. This was essentially Georgi Mirskii's point when he argued for the development of a Soviet foreign policy based on normal great power interests and considerations. In the South Asian context, there has been a turning to classical balance of power analyses in which India is given the key role.

Two Soviet scholars, writing in 1990, state that "The 1990s are going to be the time when India emerges as a major regional power of Asia."[18] Some of the reasons given for this observation are worth noting. First, the absence of bipolarity and the developing multipolarity means the countries of the region will determine the regional power system. Second, in a kind of Hobbesian logic, the absence of "supranational structures" means there are no limitations on regional power competition. Finally, the authors note that "the regional strategy of the new centers of force proceeds from the size of their military and their general economic and external economic potential ..."[19] It will be India then that predominates in South Asia in the twenty-first century.

Beyond New Thinking and the Soviet Union

In a 1985 *Mirovaia ekonomika i mezhdunarodnye otnosheniia* review article, Nodari Simoniia commented, "One gets the impression that the authors have cast off from one bank, but have not yet resolved to touch shore at the other." In some ways, the same could be said of Soviet views of international and regional relations at the end of the regime. Some scholars and policymakers "touched shore" as neo-realists. They spoke in the language of national interest, balance of power, and multipolarity. However, by emphasizing global, human connections, the New Thinking was a challenge to realism as well. Many of the analysts who rejected both the old Soviet thinking and realism have not yet "touched shore." As this study has tried to show, however, the "casting off" was in many ways the essential part of the challenge.

With the coming to power of Mikhail Gorbachev in 1985, questions were raised about the future of Soviet policy in South Asia. Given concerns about the domestic Soviet economy and the political situation in those countries of South Asia, there was little possibility for a turn-about in Soviet relations with the peripheral countries of the region, but Afghanistan and India were not such clear cases. However, India received more credit extensions from the USSR in the Gorbachev era than ever before. The future of the Soviet relationship with Afghanistan seemed less clear under Gorbachev. A downturn in relations was made inevitable by Gorbachev's decision to withdraw troops, but the withdrawal certainly did not end the fighting in Afghanistan or restore stability to the region. Given the interconnectedness of domestic Soviet politics and foreign policy and the redefinition of Soviet interests in South Asia and internationally, India and

Afghanistan could not have expected the kind of generous support that they in the past received from Moscow, even if Gorbachev had remained in power. However, long-standing ties, particularly in the economic sphere, left hope for continued close relations with those countries.

The post-Soviet period in Moscow thus far seems to confirm the importance of the New Thinking in foreign policy and the continuity of certain themes introduced by Gorbachev. Yeltsin and his Foreign Minister, Kozyrev, have not sought to turn back the New Thinking or to dramatically reorient Russian foreign policy. Russia, like Gorbachev's Soviet Union, will continue to function as a major power, enjoying relations with the countries of South Asia, and maintaining close ties to India. Like Gorbachev's Soviet Union, Russia for the time being will be unable to afford a return to the activist policies of Khrushchev or Brezhnev, and there is little in the rhetoric from this regime that suggests an interest in doing so (although concerns about a conservative or nationalist backlash are evident). Given that Russia and its allies in Central Asia share an interest in the stability of Central Asia and that Russia is the predominant military power to emerge from the ruins of the USSR, however, Moscow could find itself the reluctant peacemaker in the region.

Although Russia is the primary successor of Soviet policy in South Asia, the devolution of power in the USSR in the early 1990s and the break-up of the Soviet Union is sure to have important consequences for South Asian policy. In the early part of 1991, observers wondered about the nature of the new Commonwealth of Independent States. If a new union could be forged from the old empire, what would be the effect on relations with countries of South Asia? How would competing national interests in foreign policy be resolved? Part of the answer to these questions seemed to lie in an examination of the perceptions of analysts and policymakers in different republics. It appeared unlikely, for example, that Boris Yeltsin and his "new thinking" foreign policy specialists would continue to support the regime in Kabul. The more conservative republics of Tajikistan and Uzbekistan, however, had different views and different interests in the outcome of the political crisis in Afghanistan. Had the Commonwealth functioned to coordinate foreign policy, disagreements seemed likely.

It rapidly became clear, however, that the Commonwealth of Independent States would not simply be a replacement for the old Soviet Union. The republics began pursuing their own foreign policies and developing their own foreign policy establishments with great energy. Particularly for former republics where this process is not very advanced, long-standing contacts with India especially will help ensure that relations continue. Central Asian republics will, of course, be particularly interested in Afghanistan. Historical and cultural ties in the region suggest the development of close economic and political relations. However, despite the long-awaited collapse of the Najibullah government, peace still has not come to Afghanistan. The disintegration of the USSR, unfortunately marked by violence in some of the southern former republics, most notably Tajikistan, does not bode well for this unstable region. Until the political turmoil within the various countries of the region subsides, there may be as much conflict as cooperation.

With Moscow no longer able to speak for all the republics' interests, how policymakers in Russia and the republics perceive conditions in South Asia and their ability to exploit opportunities there will continue to be a critical factor in foreign policy towards the region.

Notes

1 Introduction: South Asia in the USSR's Third World policy

1 This tactic, however, left a very sour taste in the mouths of most Indians when independence arrived, leaving the Communist Party with few supporters in India. See John Kautsky, *Moscow and the Communist Party of India*, London: Chapman and Hall, 1956.

2 The Indian communists divided into the Communist Party of India (CPI) which had close ties to Moscow and the Communist Party (Marxist). The Indian communists (CP[M]) divided again in 1967, with the pro-Peking elements, mainly Naxalites, forming their own party, the Communist Party (Marxist–Leninist) which was recognized by Beijing as the legitimate communist organization in India. See B. N. Pandey, *South and Southeast Asia, 1945–1979: Problems and Policies*, New York: St. Martin's Press, 1980: 147–9.

3 Naturally, Soviet relations with Bangladesh were not opened until after the 1971 war.

4 Strobe Talbott (ed. and trans.), *Khrushchev Remembers*, Boston: Little, Brown and Company, 1974: 308.

5 As another instance of the importance of personal diplomacy during his 1960 trip to the USSR, one of the key Pakistani negotiators, Ayub Khan, had found Premier Kosygin interested in improving relations between Pakistan and the Soviet Union. Reportedly, Ayub insisted that no meetings be held without the presence of a Soviet representative, namely Kosygin. See G. W. Choudhury, *India, Pakistan, Bangladesh, and the Major Powers*, New York: Free Press, 1975: 51.

6 See Elizabeth Kridl Valkenier, *The USSR and the Third World: An Economic Bind*, New York: Praeger, 1983.

7 See, for example, Francis Fukuyama, *Moscow's Post-Brezhnev Reassessment of the Third World*, R-3337-USDP, Santa Monica: Rand Corporation, February, 1986; Stephen Sestanovich, "Do Soviets Feel Pinched by Third World Adventurism?" *Washington Post*, May 20, 1984; Harry Gelman, "The Soviet Union in the Less Developed World: A Retrospective Overview and Prognosis," in Andrzej Korbonski and Francis Fukuyama (eds.), *The Soviet Union and the Third World: The Last Three Decades*, Ithaca: Cornell University Press,

1987; and Alvin Z. Rubinstein, *Soviet Policy towards Turkey, Iran, and Afghanistan*, New York: Praeger, 1982.
8 Karen Dawisha, *"Perestroika, Glasnost'*, and Soviet Foreign Policy," *Harriman Institute Forum*, vol. 3, no. 1 (January, 1990).
9 They were especially evident in what has been called by Francis Fukuyama, Moscow's post-Brezhnev policy reassessment. See Fukuyama, *Moscow's Post-Brezhnev Reassessment of the Third World*.

2 Soviet perceptions of the Third World and South Asia

1 See for example, Francis Fukuyama, *Moscow's Post-Brezhnev Reassessment of the Third World*, R–3337 USDP, Santa Monica: Rand Corporation, 1986; Galia Golan, *The Soviet Union and National Liberation Movements in the Third World*, Boston: Unwin Hyman, 1988; Jerry Hough, *The Struggle for the Third World: Soviet Debates and American Options*, Washington, DC: Brookings Institution, 1986; Margot Light, *The Soviet Theory of International Relations*, New York: St. Martin's Press, 1988; Daniel Papp, *Soviet Perceptions of the Developing World in the 1980s: The Ideological Basis*, Lexington: Lexington Books, 1985; and Elizabeth Kridl Valkenier, *The Soviet Union and the Third World: An Economic Bind*, New York: Praeger, 1983.
2 For an excellent discussion of censorship and control of print media in particular, see Lilita Dzirkals, Thane Gustafson, and A. Ross Johnson, *The Media and Intra-Elite Communication in the USSR*, R-2869, Santa Monica: RAND, 1982.
3 Golan, *The Soviet Union*: 7.
4 See, for example, Rajan Menon, *Soviet Power and the Third World*, New Haven: Yale University Press, 1986, and Mark Katz, *The Third World in Soviet Military Thought*, Baltimore: Johns Hopkins University Press, 1982.
5 For an excellent, concise discussion of correlation of forces in the Third World, see Menon, *Soviet Power*.
6 Although this theme certainly predated the period of this study, two fine contemporary examples can be found in Colonel V. Solovev, "Army of Internationalists," *Soviet Military Review*, no. 4 (April, 1980) and A. Iskenderov, "The National Liberation Movement in Our Time," in *The Third World*, Moscow: Progress Publishers, 1970.
7 See Michael MccGwire, *Soviet Military Power*, Washington, DC: Brookings Institution, 1986.
8 Menon, *Soviet Power*: 68.
9 See, for example, Colonel G. Malinovskii, "Lokal'nie voini v zone natsional'no-osvoboditel'nogo dvizheniia," *Voenno-istoricheskii zhurnal*, no. 5 (May, 1974): 91–98.
10 See Major V. Ivanov, "The Rapid Deployment Force: A Tool for U.S. Aggression," *Zarubezhnoe voennoe obozrenie*, no. 4 (April, 1980): 9–13, in *Joint Publications Review Service (JPRS)*, no. 76290 (August 25, 1980): 81.
11 See Marshall V. D. Sokolovskii, *Soviet Military Strategy*, 3rd ed., New York: Crane, Russak, 1975.

12 See, for example, Georgi Mirskii, *Tretii mir: obshchestvo, vlast', armiia*, Moscow: Nauka, 1976.
13 See, for example, Andrei Gromyko and Boris Ponomarev (eds.), *Soviet Foreign Policy*, vol. II, *1945–1980*, Moscow: Progress, 1981; Shalva P. Sanakoev, "The World Today: Problems of the Correlation of Forces," *International Affairs* (Moscow), 11: 40–50; and Sanakoev and Nikolai Kapchenko, *O teorii vneshnei politiki sotsializma*, Moscow: Mezhdunarodnye otnosheniia, 1977.
14 Karen Dawisha, "The Correlation of Forces and Soviet Policy in the Middle East," in Robbin F. Laird and Erik P. Hoffmann, *Soviet Foreign Policy in a Changing World*, New York: Aldine de Gruyter, 1986: 760.
15 As discussed in chapter 6, this was the case with the USSR and the Indian Communist Party in the late 1970s, when Prime Minister Indira Gandhi took steps to curtail those relations.
16 See Rajan Menon, *Soviet Power*, 24, for a brief discussion of the meaning of national liberation; see Galia Golan, *Soviet Union*, for a more detailed analysis.
17 Boris Ponomarev, "The Liberation Movement is Invincible," in *Developing Countries in the Contemporary World* (Moscow, 1981): 12.
18 Rostislav Ulianovskii, *Present Day Problems of Asia and Africa*, Moscow: Progress Publishers, 1980: 27.
19 Ibid.: 148.
20 See Babajan Gafurov and Georgi F. Kim, *Lenin and National Liberation in the East*, Moscow: Progress, 1978, for a discussion of the class composition of national liberation movements. Gafurov served as head of the Tajik Communist Party from 1946 to 1956 and as director of the Academy of Science's Institute of Oriental Studies until 1977; Kim served as the deputy director of the same institute.
21 Karen Brutents, *National Liberation Revolutions Today*, vol. II, Moscow: Progress Publishers, 1977: 9–55.
22 Rostislav Ulianovskii, "O natsional'noi i revoliutsionoi demokratii: Puti evoliutsii," *Narody Azii i Afriki*, vol. 2 (1984).
23 Nodari Simoniia, "Voprosy formatsionnogo perekhoda v antagonisticheskikh obshchestvakh Vostoka v sovremennuiu epokhu," *Narody Azii i Afriki*, vol. 2 (1983).
24 Rostislav Ulianovskii, *Sotsializm i osvobodivshiesia strany*, Moscow: Nauka, 1972: 412.
25 Karen Brutents, *The Newly Free Countries in the Seventies*, Moscow: Progress, 1979: 46.
26 See G. Kim, "The National Liberation Movement Today," *International Affairs* (Moscow), no. 4 (April, 1981): 32–33. In this article, Kim also makes the argument that not all countries on *socialist* paths of development may skip stages of development.
27 See Nodari Simoniia, "Newly Free Countries: Problems of Development," *International Affairs* (Moscow), vol. 5 (1982): 83–91, and an earlier version of this scheme in "Metodologicheskie problemy analiza ekonomicheskogo

razvitiia v osvobodivshikhsia stran," in *Ekonomika razvivaiushchikhsia stran: Teorii i metody issledovaniia*, Moscow: Nauka, 1979: 200–2.

28 V. Sheinis, "The Differentiation of the Developing Countries," in *Economic Development of the Newly Free Countries*, Moscow, 1983: 32–57.

29 See Aleksei Levkovskii, *Tretii mir v sovremennom etape: Nekotorye problemy sotsial'no-ekonomicheskogo razvitiia mnogoukladnykh gosudarstv*, Moscow: Nauka, 1970, and for a more recent example, *Sotsialnaia struktura razvivaiushchikhsia stran*, Moscow: Mysl', 1978.

30 Valkenier, *The Soviet Union and the Third World*: 85–86.

31 Glerii Shirokov, "Industrialization and the Changing Pattern of India's Social and Economic System," in V. Pavlov, V. Rastiannikov, and G. Shirokov, *India: Social and Economic Development (18th–20th Centuries)*, Moscow: Progress, 1975: 187.

32 See Glerii Shirokov, *Traditsionnye struktury i ekonomicheskii rost v Indii*, Moscow: Nauka, 1984. In particular, see chapter 4.

33 An example of a major work blaming imperialism for causing ethnic conflict is that of V. V. Zagladin and F. D. Ryzhenko, *Sovremennoe revoliutsionnoe dvizhenie*, Moscow: Politizdat, 1973. M. Lazarev has a more comprehensive analysis in "Sovremennyi etap natsional'nogo razvitiia stran zarubezhnogo Vostoka," *Aziia i Afrika segodnia*, no. 12 (1979): 22–25, which views ethnic conflict as a product of economic disparities and also recognizes the political content of ethnic relations. See Golan, *Soviet Union*, for an excellent discussion of different approaches to ethnicity in the Third World.

34 For an excellent discussion of earlier Soviet writings on India and the Third World, see Stephen Clarkson, *The Soviet Theory of Development: India and the Third World in Marxist–Leninist Scholarship*, Toronto: University of Toronto Press, 1978.

35 See Valkenier, *The Soviet Union and the Third World*: 95.

36 R. G. Landa, "Rol' gosudarstvennogo menedzhmenta v sotsial'noi evoliutsii Afro-Aziatskikh stran kapitalisticheskoi orientatsii," *Narody Azii i Afriki*, vol. 4 (1985): 30–38.

37 O. V. Maliarov, "Rol' gosudarstva v kapitalisticheskoi transformatsii kolonial'noi sotsial'no-ekonomicheskoi struktury," *Narody Azii i Afriki*, vol. 5 (1985): 9–20.

38 Ibid.: 10.

39 See Sergei Kamenev, *Pakistan: Gosudarstvennye finansy i ekonomicheskoe razvitie*, Moscow: Nauka, 1982.

40 Nikolai Dlin, *Spetsifika sotsial'no ekonomicheskogo razvitiia nesotsialisticheskikh stran Azii*, Moscow: Nauka, 1978: 137.

41 See Maliarov, "Rol' gosudarstva."

42 Valkenier, *The Soviet Union and the Third World*: 79.

43 See M. G. Pikulin and R. T. Rashidov, *Promyshlennost' i rabochee klass Afghanistana*, Tashkent: FAN, 1984; and I. B. Red'ko, *Politicheskaia istoriia Nepala*, Moscow: Nauka, 1980.

44 See A. N. Zakhozhaia, *Bangladesh: Stanovlenie i razvitie gosudarstvennosti*, Moscow: Nauka, 1984.

45 V. Pavlov, V. Rastiannikov, and G. Shirokov, *India: Social and Economic Development (18th–20th Centuries)*, Moscow: Progress, 1975: 131.

46 See V. I. Lenin, *Imperialism, the Highest Stage of Capitalism*, in Lenin, *Collected Works*, vol. 22, London: Lawrence and Wishart; Moscow: Progress, 1964: 185–304.

47 See A. P. Butenko, *Sotsializm i mezhdunarodnye otnosheniia*, Moscow: Nauka, 1975, for a discussion of capitalist aid to the developing countries and the role of the socialist system in assisting the Third World; see also V. Vasilkov, "Africa: U.S. Imperial Policy in Action," *International Affairs*, vol. 6 (1986), which also recognizes the need in the Third World for financial assistance from the West.

48 V. V. Rymalov, "The Crisis of the World Capitalist System and the Developing Countries," *International Affairs*, vol. 3 (1986): 63–72.

49 V. Vasilkov, "Africa": 73.

50 See, for example, A. Glinkin, "Latinskaia Amerika: Vneshniaia politika i ekonomicheskaia zavisimost'," *Latinskaia Amerika*, vol. 8 (1981): 41–53.

51 V. V. Vigand, "Ekspluatatsiia Afriki inostrannym chastnym kapitalom," *Narody Azii i Afriki*, vol. 1 (1986): 21–30.

52 See Nodari Simoniia, "The Charter of Freedom and Independence," *International Affairs*, vol. 1 (1986): 54.

53 Lev Klochkovskii, *Economic Neocolonialism*, Moscow: Progress, 1975: 58.

54 Nodari Simoniia, "Aid in the Strategy of Neocolonialism," in *NIEO*, Moscow, 1985: 77.

55 G. Shirokov, "Interstructural Relations in Developing Countries' Economies," in *Developing Countries in the Contemporary World*: 36.

56 See World Bank, *World Development Report, 1984*. No figures are available for Afghanistan.

57 Liubov Chistiakova, "South and South-East Asia: Structural Factors of Inflation," *Economic Development of the Newly Free Countries*, Moscow: "Social Sciences Today," 1983: 137.

58 See Shirokov, "Interstructural Relations."

59 See *Rabochii klass Azii*, Moscow: Nauka, 1985, particularly the chapter on Nepal: 177–87.

60 It may not be surprising then that scholars writing on the Green Revolution did not criticize it as seriously as they might have. Indeed, the Green Revolution has been portrayed as a positive force, a means towards the capitalization of the agrarian economy that could help transform the range of socioeconomic relations. See, for example, Pavlov, Rastiannikov, and Shirokov, *India*, chapter 2.

61 Soviet scholars of India and South Asia were at the forefront of some of the most innovative and sophisticated analyses on Third World development. As the next chapter will show this had to do with the longevity and closeness of the Indo-Soviet relationship which has permitted a large number of scholars and policymakers to visit the country and discuss a variety of issues with the very large and well-educated Indian policymaking and research establishments. It also had to do with the importance the

USSR placed on its relationship with India not only in South Asia but also in the Third World at large. Making that relationship work had been a top priority for Soviet policymakers for many years, and as subsequent chapters will show, the USSR had been willing to make some important concessions to maintain its excellent ties to New Delhi. That scholars, therefore, had been talking about the prospects for cottage industries and by the mid-1980s, private sector development in India for some time should have come as no surprise.

62 As W. Raymond Duncan and Carolyn McGiffert Ekedahl note, in his January 1986 disarmament proposals, Gorbachev also indicated his interest in "breaking with the past" to improve East–West relations. *Moscow and the Third World under Gorbachev*, Boulder: Westview, 1990: 88.

63 See Light, *Soviet Theory of International Relations*, for an excellent discussion of the significance of the New Thinking.

64 Edvard Shevardnadze was the most vocal proponent of this view and was opposed in 1988 most notably by Egor Ligachev. For a concise discussion of the debate see Marie Mendras, "Soviet Foreign Policy: In Search of Critical Thinking," in Tsuyoshi Hasegawa and Alex Pravda (eds.), *Perestroika: Soviet Domestic Politics and Foreign Policies*, London: Royal Institute of International Affairs/Sage, 1990: 206–21.

65 For a more recent discussion of positive interactions between states of different social systems, see Oleg Bykov, "Kontseptsiia mirnogo sosushchestvovaniia v svete novogo myshleniia," *MEiMO*, vol. 2 (1990): 5–17.

66 Evgenii Primakov, "A New Philosophy in Soviet Foreign Policy," *Pravda* (July 10, 1987): 4.

67 Rajan Menon offers a fine analysis of Soviet thinking about the Third World and use of the military instrument in Soviet foreign policy in this period in *Soviet Power in the Third World*.

68 Mikhail Gorbachev, *Perestroika: New Thinking for Our Country and the World*, New York: Harper and Row, 1988: 127.

69 See Jonathan C. Valdez, *Socialist Internationalism, Contradictions, and East Europe: The Ideology of Soviet Influence, 1969–1988* (Cambridge: Cambridge University Press, 1992), for an excellent discussion of the affects of making human interests a priority on socialist internationalism with regard to Soviet policy in Eastern Europe.

70 Viacheslav Dashichev, "East–West Quest for New Relations: The Priorities of Soviet Foreign Policy," *Literaturnaia Gazeta* (May 18, 1988), in Isaac J. Tarasulo (ed.), *Gorbachev and Glasnost': Viewpoints from the Soviet Press*, Wilmington, Delaware: Scholarly Resources, 1989: 225–37.

71 "Sovremennyi kapitalizm i razvivaiushchiisia mir: kharakter i perspektivy vzaimootnoshenii," *MEiMO*, vol. 5 (1988): 123–41.

72 See Glerii Shirokov, "Proizvoditel'nye sily i stanovlenie imperializma," *Narody Azii i Afriki*, vol. 5 (1989): 6–14; Iurii Krasin, "Leninskoe nasledie potrebnost' v novom videnii," *MEiMO*, vol. 4 (1990): 5–15.

73 Anatolii Elianov, "Problemy modernizatsii sotsial'no-ekonomicheskikh struktur v 'tret'em mire'," *MEiMO*, vol. 7 (1988): 16–32.

74 See, for example, Pavel Khvoinik, "Imperializm: termin i soderzhanie," *MEiMO*, vol. 1 (1990): 5–19.

75 Gorbachev, *Perestroika*: 124–25.

76 Dashichev, "East–West Quest for New Relations": 237.

77 See Viktor Spandar'ian and Nikolai Shmelev, "Problemy povysheniia effektivnosti vneshneekonomicheskikh sviazei SSSR," *MEiMO*, vol. 8 (1988): 10–25.

78 See, for example, *Izvestiia* (December 24, 1987), article by Dmitrii Volskii.

79 Georgi Mirskii, "K voprosu o vybore puti i orientatsii razvivaiushchikhsiia stran," *MEiMO*, vol. 5 (1987): 70–81.

80 Aleksei Kiva issues a similarly pessimistic assessment in "Sotsialisticheskaia orientatsiia: teoreticheskii potentsial kontseptsii i prakticheskie realii," *MEiMO*, vol. 11 (1990): 62–72.

81 Alexei Kiva, "Sotsialisticheskaia orientatsiia: ozhidaniia i real'nost'," *Narody Azii i Afriki*, vol. 6 (1988): 49–58.

82 *Izvestiia*, July 11, 1987.

83 Leonid Vasiliev, "Izuchenie Vostoka i problemy perestroiki," *Narody Azii i Afriki*, vol. 3 (1989): 49–66.

84 Nikolai Shmelev, "'Tretii mir'i mezhdunarodnye ekonomicheskie otnosheniia," *MEiMO*, vol. 9 (1987): 12–24.

85 O. V. Maliarov, "Gosudarstvenno-kapitalisticheskii uklad v protsesse kapitalisticheskoi evoliutsii kolonial'noi ekonomiki," *MEiMO*, vol. 2 (1988): 3–15.

86 See Nikolai Karagodin, "Razvivaiushchiesia strany: ekonomicheskia politika gosudarstva i miroxoziaistvennye pozitsii," *MEiMO*, vol. 11 (1988): 46–61.

87 Igor' Zevelev and Aleksei Kara-Murza, "Gosudarstvo i puti obshchestvennogo progressa v stranakh Azii i Afriki," *MEiMO*, vol. 4 (1989): 103.

88 Georgi Mirskii, "Avtoritarizm i vlast' voennykh v 'tret'em mire," *MEiMO*, vol. 7 (1989): 45–54.

89 See Leonid Vasiliev, "Izuchenie Vostoka i problemy perestroiki," *Narody Azii i Afriki*, no. 3 (1989): 49–66.

90 Maliarov, "Gosudarstvenno – kapitalisticheskii uklad ... ": 3–15.

91 Stanislav Zhukov, "Sfera uslug i ekonomicheskii rost v razvivaiushchikhsia stranakh," *MEiMO*, vol. 4 (1988): 34–48.

92 Valentin Uliakhin, "Podpriadnyi biznes v stranakh Azii," *Narody Azii i Afriki*, vol. 3 (1989): 3–14, and "Strany Azii – politika gosudarstva v otnoshenii melkogo biznesa," *Narody Azii i Afriki*, vol. 4 (1989): 4–13.

93 For an excellent article debunking the notion of the USSR as a model of development, see Muzaffar Olimov, "Etalon nekapitalisticheskogo razvitiia?" *Narody Azii i Afriki*, vol. 4 (1989): 18–26.

94 See Leon Zevin, "Nekotorye voprosy ekonomicheskogo sotrudnichestva SSSR s razvivaiushchimisia stranami," *MEiMO*, vol. 3 (1988): 41–51; Sergei Kostrikov and Igor' Tarasov, "Tretii mir: poniatie i real'nost'," *MEiMO*, vol. 11 (1990): 21–32.

95 Gennadi Musaelian and Aleksandr Sukhoparov, "Afghanistan: Following the Road of Goodwill," *International Affairs*, no. 1 (January, 1988): 124.

96 "Afghanistan: Preliminary Results," *Ogonek*, no. 30 (1988) in Isaac J. Tarasulo, *Gorbachev and Glasnost: Viewpoints from the Soviet Press*, Wilmington, DE: SR Books, 1989: 238–47.
97 Kim Tsagalov, "Na vesakh istorii," *Narody Azii i Afriki*, vol. 3 (1990): 21–31.
98 A. V. Viktorov, "Natsional'noe primirenie v Afganistane: novyi podkhod NDPA k natsional'noi burzhuazii," *Narody Azii i Afriki*, vol. 2 (1989): 25–36.
99 Scholars still tended to be highly supportive of the longstanding Soviet–Indian relationship. See, for example, G. I. Georgiev, "Sovetsko–Indiiskoe sotrudnichestvo v razvitii natsional'noi promyshlennosti Indii," *Narody Azii i Afriki*, no. 4 (1987): 13–25.
100 See, for example, A. Antonov, "Sri Lanka: tragediia ostrova," *Aziia i Afrika segodnia*, no. 5 (1990): 29–33, which looks at the conflict between Tamils and Sinhalese and its impact on Sri Lanka; A. Krylov, "Sectarianism: istoki i tendenstii," *Aziia i Afrika segodnia*, no. 7 (1989): 2–6, which examines the problem of inter-sectarian conflict including India and Sri Lanka.
101 See, for example, an article by O. V. Pleshov in *Narody Azii i Afriki*, no. 1 (1987) entitled "'Islamizatsiia' v Pakistane: motivy i sredstva osushchestvleniia," which makes the link between the clergy and the dominant military in Pakistan in the 1980s. See also the *Ogonek* interview with Major General Tsagalov in Isaac J. Tarasulo, *Gorbachev and Glasnost*.

3 The Soviet Union in South Asia: objectives and instruments

1 See Leo Rose, "South Asia and the Outside World," in A. J. Wilson and D. Dalton (eds.), *The States of South Asia: Problems of National Integration*, Honolulu: University of Hawaii Press, 1982: 313–27.
2 Rostislav Ulianovskii, *Sotsializm i osvobodivshiesia strany*, Moscow: Nauka, 1972: 412.
3 V. Pavlovskii, "Collective Security: The Way to Peace in Asia," *International Affairs*, no. 7 (July, 1972): 25.
4 W. Howard Wriggins, "U.S. Interests in South Asia and the Indian Ocean," in Lawrence Ziring (ed.), *The Subcontinent in World Politics: India, its Neighbors and the Great Powers*, New York: Praeger, 1982: 211.
5 Alexei Kiva, "Socialist-Oriented Countries: Some Development Problems," *International Affairs*, no. 10 (October, 1984): 22.
6 In a very direct article, a scholar at the Institute for the World Socialist System wrote of the extreme difficulties of undeveloped countries, without a well developed capitalist base, to make the transition to socialism. A. N. Butenko, "Nekotorye teoreticheskie problemy perekhoda k sotsializmu stran c nerazvitoi ekonomikoi," *Narody Azii i Afriki*, no. 5 (1982): 70–79.
7 K. Mikhailov, "Provocatory Campaign over Afghanistan," *International Affairs*, no. 3 (March, 1980): 100.
8 In the late 1980s, Soviet scholars would make similar arguments about the rationale for the Soviet intervention. See, for example, "Interview with Evgenii Ambartsumov," in FBIS–SOV–89–157 (August 16, 1989); and

Nodari Simoniia, "Looking to the Future Without Prejudices," *New Times* (August, 1990): 16.

9 On October 16, 1980, Leonid Brezhnev finally declared the Afghan revolution to be irreversible.

10 Alexander Prokhanov, "Afghanistan," *International Affairs*, no. 8 (August, 1988): 21.

11 Leonard S. Spector, *The New Nuclear Nations*, New York: Vintage Books, 1985: 11.

12 Michael MccGwire, *Military Objectives in Soviet Foreign Policy*, Washington, DC: Brookings, 1987: 184–85.

13 For a discussion of the Soviet desire to avoid confrontation with the US in the Third World, see Roy Allison and Phil Williams (eds.), *Superpower Competition and Crisis Prevention in the Third World*, Cambridge: Cambridge University Press, 1990.

14 MccGwire, *Military Objectives*: 204.

15 Geoffrey Jukes, "Soviet Naval Policy in the Indian Ocean," in Larry Bowman and Ian Clark (eds.), *The Indian Ocean in Global Politics*, Boulder: Westview, 1981: 178.

16 This objective nicely complemented the increased use in the USSR of "economic advantage" and cost/benefit approaches to international trade relations insofar as it offered the USSR an excellent means to earn hard currency from the Third World.

17 See, for example, Georgi Mirskii, *Tretii mir: obshchestvo, vlast' armiia*, Moscow: Nauka, 1976; Maj. Gen. V. Mozolev, "The Role of the Army in the Developing Countries," *Voenno-istoricheskii zhurnal*, no. 4 (1980): 60–68, in *Joint Publications Review Service (JPRS)* no. 76107 (July 24, 1980): 68–78.

18 See United States Arms Control and Disarmament Agency, *World Military Expenditures and Arms Transfers*, and Stockholm International Peace Research Institute, *SIPRI Yearbook*, various years.

19 *SIPRI Yearbook 1991: World Armaments and Disarmament*, Oxford: Oxford University Press, 1991: 214.

20 *SIPRI Yearbook 1990*.

21 See Jyotirmoy Banerjee, "Moscow's Indian Alliance," *Problems of Communism*, vol. 36 (January–February, 1987): 1–12; and *SIPRI Yearbook 1991*: 212.

22 V. Svetozarov, "The Afghan Revolution: Fifth Anniversary," *International Affairs*, no. 5 (May, 1985): 44. Also, as Marshal Ustinov noted, "the entry of the Soviet army contingent into the territory of the Democratic Republic of Afghanistan ... frustrated the plans of international and domestic reaction to suppress the Afghan revolution and transform Afghanistan into an outpost of imperialism on our country's southern borders," in "True to the Party's Cause," *International Affairs*, no. 5 (May, 1981): 23.

23 The USSR faced little competition in Afghanistan: since the 1950s, the United States, for example, had refused to supply Kabul with arms.

24 V. P. Lukin, "The USSR and the Asia-Pacific Region." Paper presented at the 31st Annual Conference of the International Institute for Strategic Studies, Oslo, September, 1989.

25 See Elizabeth Kridl Valkenier, *The Soviet Union and the Third World: An Economic Bind*, New York: Praeger, 1983: 11–20.

26 See, for example, A. Nizamov, "India at the Start of the 1980s," *International Affairs*, no. 3 (March, 1980): 14–19.

27 Even the conservative journal *International Affairs* ran an article in which it was warned that the productivity of the state sector should not be over-rated. See V. Shurygin, "India: A Time of Important Decisions," *International Affairs*, no. 11 (1975): 55–62.

28 Calculated from Gu Guan-fu, "Soviet Aid to the Third World, an Analysis of its Strategy," *Soviet Studies*, vol. 35, no. 1 (January, 1983): 75.

29 This was the case for Sri Lanka. Interviews with the head of the socialist aid desk of the Department of External Affairs conducted in Colombo in the summer of 1983 revealed that credits were tied to Soviet products unsuitable for Sri Lanka and that when industrial products were bought, spares were often not available. Additionally, it was widely believed that the USSR was pursuing an aid policy designed to benefit its own economic interests, failing to take into account the needs of the developing economy.

30 W. Raymand Duncan and Carolyn McGiffert Ekedahl, *Moscow and the Third World under Gorbachev*, Boulder: Westview, 1990: 36.

31 For an excellent discussion of Indo-Soviet economic relations, including many of points mentioned in this paragraph, see Santosh Mehrotra, "The Political Economy of Indo-Soviet Relations," in Robert Cassen (ed.), *Soviet Interests in the Third World*, London/Beverley Hills: Royal Institute for International Affairs/Sage, 1986: 226–36.

32 As an article in *The Economist*, September 14, 1991: 37, succinctly described it "Trade between India and the ex-Soviet Union is designated in non-convertible rupees and is supposed to be balanced every year. Soviet military and project loans are denominated in rubles and are repaid through the export of goods from India valued at whatever exchange rate is prevailing at the time."

33 Santosh Mehrotra, "The Political Economy of Indo-Soviet Relations," in Robert Cassen (ed.), *Soviet Interests in the Third World*: 230.

34 *The Economist*, July 28, 1990: 28. Part of the discrepancy between the Indian and Soviet data can be explained by the barter/clearing arrangement system.

35 Rajan Menon, "The Military and Security Dimensions of Soviet-Indian Relations," in Robert H. Donaldson (ed.), *The Soviet Union in the Third World: Successes and Failures*, Boulder; Westview, 1981: 247.

36 Georgi Mirskii, "The New Political Thinking and Soviet Approach to Regional Conflicts." Paper presented at the International Studies Association Conference, Washington, DC, March, 1989.

37 See Margot Light, *The Soviet Theory of International Relations*, New York: St. Martin's Press, 1988: 7, for an excellent discussion of the scientific basis of Soviet foreign policy.

38 His visits were followed in 1985 with those of Indian Defense Minister Rao.

39 See G. W. Choudhury, *India, Pakistan, Bangladesh, and the Major Powers*, New York: Free Press, 1975: 205.

40 The Indian communists [CP(M)] divided again in 1967, with the pro-Beijing elements, mainly Naxalites, forming their own party, the Communist Party (Marxist–Leninist) which is recognized by Beijing as the legitimate communist organization in India. See B. N. Pandey, *South and Southeast Asia, 1945–1979: Problems and Policies*, New York: St. Martin's Press, 1980: 147–49.

41 *Documents of the Eleventh Party Congress of the Communist Party of India*, New Delhi: CPI Publications, 1978.

42 See Louis Dupree, *Afghanistan*, Princeton: Princeton University Press, 1980, and Henry Bradsher, *Afghanistan and the Soviet Union*, Durham: Duke University Press, 1985.

43 See Bradsher, *Afghanistan and the Soviet Union*: 68–70.

44 *Ibid.*: 72.

45 See Karen Dawisha, "*Perestroika, Glasnost* and Soviet Foreign Policy," *The Harriman Institute Forum*, vol. 3, no. 1 (January, 1990), for a discussion of a weakening of the party's role in foreign policymaking in the late 1980s.

46 *New York Times*, December 2, 1986.

47 See Thomas P. Thornton, "Gorbachev's Courtship of India," *Roundtable*, vol. 304 (1987), for a discussion of the results of the visit.

48 Although Indian trade statistics indicate an increase in trade in the late 1980s, Soviet trade statistics show trade with India stagnating in the late 1980s, dropping to 2,191 million rubles total in 1986 and 2,178.5 million rubles in 1987, but increasing in 1988 and 1989 (to 2,252 and 2,917.8, respectively).

49 *Vneshniaia torgovlia SSSR*. Various years.

50 According to *Vneshnie ekonomicheskie sviazi SSSR*, in 1988, Soviet exports made up 72% of total trade; in 1987 – 69.5%; in 1986 – 68.9%; and in 1985 – 62.9%.

51 *Vneshniaia torgovlia SSSR* and *Vneshnie ekonomicheskie sviazi SSSR*, various years.

52 *Ibid.*

53 *Ibid.*

54 M. Siddieq Noorzoy, "Soviet Economic Interests in Afghanistan," *Problems of Communism*, vol. 36 (May–June, 1987): 54.

55 *The Economist*, 25 September – 1 October, 1982: 82.

56 Leon Zevin, *Economic Cooperation of Socialist and Developing Countries: New Trends*, Moscow: Nauka, 1976; also *Sotrudnichestvo sotsialisticheskikh i razvivaiushchikhsia stran: novyi tip mezhdunarodnykh otnoshenii*, Moscow: Nauka, 1980.

57 Calculated from *U.N. Statistical Yearbook of International Trade, 1980* and *U.N. Statistical Yearbook, 1985*. GDP for Afghanistan is not available.

58 Mehrotra, "The Political Economy of Indo-Soviet Relations:" 228.

59 See Peter Lyon, "The Soviet Union and South Asia in the 1980s," in Robert Cassen (ed.), *Soviet Interests in the Third World*: 35, 36, 37.

60 *Ibid.*: 37.

61 Aleksander Alekseev, "The USSR–India: Cooperation for the Benefit of the Peoples," *International Affairs* (May 1987): 49.

62 For a quantitative analysis of Soviet trade with India and Pakistan see Warren Phillips and Linda Racioppi, "The USSR in Asia and the Middle East: A Quantitative Analysis of Economic Relations with Selected Third World Countries." Paper presented to International Studies Association Conference, Washington, DC, April 10–14, 1990.

63 Karen Dawisha, *Soviet Foreign Policy towards Egypt*, London: Macmillan, 1979: 178.

64 Rajan Menon, *Soviet Power and the Third World*, New Haven: Yale University Press, 1986: 173, for example, says that: "it should hardly be surprising that arms transfers are the *key* instrument of Soviet policy toward the Third World" (italics, mine).

65 See *SIPRI Yearbook 1991*.

66 However, the USSR had sold arms to Pakistan in the mid-1960s. Those transfers were designed in part to enhance the thaw in Soviet–Pakistani relations that occurred after the Tashkent conference in the hope that Pakistan would not turn to China after losing arms assistance from the United States after the 1965 war with India, and in part to cue India that their warm relationship would not deter the USSR from pursuing its interest in other countries of the region.

67 See US Arms Control and Disarmament Agency, *World Military Expenditures and Arms Transfers*, various years, and Stockholm International Peace Research Institute, *SIPRI Yearbook*, various years.

68 The US Arms Control and Disarmament Agency puts the percentage of Afghan arms imports attributable to former Warsaw Treaty Organization members at approximately 90%. *World Military Expenditures and Arms Transfers*.

69 Also, during the early 1980s, the USSR and India reached advance agreement for purchase and possible production of the MiG-31 Foxhound. See S. Nihal Singh, "Why India Goes to Moscow for Arms," *Asian Survey*, vol. 24, no. 7 (July, 1984): 713–14.

70 See Mehrotra, "The Political Economy of Indo-Soviet Relations": 224.

71 India also received a license to produce Atoll missiles in 1964.

72 See *SIPRI Yearbook*, 1970–86. According to Dilip Mukerjee, "Indo-Soviet Economic Ties," *Problems of Communism*, vol. 36 (January–February, 1987): 16, India may also produce the MiG-29.

73 *SIPRI Yearbook 1991*: 256.

74 Jyotirmoy Banerjee, "Moscow's Indian Alliance," *Problems of Communism*, vol. 36 (January–February, 1987): 5.

75 US Department of State, *Warsaw Pact Aid to Non-Communist LDCs, 1984*, May, 1986: 20.

76 *Ibid*: 21.

77 Rajan Menon, "The Military and Security Dimensions of Soviet-Indian Relations": 246.

78 See Menon, *Soviet Power and the Third World* for an excellent discussion of the constraints on Soviet power projection.

79 Alvin Z. Rubinstein, "Soviet Geopolitical Involvement in the Arc of Crisis,"

in Hafeez Malik (ed.), *International Security in Southwest Asia*, New York: Praeger, 1984: 191.

80 Rajan Menon argues that "the lack of doctrinal emphasis on power projection, and the absence of any indication that strategic amphibious assaults outside the umbrella of shore-based aircraft are being prepared for, suggests that the Soviet naval infantry is not intended for distant intervention." *Soviet Power in the Third World*: 111.

81 Jukes, "Soviet Naval Policy in the Indian Ocean": 175–77.

82 For a discussion of the US and Soviet roles in the Indian Ocean, see Dieter Braun, *The Indian Ocean: Region of Conflict or 'Peace Zone'?* New York: St. Martin's, 1983: 64.

83 For example, Menon, *Soviet Power in the Third World*.

4 Stability and change in Soviet–South Asian relations, 1970–1978

1 The USSR had often stressed its commitment to revolutionary democratic regimes and countries of socialist orientation. Until 1978, no country in South Asia fit into either of these categories; nonetheless, the commitment of South Asian countries to socialism, however defined, and an anti-imperialist foreign policy was supported by the Soviet Union.

2 Boris Ponomarev, "The International Significance of the Berlin Conference," *Kommunist*, no. 11 (July 1976), quoted in Francis Fukuyama, Scott Bruckner, and Sally Stoecker, "Soviet Political Perspectives on Power Projection," *RAND* N–2430–A (March, 1987): 56.

3 See Stanley Wolpert, *Roots of Confrontation in South Asia*, New York: Oxford University Press, 1982: 126–27.

4 The Awami position from this point on called for separate currency, a separate militia, Bengali language, control of taxation, revenues, and foreign exchange. For a concise discussion of the events of 1966 see Wolpert, *Roots of Confrontation*.

5 For an excellent discussion of the negotiations see Richard Sisson and Leo Rose, *War and Secession: Pakistan, India, and the Creation of Bangladesh*, Berkeley: University of California, 1990: 91–133.

6 US Senate, *Congressional Record*, May 18, 1971: S7128–7129.

7 Sisson and Rose, *War and Secession*: 153.

8 S. M. Burke, *Mainsprings of Indian and Pakistani Foreign Policies*, Minneapolis: University of Minnesota Press: 208.

9 See David H. Bayley, "India: War and Political Assertion," *Asian Survey*, vol. 12, no. 2 (February, 1972): 92; Robert LaPorte, "Pakistan in 1971: The Disintegration of a Nation," *Asian Survey*, vol. 12, no. 2 (February, 1972): 102.

10 On the night of March 25, 1971 alone estimates of the number of Bengalis killed range from "thousands to hundreds of thousands." See Wolpert, *Roots of Confrontation*: 136.

11 K. G. Antonova, G. Bongard-Levin, G. Kotovskii, *A History of India*, 2 vols., Moscow: Progress, 1979, vol. 2: 325.

12 See *Pravda* (April 1, 1971) in *USSR and the Third World*, vol. 1, no. 4 (March 22 – April 25, 1971): 172.
13 See A. Ulanskii, *New Times*, no. 14 (April 14, 1971): 8–9.
14 New Delhi Radio (April 1, 1971) in *USSR and the Third World*, vol. 1, no. 4 (March 22 – April 25, 1971): 172.
15 Moscow Radio (April 4, 1971) in *USSR and the Third World*, vol. 1, no. 4 (March 22 – April 25, 1971): 172.
16 *Pravda* (April 4, 1971) in *USSR and the Third World*, vol. 1, no. 4 (March 22 – April 25, 1971): 172–73.
17 Pakistan Radio (April 6, 1971) in *USSR and the Third World*, vol. 1, no. 4 (March 22 – April 25, 1971): 173; Sisson and Rose, *War and Secession*: 240–41.
18 Sisson and Rose, *War and Secession*: 241.
19 *NCNA* (March 22, 1971) in *USSR and the Third World*, vol. 1, no. 4 (March 22 – April 25, 1971): 174.
20 See Peking Radio (April 28, 1971) in *USSR and the Third World*, vol. 1, no. 5 (April 26 – June 1, 1971): 230.
21 *Statesman Weekly* (July 24, 1971).
22 Sisson and Rose, *War and Secession*: 242.
23 Robert Jackson, *South Asian Crisis*, New York: Praeger, 1975: 49.
24 See Jackson, *South Asian Crisis*, for an excellent discussion of the American position on East Pakistan.
25 Sisson and Rose, *War and Secession*, 241.
26 See Robert H. Donaldson, "India: The Soviet Stake in Stability," *Asian Survey*, vol. 12, no. 6 (June, 1972): 484.
27 *Treaty of Peace, Friendship and Cooperation between the Republic of India and the Union of Soviet Socialist Republics*, August 9, 1971, in Zafar Imam, *Towards a Model Relationship: A Study of Soviet Treaties with India and Other Third World Countries*, New Delhi: ABC Publishing, 1983: 112–16.
28 *Ibid.*: 115.
29 See Information Service of India (August 9, 1971) in *USSR and the Third World*, vol. 1, no. 7 (1971): 355.
30 Delhi Overseas Service (August 10, 1981) in *FBIS Daily Report*, no. 156 (August 12, 1971): 4.
31 See New Delhi Radio (August 9, 1971) and Radio Moscow (August 9, 1971) in *USSR and the Third World*, vol. 1, no. 7 (July 5 – August 15, 1971): 355.
32 Karachi Radio (August 11, 1971) in *USSR and the Third World*, vol. 1, no. 7 (July 5 – August 15, 1971): 364.
33 See Sardar Abdul Kayyum, Azad Kashmir President, on Karachi Radio (August 11, 1971) in *USSR and the Third World*, vol. 1, no. 7 (July 5 – August 15, 1971): 364.
34 *Christian Science Monitor* (August 11, 1971) quoted in *USSR and the Third World*, vol. 1, no. 7 (July 5 – August 15, 1971): 356.
35 *Financial Times*, August 13, 1971, quoted in *USSR and the Third World*, vol. 1, no. 7 (July 5 – August 15, 1971): 357.
36 *Pravda*, November 7, 1971, reported in *USSR and the Third World*, vol. 1, no. 10 (October 25 – December 5, 1971): 586.

37 *Novoe vremia*, no. 46 (1971) in *USSR and the Third World*, vol. 1, no. 10 (October 25 – December 5, 1971): 586.

38 New Delhi Radio, November 15, 1971, reported in *USSR and the Third World*, vol. 1, no. 10 (October 25 – December 5, 1971): 579. Account of a Soviet parliamentary delegation visit.

39 *The Times of India*, October 25, 1971.

40 "Joint Statement on the Occasion of Mrs. Indira Gandhi's Visit to Moscow, 29 September 1971," in Jackson, *South Asian Crisis*: 194.

41 See *New York Times* reportage for early November, 1971, and Jackson, *South Asian Crisis*: 93.

42 See *New York Times*, 29 October and 7 November, 1971, and Burke, *Mainsprings of Indian and Pakistani Foreign Policies*: 210.

43 See *The Military Balance, 1971–1972*, London: International Institute for Strategic Studies, 1971.

44 *NCNA*, November 5, 1971, reported in *USSR and the Third World*, vol. 1, no. 10 (October 25 – December 5, 1971): 588.

45 Jackson, *South Asian Crisis*: 103.

46 *New York Times*, 31 December, 1971.

47 American resolution in UN S/10416.

48 Soviet resolution in UN S/10428.

49 See UN S/10410 for the complete Security Council Report on the events since July 20.

50 A second planning agreement signed in 1978 brought a clearer link between central economic plans of the two countries.

51 *Vneshniaia torgovlia SSSR v 1973g.*

52 V. Shurygin, "India: A Time of Important Decisions," *International Affairs*, no. 11 (November, 1975): 61.

53 K. Antonova, G. Bongard-Levin, and G. Kotovskii, *A History of India*, vol. 2, Moscow: Progress, 1978: 332.

54 Stephen Cohen and Richard Park, *India: Emergent Power?* New York: Crane Russak, 1978: xiv.

55 See, for example, V. Shurygin, "India: A Time of Important Decisions": 57–59.

56 See, for example, I. Shedrov's commentary in *Pravda*, June 27, 1975; also, a June 28 article noting popular support for Mrs. Gandhi's actions.

57 *Pravda*, December 26, 1975.

58 See Robert L. Hardgrave, *India Under Pressure: Prospects for Political Stability*, Boulder: Westview, 1984: 81.

59 *Izvestiia*, 5 February, 1977.

60 Moscow Radio in English, 6 March 1977, in *USSR and the Third World*, vol. 7, nos. 1 and 2 (1 January – 30 April, 1977): 5.

61 Myron Weiner, "India," in Myron Weiner and Ergun Ozbudun (eds.), *Competitive Elections in Developing Countries*, Durham: Duke University Press/American Enterprise Institute, 1987: 54.

62 *Izvestiia*, 22 March, 1977.

63 Moscow Radio, 1 April, 1977, in *USSR and the Third World*, vol. 7, nos. 1 and 2 (1 January – 30 April, 1977): 5.

64 New Delhi Radio, April 25 and 26, 1977, in *USSR and the Third World*, vol. 7, nos. 1 and 2 (1 January – 30 April, 1977): 6.
65 Santosh Mehrotra, "The Political Economy of Indo-Soviet Relations," in Robert Cassen (ed.), *Soviet Interests in the Third World*, London/Beverly Hills: Sage, 1986: 226.
66 Burke, *Mainsprings of Indian and Pakistani Foreign Policy*: 233.
67 V. Shurygin, "Bangladesh: Emergence of a Young Republic," *International Affairs*, no. 12 (December, 1974): 56.
68 "TASS Correspondent on Opposition Attacks on Bangladesh Government," in Jain, *Soviet–South Asian Relations*: 171.
69 *Pravda*, 9 March, 1973.
70 *Izvestiia*, 10 April, 1974.
71 Lawrence Ziring, "Asian Tangles and Triangles," in Ziring (ed.), *The Subcontinent in World Politics: India, Its Neighbors, and the Great Powers*, New York: Praeger, 1982: 8.
72 "Decisive Measures," in *Pravda*, 16 June 1974.
73 Dacca Radio, 18 January, 1975, in *USSR and the Third World*, vol. 5, no. 2 (6 January – 23 February, 1975).
74 See *Pravda* reportage on August 17, 18, 19, 1975.
75 See V. Shurygin article, "Trebozhnaia obstanovka v Bangladesh," in *Pravda*, November 23, 1975.
76 See *Pravda*, April 21, 1976.
77 "Soviet–Pakistan Joint Communique, 18 March 1972," in R. K. Jain, *Documents in Soviet–South Asian Relations 1947–1978*, 2 vols., Atlantic Highlands, NJ: Humanities Press, 1979: 100.
78 Burke, *Mainsprings of Indian and Pakistani Foreign Policies*, 228.
79 *Ibid.*, 230.
80 P. Kutsobin and V. Shurygin, "South Asia: Tendencies Toward Stability," *International Affairs*, vol. 4 (April, 1973): 43–48.
81 *Vneshniaia torgovlia SSSR v 1973 g.*
82 See *Pravda* reportage on May 13, 19, 20, and 25, and June 22 and 26 for India–Pakistan relations; and May 14 for negative aspects of Chinese foreign policy.
83 Vsevolod Kalinin, "Confirmed Forecasts," in *Pravda*, 11 March 1977, in Jain, *Documents in Soviet–South Asian Relations*: 141.
84 Arkady Maslennikov commentary in *Pravda*, 29 May 1970.
85 See James Jupp, *Sri Lanka – Third World Democracy*, London: Frank Cass, 1978: 311.
86 G. Kudin, "Ceylon: Repairing the Damage," *New Times*, September, 1971; Moscow Radio, April 18, 1971 in *USSR and the Third World*, vol. 1, no. 3: 162.
87 E. Menkes, "Sri Lanka: Achievements and Problems," *International Affairs*, no. 9 (September, 1976): 120.
88 A. Usvatov, "Sri Lanka's Progress and Problems," in *New Times*, no. 5 (May, 1974): 14–15.
89 *Vneshniaia torgovlia SSSR*, various years. It is important to recognize,

however, that for 1978, the year after the more conservative UNP took over, trade was down to 15.4 million rubles.

90 Interviews with officials in the Department of External Affairs, Colombo, July, 1983.

91 *Pravda*, 24 July 1977, in *USSR and the Third World*, vol. 7, no. 4: 77.

92 New Delhi Radio, September 3, 1977, in *USSR and the Third World*, vol. 7, nos. 5 and 6; Moscow Radio, September 8, 1977, in *ibid.*

93 Alexei Iudashev, "Overcoming the Colonial Legacy," *New Times*, February 1978, in Jain, *Soviet–South Asian Relations*: 372–74.

94 Leo Rose and John T. Scholz, *Nepal: Profile of a Himalayan Kingdom*, Boulder: Westview, 1980: 128.

95 "Home Thoughts from Abroad," *Far Eastern Economic Review*, no. 25 (June 6, 1971): 9.

96 *Izvestiia*, February 18, 1971, in *USSR and the Third World*, vol. 1, no. 3 (February 15 – March 12, 1971): 107.

97 NCNA, July 31, 1975, in *USSR and the Third World*, vol. 5, nos. 6–8 (July 7 – December 31, 1975): 316.

98 Moscow radio, June 6, 1976, in *USSR and the Third World*, vol. 6, nos. 2 and 3 (April 1 – July 31, 1976): 105.

99 *Pravda*, February 28, 1971, in *USSR and the Third World*, vol. 1, no. 3 (February 15 – March 21, 1971): 98.

100 See Louis Dupree, *Afghanistan*, Princeton: Princeton University Press, 1980: 522.

101 *Novoe vremia*, no. 9 (February 26, 1971) in *USSR and the Third World*, vol. 1, no. 3 (February 15 – March 21, 1971): 98.

102 "Always on the Boil," *The Economist*, December 19, 1970: 43–44.

103 Iv. V. Gankovskii, N. M. Gurevich, S. F. Levin, and V. N. Moskalenko, *A History of Afghanistan*, Moscow: Progress, 1985: 291.

104 *Pravda*, April 20, 1975, in *USSR and the Third World*, vol. 5, no. 4, 1975: 131.

105 *Izvestiia*, July 18, 1975, in *USSR and the Third World*, vol. 1, nos. 6–8 (July 7 – December 31, 1975): 278.

106 Henry Bradsher, *Afghanistan and the Soviet Union*, Durham: Duke University Press, 1985: 64.

107 *Pravda*, June 2, 1975.

108 Kabul Radio, February 2, 1975 and March 2, 1975, in *USSR and the Third World*, vol. 5, no. 3, 1975: 87.

109 See Bradsher, *Afghanistan and the Soviet Union*, 64; *Izvestiia*, December 11, 1975 (pp. 1–3) in *FBIS/SU*, December 17, 1975: J1–3.

110 *Pravda*, December 9, 1975.

111 *Vneshniaia torgovlia SSSR*, 1973 and 1975.

112 See, for example, Georgi Kim's characterization of Pakistan as engaging in "modernization" from above while India is said to have "mass democratic capitalism from below," in "The National Liberation Movement Today," *International Affairs* (Moscow), no. 4 (April, 1981): 32–33. Similarly, Nodari Simoniia's reference to "democratic capitalism" in India versus "bureaucratic capitalism" in Pakistan, in "Metodologicheskie problemy analiza

ekonomicheskogo razvitiia v osvobodivshikhsia stran," in *Ekonomika razvivaiushchikhsia stran: teorii i metody issledovaniia*, Moscow: Nauka, 1979: 200–2.

113 Even articles in *International Affairs* were wary of overestimating the socialist potential of any of these countries.

5 Soviet–South Asian relations in the wake of Afghanistan, 1978–1985

1 The PDPA was formed in 1965, but the two factions which comprised it were dissimilar in many ways. The Parcham was a largely urban, Dari-speaking intellectual socialist organization whereas the Khalq, the larger of the factions, was mainly Pushtun, worker and peasant based, with close ties to the Afghan army. These differences made it difficult for the factions to collaborate, and so the PDPA was wracked by tensions ever since its formation in 1965. See Louis Dupree, *Afghanistan*, Princeton: Princeton University Press, 1980 and Anthony Arnold, *Afghanistan's Two Party Communism*, for more complete discussions of the factions.

2 Dupree, *Afghanistan*: 770

3 See, for example, N. M. Gurevich, "Predrevoliutsionnyi krizis v Afganistane," *Narody Azii i Afriki*, no. 4 (1982): 28–37; L. Mironov and G. Poliakov, "Afghanistan: The Beginning of a New Life," *Narody Azii i Afriki*, no. 3 (March, 1979): 46–54.

4 See Louis Dupree, "Red Flag Over the Hindu Kush Part II: The Accidental Coup, or Taraki in Blunderland," *AUFS Reports*, no. 45, 1975.

5 Moscow in Dari to Afghanistan, 15 May, 1978, FBIS-SOV-78-97: J1.

6 Bradsher, *Afghanistan and the Soviet Union*, Durham, NC: Duke University Press, 1985: 86.

7 *Ibid.*: 3.

8 For an interesting and critical examination of the ability of Third World vanguard parties to rule, see A. V. Kiva and P. M. Shastitko, "Istoricheskii opyt Bol'shevizma i revoliutsionnaia demokratiia Afro-Aziatskikh stran," *Narody Azii i Afriki*, no. 6 (1983): 3–11.

9 In addition, the Ministry of Defense was headed by Abdul Qader, a nationalist with no formal ties to either faction. Some analysts, however, have identified Qader as Parchami or Parchami-sympathizer. See Anthony Arnold, *Afghanistan: The Soviet Invasion in Perspective*, Stanford: Hoover Institution Press, 1985: 74.

10 See *ibid.*: 74; also *Kabul Times*, September 23, 1978.

11 Bradsher, *Afghanistan*: 88.

12 Just one month after the revolution, for example, there were charges that the Western press were trying to provoke "religious fanaticism and a counterrevolutionary mood within Afghanistan itself." Moscow in Czech and Slovak to Czechoslovakia, 16 May, 1978 in FBIS-SOV-78-96 (17 May, 1978): J3. For later coverage of "external threats" see Soviet reportage of Afghan rallies against Pakistani subversion and "all other machinations of internal and external reaction which, supported by imperialist quarters, are

hatching plans of aggression against the Democratic Republic." TASS in English, 3 June, 1979, FBIS-SOV-79-108 (4 June 1979): D1.

13 See Louis Dupree, "Red Flag Over the Hindu Kush Part III: Rhetoric and Reforms, or Promises! Promises!" *AUFS Reports*, no. 23, 1980.

14 See Bhabani Sen Gupta, *Afghanistan: Politics, Economics and Society*, Boulder: Lynne Rienner, 1986: 48–49; John C. Griffiths, *Afghanistan: Key to a Continent*, Boulder: Westview Press, 1981: 186.

15 See Amnesty International, "Violations of Human Rights and Fundamental Freedoms in the Democratic Republic of Afghanistan" (May, 1979) reported in Bradsher, *Afghanistan and the Soviet Union*: 90. Dupree estimates that by September, 1979, 8–10,000 people had been executed by the PDPA government. See "Red Flag Over the Hindu Kush Part VI: Repressions, or Security Through Terror," *AUFS Report*, no. 29, 1980: 9.

16 The following discussion is based on the analyses of Louis Dupree, "Red Flag Over the Hindu Kush Part III", and Anthony Hyman, *Afghanistan under Soviet Domination, 1964–1981*, New York: St. Martin's Press, 1982: 86–92. Hyman argues that these three reforms were linked by the regime, the PDPA seeing the three as mutually supporting and therefore, trying to accomplish all simultaneously.

17 See Dupree, "Red Flag Over the Hindu Kush Part III": 6–7.

18 See *ibid.*, and Hyman, *Afghanistan under Soviet Domination*, 1982.

19 See Nancy Hatch Dupree, in "Red Flag Over the Hindu Kush Part III": 7.

20 See ANIS (March 17, 1979) in *JPRS* No. 73630 (June 6, 1979): 22–23.

21 Hyman, *Afghanistan under Soviet Domination*: 92.

22 Moscow in Czech and Slovak to Czechoslovakia, 16 May, 1978 in FBIS-FOV-78-96 (17 May, 1978): J3; A. Usvatov, "Afghanistan Becomes a Democratic Republic," *Novoe vremia*, no. 2 (12 May, 1978) in FBIS-SOV-78-97 (18 May, 1978): J3.

23 See, for example, Boris Ponomarev, "The Liberation Movement is Invincible," in *Developing Countries in the Contemporary World*, Moscow: Social Sciences Today, 1981. Articles lauding the early reforms announced by the PDPA continued to appear into the Gorbachev era: see V. Semionov, "Revolutionary Afghanistan: Eight Years Later," *International Affairs*, no. 5 (May, 1986): 46–52.

24 An example of the general charges made is found in this quote by A. V. Stepanov: "The revolutionary reforms in Afghanistan came up against violent resistance on the part of the deposed exploiter classes which were given extensive support by international reaction and imperialism." "Afghanistan on the Path of Revolutionary Change," *International Affairs*, no. 5 (May, 1984): 25. Additionally, some press reports detailed how the CIA was aiding the mujaheddin in Iran and Pakistan; others focused on the role of China in supplying arms.

25 Some scholars, such as Thomas Hammond (*Red Flag Over Afghanistan: The Communist Coup and the Soviet Invasion and Its Consequences*. Boulder: Westview, 1984) argue that Brezhnev demanded that Taraki oust Amin in an

effort to halt the deteriorating situation in the country and to allow a broader basis for representation in the government.

26 *Pravda*, September 11, 1979 in *CDSP*, 31-37–17.

27 Hammond, *Red Flag Over Afghanistan*: 80.

28 Puzanov was recalled and replaced by F. A. Tabeev in late November.

29 See Bradsher, *Afghanistan*: 123.

30 Paputin was reported to have committed suicide (presumably for having failed in his mission) on December 28; the circumstances of death, however, are not fully known.

31 Selig Harrison, "Inside the Afghan Talks," *Foreign Policy*, no. 72 (Fall, 1988): 35. Others have included Andropov among the guilty. See "Afghanistan: One Year On," *International Affairs*, no. 3 (March, 1990): 88.

32 Joseph J. Collins, *The Soviet Invasion of Afghanistan: A Study in the Use of Force in Soviet Foreign Policy*, Lexington, MA: Lexington Books, 1986: 78.

33 *Financial Times*, 4 January, 1980 and 18 January, 1980.

34 Collins, *The Soviet Invasion*: 79. The first troops sent in were Category Three (the lowest state of readiness) from Central Asia.

35 Jiri Valenta, "From Prague to Kabul: The Soviet Style of Invasion," *International Security*, vol. 5 (Fall, 1980): 114–40.

36 See, for example, Associated Press Report, December 8, 1979 in *USSR and the Third World*, vol. 10, no. 1 (1 December – 31 January, 1980): 2; *The Times*, 22 December, 1979; *Daily Telegraph*, 23 December, 1979.

37 New China News Agency, 30 December, 1979, in *USSR and the Third World*, vol. 10, no. 1 (1 December – 31 January, 1980): 10.

38 *Ibid*.: 10.

39 The delegations opposing the resolution were the USSR, Byelorussia, Ukraine, Afghanistan, Angola, Bulgaria, Cuba, Czechoslovakia, Ethiopia, German Democratic Republic, Grenada, Hungary, Laos, Mongolia, Mozambique, Poland, and People's Democratic Republic of Yemen.

40 See *Pravda*, January 7, 1980 and January 11, 1980.

41 Tehran Radio, December 28, 1979, *USSR and the Third World*, vol. 10, no. 1 (1 December, 1979 – 31 January, 1980): 7.

42 Karachi Radio, 30 December, 1979, *USSR and the Third World*, vol. 10, no. 1 (1 December, 1979 – 31 January, 1980): 7.

43 Vladilen Baikov, "A Springboard for Interference," TASS International Service in Russian, January 6, 1980 in FBIS-SOV-80-004 (7 January, 1980): D5.

44 See *USSR and the Third World* and FBIS (Soviet Union and South Asia series) for January, 1979.

45 S. Nihal Singh, *The Yogi and the Bear: The Story of Indo-Soviet Relations*, Riverdale, MD: Riverdale Publishing Co., 1986: 160.

46 *Pravda*, 21 July, 1980.

47 Iurii Kornilov and Ravil Musin commentary, *TASS*, January 5, 1980, FBIS-SOV-80-004 (January 7, 1980): D4.

48 TASS in English, 4 January, 1980, FBIS-DOV-80-004 (7 January, 1980): D1.

49 See S. Nihal Singh, *The Yogi and the Bear: The Story of Indo-Soviet Relations*, Riverdale, MD: Riverdale Publishing Co., 1986: 159.

50 Shirokov article, *Pravda*, August 3, 1979, and Shurygin article, *Pravda*, November 21, 1979, in *USSR and the Third World*, vol. 9, nos. 4, 5, 6: 60.
51 Refugees also fled to Iran and a few to India, but the lion's share went to Pakistan.
52 Prior to the Soviet invasion, the number of Soviet civilian advisors was placed by one source at approximately 5,000. Bhabani Sen Gupta, *Afghanistan: Politics, Economics and Society*, Boulder: Lynne Rienner, 1986: 70.
53 Bradsher, *Afghanistan*: 285.
54 Hammond, *Red Flag Over Afghanistan*: 151.
55 Agence France Presse, July 27, 28, and August 2, 1980, in *USSR and the Third World*, vol. 10, nos. 1–2 (1 June – 6 November, 1980): 67.
56 Collins, *The Soviet Invasion*: 140.
57 Babrak warned in 1984, "Fist and sword do not have a place in the party ... The equipment and military means given to you are not to be used in the party," quoted in Arnold, *Afghanistan: The Soviet Invasion in Perspective*: 104.
58 Sen Gupta, *Afghanistan: Politics, Economics and Society*: 118.
59 Tehran Radio, January 28, 1980, and *Financial Times*, February 6, 1980, in *USSR and the Third World*, vol. 10, nos. 2–3 (1 February – 31 May, 1980): 29.
60 Kabul Radio, February 23–24, 1980, in *USSR and the Third World*, vol. 10, nos. 2–3 (1 February – 31 May, 1980): 29.
61 L. Mironov, "Kontrrevoliutsia ne preidet!" *Pravda*, February 24, 1980: 5.
62 See *Pravda*, February 21–24, 1980.
63 The Parcham-led government even changed the colors of the flag from all red to red, black and green (for Islam) against the protestations of many Khalqis.
64 Sen Gupta, *Afghanistan: Politics, Economics and Society*: 118.
65 One type of preparatory meeting that the regime used to attempt to coopt tribes was the traditional *jirgah*; however, many tribal leaders would not participate and many of those who did, did so without enthusiasm.
66 Bradsher, *Afghanistan*: 235.
67 Agence France Presse, 26 April, 1980, in *USSR and the Third World*, vol. 10, nos. 2–3 (1 February – 31 May, 1980): 27.
68 Karl E. Jentoft, "Soviet Domestic Writings on Afghanistan: A Content Analysis, December 1979 – March, 1988" (unpublished manuscript) shows that the foreign intervention theme was the most prevalent in Soviet interpretation of the Afghan war.
69 Collins, *The Soviet Invasion*: 145.
70 *Ibid.*, put the number in 1984 at about 120,000; the *Daily Telegraph* on March 13, 1984, put it at over 185,000, while rebel leader Burhanuddin Rabbani estimated Soviet troops at over 200,000, according to *The Times* on April 24, 1984.
71 See Hyman, *Afghanistan under Soviet Domination*, for an excellent discussion of Kalakani and the SAMA as well as other opposition groups.
72 NCNA, 18 November, 1981, in *USSR and the Third World*, vol. 12, nos. 1–2 (7 November, 1981 – 6 March, 1982): 1.
73 Kabul Radio, September 17, 1982, in *USSR and the Third World*, vol. 13, nos. 1–2 (7 July – 6 November, 1982): 50.

74 For example, rebels blew up the oil pipeline in Samangan Province, attacked Bagram airforce base outside Kabul, set off explosions in Kabul, and attacked military convoys outside Kabul.
75 Karachi Radio, February 22, 1984, in *USSR and the Third World*, vol. 14, nos. 2–3 (7 January – 6 May, 1984): 6.
76 *Vneshniaia torgovlia SSSR*, various years.
77 Calculated from *U.N. International Trade Statistics Yearbook*, various years.
78 *Financial Times*, May 29, 1980; *New York Times*, May 29, 1980.
79 New Delhi Radio, 28 March, 1980, in *USSR and the Third World*, vol. 10, nos. 2–3 (1 February – 31 May, 1980): 37.
80 New Delhi Radio, May 28, 1980 in *USSR and the Third World*, vol. 10, nos. 2–3 (1 February – 31 May, 1980): 37.
81 V. Shurygin, "Vazhnyi shag," *Pravda*, July 9, 1980: 5.
82 See *Pravda*, June 7, 1980; *TASS*, June 3, *USSR and the Third World*, vol. 10, nos. 4–6 (1 June – 6 November, 1980): 71.
83 *ISI*, June 17, 1980, *USSR and the Third World*, vol. 10, nos. 4–6 (1 June – 6 November, 1980): 72.
84 Foreign Minister Huang Hua was scheduled to visit New Delhi in the fall of 1980, but this was postponed until June of 1981 due to India's action on Kampuchea. An NCNA report called the Indian recognition "stupid." NCNA, July 9, 1980, *USSR and the Third World*, vol. 10, nos. 4–6 (1 June – 6 November, 1980): 74.
85 One review article that focused on China's collusion with US imperialism observed that "the U.S. and China had 'parallel interests' in the some areas of the world ... particularly Asia." P. Artemyev, "Peking: Partnership with Imperialism," *International Affairs*, no. 6 (June, 1981): 125–6.
86 V. Shurygin, "Kholodnyi vetry iz-za Gimalaev," *Pravda*, August 7, 1980: 4.
87 Robert C. Horn, "The Soviet Union and South Asia: Moscow and New Delhi Standing Together," in Andrzej Korbonski and Francis Fukuyama (eds.), *The Soviet Union and the Third World: The Last Three Decades*, Ithaca, NY: Cornell University Press, 1987: 223.
88 Singh, *The Yogi and the Bear*: 174.
89 NCNA, 13 December, 1980 and 13 January, 1981, in *USSR and the Third World*, vol. 11, nos. 1–2 (7 November, 1980 – 6 March, 1981): 9.
90 New Delhi Radio, 23 December, 1980 in *USSR and the Third World*, vol. 11, nos. 1–2 (7 November, 1980 – 6 March, 1981): 9.
91 All India Radio, November 15, 1980 in *USSR and the Third World*, vol. 11, nos. 1–2 (7 November, 1980 – 6 March, 1981): 13.
92 New Delhi Radio, 15 December, 1980, in *USSR and the Third World*, vol. 11, nos. 1–2 (7 November, 1980 – 6 March, 1981): 13.
93 Singh, *The Yogi and the Bear*: 183.
94 See *SIPRI Yearbooks* for 1979 and 1980. India had obtained the license on the Jaguar fighter from Britain in 1979 as well.
95 New Delhi Radio, February 26, 1981, in *USSR and the Third World*, vol. 11, nos. 5–6 (7 July – 6 November, 1981): 76.
96 *Pravda*, August 8, 1981, in *USSR and the Third World*, vol. 11, nos. 5–6 (7 July – 6 November, 1981): 76.

97 Evgenii Nikolaev's Commentary on India–Pakistan Talks, Moscow, 3 February, 1982, *FBIS-SOV-82-024* (5 February, 1982): D1.

98 *TASS*, December 16, 1981; New Delhi Radio, December 25, 1981 and *TASS*, December 30, 1981, in *USSR and the Third World*, vol. 12, nos. 1–2 (7 November, 1981 – 6 March, 1982): 4.

99 New Delhi Radio, November 16, 1981, in *USSR and the Third World*, vol. 12, nos. 1–2 (7 November, 1981 – 16 March, 1982): 4.

100 Unattributed report, *USSR and the Third World*, vol. 12, nos. 3–4 (7 March – 6 July, 1982): 23.

101 See Singh, *The Yogi and the Bear*: 187–89.

102 V. Korovikov, V. Shirokov, and A. Nikolaev, "At the Indian Communists' Forum," *Pravda*, 25 March, 1982: 4, in FBIS-SOV-82-063 (1 April, 1982): D4, D6.

103 Singh, *The Yogi and the Bear*: 189.

104 Craig Baxter, Yogendra K. Malik, Charles H. Kennedy, and Robert C. Oberst, *Government and Politics in South Asia*, Boulder: Westview, 1987: 151.

105 TASS, 10 February, 1982, FBIS-SOV-82-030 (12 February, 1982): D5.

106 Segei Karmalito for TASS, 13 February, 1982, FBIS-SOV-82-032 (17 February, 1982): D1.

107 Indira's older son, Sanjay, who had been very active in politics, acted as a close advisor to his mother, and had made a name for himself particularly during the Emergency Rule, had been killed in a plane crash in 1980.

108 For a Soviet perspective see P. V. Kutsobin, "Politischeskaia bor'ba v Indii na sovremennom etape," *Narody Azii i Afriki*, no. 4 (1985): 39–48.

109 *Financial Times*, 19 October, 1983.

110 For a concise discussion of some of the problems in Indo-Soviet trade from the Soviet perspective see Aleksander Alekseev, "The USSR–India: Cooperation for the Benefit of the Peoples," *International Affairs* (May, 1987): 49.

111 See Richard P. Cronin, "Pakistani Capabilities to Meet the Soviet Threat from Afghanistan," in Theodore L. Eliot, Jr. and Robert L. Pfaltzgraff (eds.), *The Red Army on Pakistan's Border: Policy Implications for the United States*, Washington: Pergamon Brassey's Center for Asian Pacific Affairs, the Asia Foundation, and Institute for Foreign Policy Analysis, Inc., 1986: 24–25.

112 *Time*, January 28, 1980: 2.

113 Cronin, "Pakistani Capabilities": 27.

114 Thomas Perry Thornton, "Between the Stools?: U.S. Policy towards Pakistan During the Carter Administration," *Asian Survey*, October, 1982: 972–73.

115 *Pravda*, 30 July, 1982 in *USSR and the Third World*, vol. 13 nos. 1, 2 (7 July – 6 November, 1982): 60.

116 V. Svetlov, "Snova osechka," *Pravda*, 31 January, 1980: 5.

117 *TASS*, 5 February, 1980, in *USSR and the Third World*, vol. 10, nos. 2–3 (1 February – 31 May, 1980): 45.

118 For details on the negotiations leading to the agreement see, Richard

P. Cronin, "Congress and Arms Sales and Security Assistance to Pakistan," in US Congress, House Committee on Foreign Affairs, *Congress and Foreign Policy–1981*, Washington: US Government Printing Office, 1982: 107–10.

119 These charges were repeated throughout the early 1980s. See *Pravda*, November 30, 1981, in *USSR and the Third World*, vol. 11, nos. 1, 2 (7 November, 1980 – 6 March, 1981): 19; Moscow Radio, March 12, 1981, in *ibid*, vol. 11, no. 3, 4 (7 March – 6 July, 1981): 53; *Pravda*, July 30, 1982, in *ibid*, vol. 13, nos. 1, 2 (7 July – 6 November, 1982): 60; *Pravda*, 24 September and 3 November, 1983, in *ibid*, vol. 13, no. 6 (7 September – 6 November, 1983): 10.

120 Total trade turnover in 1980 was 176.6 million rubles, whereas in 1985, it had slipped to 117.6 million rubles. See *Vneshniaia torgovlia SSSR* for 1980 and 1985.

121 Calculated from *U.N. International Trade Statistics Yearbook*, various years.

122 Singh, *The Yogi and the Bear*: 196.

123 Karachi Radio, April 28, 1980, in *USSR and the Third World*, vol. 10, nos. 2–3 (1 February – 31 May, 1980): 46.

124 Karachi Radio, 13 November, 1980, in *USSR and the Third World*, vol. 11, nos. 1–2 (7 November, 1980 – 6 March, 1981): 19.

125 Karachi Radio, 14 May, 1981, in *USSR and the Third World*, vol. 11, nos. 3–4 (7 March – 6 July, 1981): 53.

126 TASS, 6 October, 1983, in *USSR and the Third World*, vol. 13, no. 6 (7 September – 6 November, 1983): 10; Moscow Radio, 24 January, 1984, in *USSR and the Third World*, vol. 14, nos. 2–3 (7 January – 6 May, 1984): 16.

127 The deputy ambassador, Viktor Beliaev, also noted that the USSR never uses economic sanctions to achieve its political objectives. Nawa-i-Waqu, 26 March, 1982, in *FBIS-SOV-82-061* (30 March, 1982): D1.

128 Pakistan began repaying the USSR for the mill with the export of goods worth Rs381 million in 1983. Karachi Radio, April 26, 1983, in *USSR and the Third World*, vol. 13, nos. 3, 4, 5 (7 March – 6 September, 1983): 20.

129 Agence France Presse, 6 April, 1980, in *USSR and the Third World*, vol. 10, nos. 2–3 (1 February – 31 May, 1980): 44.

130 Dacca Radio, 8 April, 1980, in *USSR and the Third World*, vol. 10, nos. 2–3 (1 February – 31 March, 1980): 34.

131 *Vneshniaia torgovlia*, 1980 and 1985.

132 Dacca Radio, 23 June, 1981, in *USSR and the Third World*, vol. 11, nos. 5–6 (7 July – 6 November, 1981): 76.

133 Peter J. Bertocci, "Bangladesh in 1985: Resolute Against the Storms," *Asian Survey*, vol. 26, no. 2 (February, 1986): 232.

134 *Vneshniaia torgovlia*, 1980 and 1985.

135 Calculated from *U.N. International Trade Statistics Yearbook*.

136 See V. Baikov, "Na chuzhdoi volne," *Pravda*, November 2, 1982: 5.

137 Moscow Radio, September 9, 1983, in *USSR and the Third World*, vol. 13, no. 6 (7 September – 6 November, 1983): 11.

138 *Vneshniaia torgovlia*, 1980 and 1985.

139 Calculated from *U.N. International Trade Statistics*.

140 See Lok Raj Baral, "Nepal's Security Policy and South Asian Regionalism" *Asian Survey*, vol. 26, no. 11 (November, 1986), for an excellent discussion of the security implications for Nepal of her relations with India and China.
141 *Ibid.*: 1213.
142 *Rising Nepal*, February 12, 1983.
143 Bhabani Sen Gupta, *Glimpses of Gorbachev's Soviet Union*, New Delhi: Center for Policy Research, 1986: 2.
144 W. Raymond Duncan and Carol McGiffert Ekedahl, *Moscow and the Third World under Gorbachev*, Boulder, Westview, 1990: 39.
145 Singh, *The Yogi and the Bear*: 178.
146 Discussion with Soviet scholars in the United States, October, 1987.

6 Soviet policy towards South Asia in the Gorbachev era

1 "Gorbachev CPSU Central Committee Political Report," in *Foreign Broadcast Information Service* (FBIS) – Soviet Union (SOV)–86–038 (February 26, 1986).
2 *Ibid.*: 31.
3 "Speech by M. S. Gorbachev at the Ceremonial Meeting Devoted to the Presentation of the Order of Lenin to Vladivostok," *Pravda* (July 29, 1986), translated in *CDSP*, vol. 38, no. 30 (August, 1986): 6.
4 *Ibid.*
5 The approach introduced at the 27th Party Congress and developed at Vladivostok and elsewhere was reinforced in the Central Committee Theses of the 19th Party Conference held in 1988 which attacked Brezhnev's foreign policy for its dogmatism, inflexibility, and failure to comprehend the changing world environment. See *Pravda*, May 27, 1988.
6 "Mikhail Gorbachev Addresses the United Nations," in Isaac J. Tarasulo, *Gorbachev and Glasnost: Viewpoints from the Soviet Press*, Wilmington, DE: Scholarly Resources, 1989: 329–52.
7 See Gail Lapidus, "The USSR and Asia," *Asian Survey*, vol. 27, no. 1 (January, 1987): 1–10, for a concise discussion of personnel changes and its effect on Soviet policy in Asia.
8 Karen Dawisha, "*Perestroika, Glasnost*, and Soviet Foreign Policy," *Harriman Institute Forum*, vol. 3, no. 1 (January, 1990): 2.
9 See, for example, Usman Usmanov, "Diplomacy of Tajikistan," *International Affairs*, no. 1 (January, 1990): 31–39, for an overview of Tajik foreign policy. In discussing the problem of developing and implementing a foreign policy for Tajikistan, Mr. Usman notes, "Behind the doors with the impressive-sounding sign of Ministry of Foreign Affairs of the Tajik SSR there are only ... seven people, including the Minister. Just five years ago this number would have been quite sufficient."
10 The Soviet press gave extensive daily coverage of the visit.
11 He was accompanied by Foreign Minister Edvard Shevardnadze, International Department Head Anatolii Dobrynin, Vladimir Kamentsev (then Deputy Chair of the Council of Ministers), and Chief of Staff Sergei Akhromeev, among others. *Washington Post*, November 26, 1986.

12 Jyotirmoy Banerjee points out that the two men had met three times during 1985. "Moscow's Indian Alliance," *Problems of Communism*, vol. 36 (January–February, 1987): 1.

13 Dilip Mukerjee, "Indo-Soviet Economic Ties," *Problems of Communism*, vol. 36 (January–February, 1987): 13.

14 Banerjee, "Moscow's Indian Alliance": 4.

15 "The Delhi Declaration," in *New Times*, no. 49 (1986): 1.

16 Mark Urban, *War in Afghanistan*, Basingstoke: Macmillan, 1988, 2nd ed. New York: St. Martin's, 1990: 163.

17 See *ibid* for a very complete detailing of the Zhawar and other campaigns.

18 *New York Times*, July 12, 1985.

19 For example, Louis Dupree, "Post-Withdrawal Afghanistan," and Geoffrey Jukes, "The Soviet Armed Forces and the Afghan War," in Amin Saikal and William Maley (eds.), *The Soviet Withdrawal from Afghanistan*, Cambridge: Cambridge University Press, 1989, both credit Blowpipes and Stingers with making "the air uncomfortable for Soviet pilots" (Dupree, p. 35); whereas Urban, *War in Afghanistan*, argues that the missiles had little military effect.

20 *Pravda*, April 2, 1987: 6.

21 *Pravda*, January 12, 1986.

22 *Pravda*, December 13, 1986.

23 *Pravda*, January 2, 1987: 4.

24 William Maley, "The Geneva Accords of April 1988," in Saikal and Maley (eds.), *The Soviet Withdrawal from Afghanistan*: 14.

25 Selig Harrison, "Inside the Afghan Talks," *Foreign Policy*, no. 72 (Fall, 1988): 31.

26 See Harrison, "Inside the Afghan Talks," for a more complete discussion of the American decision.

27 Edvard Shevardnadze, Interview with BAKHTAR news agency, *Pravda*, January 7, 1988: 4, translated in *CDSP*, vol. 40, no. 1 (1988): 14.

28 *Pravda*, March 16, 1988: 1.

29 Interview with Edvard Shevardnadze in *Pravda* (April 1, 1988): 5.

30 Rosanne Klass, "Afghanistan: The Accords," *Foreign Affairs*, vol 66 (Summer, 1988): 922.

31 See William Maley, "The Geneva Accords," for a fine, concise discussion of the limitations of the accords.

32 *Department of State Bulletin*, vol. 88, no. 2135 (June, 1988): 55.

33 See Urban, *War in Afghanistan*: 268–69, for a discussion of Massud's tactics.

34 "Soviet Position on Afghanistan," in *Pravda*, November 5, 1988: 4.

35 William Maley, "The Geneva Accords": 25.

36 "The Geneva Accords on Afghanistan," *International Affairs*, no. 7 (July, 1990): 66.

37 See Mohammad Ayoob, "India in South Asia: The Quest for Regional Predominance," *World Policy Journal*, vol. 7, no. 1 (Winter 1989–90): 107–34, for a discussion of the notion of predominance in South Asian regional politics.

38 See *Vneshnie Ekonomicheskie Sviazi SSSR*.

39 *Izvestiia*, December 7, 1988: 8.

40 *Izvestiia*, December 27, 1988: 5.

41 *Izvestiia*, January 10, 1989: 10.

42 *Pravda*, December 3, 1988.

43 Rasul B. Rais, "Pakistan in the Regional and Global Power Structure," *Asian Survey*, vol. 31, no. 4 (April, 1991): 390.

44 For example, demonstrations against Najib were staged, presumably by Karmal loyalist, Anahita Ratebzad. See Urban, *War in Afghanistan*: 198.

45 See Anthony Arnold, *Afghanistan's Two Party Communism*, Stanford: Hoover Institution, 1983.

46 See FBIS-NES-90-044 (March 6, 1990): 33.

47 FBIS-NES-90-048 (March 12, 1990): 42.

48 *Ibid.*

49 The Supreme Council was established in February, 1989, with responsibility for defending Afghanistan after the Soviet pull-out.

50 BAKHTAR in English, 23 March 1990 in FBIS-NES-90-057: 38.

51 Najibullah, however, also claimed that a multiparty system had in fact been established in Afghanistan in 1987. See FBIS-NES-90-057: 38.

52 FBIS-NES-90-128: 43.

53 FBIS-NES-90-127: 35.

54 The Congress was denounced by most opposition leaders as a hoax.

55 A night curfew remained in force in Kabul even after May.

56 *Far Eastern Economic Review*, December 7, 1989: 19.

57 V. Skosyrev, "The Burden of the Afghan War," *Izvestiia*, November 20, 1990: 7, translated in *CDSP*, vol. 42, no. 48 (1990): 24.

58 For example, commemorating the 26th anniversary of the founding of the Homeland Party on January 1, 1991, Najibullah said, "The reality of the Afghanistan issue is such that no group or political force alone is able to bring peace in Afghan territory." FBIS-NES-91-016: 59.

59 Most refugees did not return home to ascertain the effectiveness of the decree.

60 FBIS-NES-90-162 (August 21, 1990): 43.

61 See Usman Usmanov, "Diplomacy of Tajikistan," for a discussion of Tajik economic relations with Afghanistan.

62 See, for example, "Afghanistan: One Year On," *International Affairs*, no. 3 (March, 1990), for a sharp attack on the Soviet role and the "infantile disorder" of impatience of the PDPA.

63 Alexander Prokhanov, "Afghanistan," *International Affairs*, no. 8 (August, 1988): 22–23.

64 See, for example, Nodari Simoniia, "Looking to the future without Prejudices," *New Times*, no. 8 (1990): 16–17; and Vsevolod Semionov, "A New Situation in Afghanistan," *International Affairs*, no. 4 (April, 1988): 88–92, which quotes Najibullah as insisting that the revolution was not proletarian or socialist, and that the party was not communist.

65 FBIS-NES-90-157: 57.

66 *Christian Science Monitor*, November 26, 1986.

67 *The Economist*, November 29, 1986: 34.
68 The meeting allowed Gorbachev and Gandhi to criticize US military policy, particularly in the area of outer space (SDI).
69 *Soviet Military Review* (February, 1987): 53.
70 *SIPRI Yearbook*, various years.
71 See Peter J. S. Duncan, *The Soviet Union and India*, London: Royal Institute of International Affairs/Routledge, 1989: 77.
72 James Clad, "Friends in Need," *The Economist*, August 9, 1990: 46.
73 *Ibid.*: 79.
74 Thomas P. Thornton argues that Gandhi saw the plan as anti-American, and therefore, supporting it would have negative effects on India's role in the non-aligned movement. See "Gorbachev's Courtship of India," *The Roundtable*, vol. 304 (1987): 460.
75 Clad, "Friends in Need," 45.
76 A harbinger of this issue might have been seen in the credit extension agreement set at Delhi meeting. That agreement included a clause that if in-kind payment on interest due was not made, the interest would have to be repaid in hard currency.
77 Nikolai Volkov, "Cooperation with the Third World," *International Affairs*, no. 9 (September, 1989): 103.
78 Richard Sisson, "India in 1989: A Year of Elections in a Culture of Change," *Asian Survey*, vol. 30, no. 2 (February, 1990): 124.
79 Duncan, *The Soviet Union and India*: 83.
80 A. Shishelov, "India: Defending National Unity," *International Affairs*, no. 12 (December, 1986): 123.
81 Gleb Ivashentsov, "The Indian Giant," *International Affairs*, no. 8 (August, 1990): 64.
82 See A. Elianov, "Problemy modernizatsii sotsial'no-ekonomicheskikh struktur v 'tret'em mire'," *MEiMO*, no. 7 (1988): 16–32; and "Zapad-Iug: ekspluatatsiia ili sotrudnichestvo?" *MEiMO*, no. 11 (1990): 5–20.
83 See, for example, E. S. Iurlova, "Kasta v politicheskoi zhizn shtata Bikhar (Indiia)," *Narody Azii i Afriki*, no. 1 (1986): 31–40; M. Iu. Lomova-Oppokova, "Kasta, faktsia i politika v Indii," *Narody Azii i Afriki*, no. 4 (1988): 37–49.
84 A. G. Bel'skii and D. E. Furman, "Evoliutsiia Sikhskogo kommunalizma: religiozno-politicheskie aspekty," *Narody Azii i Afriki*, no. 5 (1988): 39–51.
85 *The Economist*, November 28, 1987: 33, notes that Pakistani officials also blame the war in Afghanistan for many more of Pakistan's ills.
86 Marvin Weinbaum, "Pakistan and Afghanistan," *Asian Survey*, vol. 31, no. 6 (June, 1991): 499.
87 Many sources have noted the Islamabad–Hekmatyar connection. See, for example, Amin Saikal, "The Regional Politics of the Afghan Crisis," in Saikal and Maley, *The Soviet Withdrawal*: 60.
88 Urban, *War in Afghanistan*: 209.
89 *Ibid.*: 241.
90 V. Mikhin, "Pakistan – Toeing the Washington Line," *International Affairs*, no. 2 (February, 1986): 86.

91 *Far Eastern Economic Review*, February 16, 1989: 12; "View from Islamabad," *International Affairs*, no. 10 (October, 1990): 155.

92 See "Pakistan – Toeing the Washington Line": 87.

93 Anwar H. Syed claims that Bhutto was forced by the military and the bureaucrats to accept Yaqub Khan. "The Pakistan People's Party and the Punjab," *Asian Survey*, vol. 31, no. 7 (July, 1991): 591.

94 *Pravda*, February 21, 1990: 5.

95 See O. V. Pleshov, "'Islamizatsiia' v Pakistane: motivy i sredstva osushchestvleniia," *Narody Azii i Afriki*, no. 1 (1987); and "'Ideologiia Pakistana': transformatsiia poniatiia," *Narody Azii i Afriki*, no. 3 (1988): 25–33.

96 See Bruce Matthews, "Sri Lanka in 1989: Peril and Good Luck," *Asian Survey*, vol. 30, no. 2 (February, 1990): 147.

97 Marshall R. Singer, "Sri Lanka in 1990: The Ethnic Strife Continues," *Asian Survey*, vol. 31, no. 2 (February, 1991): 144.

98 *Vneshniaia torgovlia SSSR*, various years, *Vneshnie ekonomicheskie sviazi SSSR*, various years.

99 King Birendra visited China in 1987, and in 1988, Nepal purchased some arms from China.

100 *New Times*, May 1, 1991: 20–21.

101 Iu. Vinogradov, "Conflict in Sri Lanka," *International Affairs*, no. 4 (April, 1988): 73.

102 See, for example, *Pravda*, August 3, 1987 (p. 6) article by V. Korvikov.

103 V. Georgiev, "The South Asian Association for Regional Cooperation," *International Affairs*, no. 10 (October, 1987): 144.

104 For example, the meeting between Benazir Bhutto and Rajiv Gandhi at the December 1988 meeting of the SAARC was viewed very positively by the Soviet press. See *Izvestiia*, January 3, 1989: 4.

Conclusion

1 See, for example, Boris Ponomarev, "The Liberation Movement is Invincible," in *Developing Countries in the Contemporary World* (Moscow: Social Sciences Today, 1981): 7–32.

2 See V. V. Rymalov, "The Crisis of the World Capitalist System and the Developing Countries," *International Affairs*, no. 3 (March 1986): 63–72.

3 See, for example, R. M. Mukimdzhanova, *Pakistan i imperialisticheskie derzhavy, 70e – nachalo 80kh godov*, Moscow: Nauka, 1984.

4 See Rostislav Ulianovskii, *Present Day Problems in Asia and Africa. Theory, Politics, and Personalities*, Moscow: Nauka, 1981.

5 Indeed, Gorbachev, in his speech to the 27th Congress of the CPSU, made the point that many of Third World's ills were the result of imperialism.

6 See, for example, S. L. Stoklitskii, L. D. Fridman, and P. F. Andrukovich, *Ekonomicheskie struktury Arabskikh stran*, Moscow: Nauka, 1985, and V. L. Sheinis and A. Ia. El'ianov, *Razvivaiushchiesia strany: Ekonomicheskii rost i sotsial'nyi progress*, Moscow: Nauka, 1983.

7 See Aleksei Levkovskii, *Sotsial'naia struktura razvivaiushchikhsia stran*,

Moscow: Mysl', 1979; Glerii K. Shirokov, "Interstructural Relations in Developing Countries," in *Developing Countries in the Contemporary World*, 33–46. See also Margot Light, *The Soviet Theory of International Relations*, New York: St. Martin's Press, 1988: 134–37, for a discussion of the role of the *mnogoukladnost'* literature in Soviet attempts to incorporate the Third World into their international relations theory.

8 Allen Lynch, *The Soviet Study of International Relations*, Cambridge: Cambridge University Press, 1987: xxxii.

9 However, it is not suggested that the scholars of Third World studies were responsible for the New Thinking. There is ample evidence to suggest that the essential tensions between the USSR and the West (and its attendant military and nuclear dimensions) were central to the Gorbachev foreign policy reformulation. Orientalists and Third World scholars, like Primakov, however, did play an important role in development of the New Thinking. See Lynch, *The Soviet Study of International Relations*.

10 Andrei Kozyrev and Andrei Shumikhin, "East and West in the Third World," *International Affairs*, no. 3 (March, 1989): 66.

11 Alexander Bovin, "Afghanistan: A Difficult Decade," *Izvestiia*, December 23, 1988: 5, translated in *CDSP*, vol. 40, no. 51 (1988): 10.

12 Valentin Uliakhin, "Podpriadnyi biznis v stranakh Azii," *Narody Azii i Afriki*, no. 3 (1989): 3–14; and "Strany Azii – politika gosudarstva v otnoshenii melkogo biznes," *Narody Azii i Afriki*, no. 4 (1989): 4–13.

13 Nikolai Volkov, "Cooperation with the Third World," *International Affairs*, no. 9 (September, 1990): 103–10.

14 See Colonel V. Solovev, "Army of Internationalists," *Soviet Military Review*, no. 4 (April 1980), and A. Iskenderov. "The National Liberation Movement in Our Time," *The Third World*, Moscow: Progress, 1970.

15 It was not until the Sri Lanka Freedom Party came to power in 1956 in coalition with leftist parties that the USSR and Sri Lanka even opened diplomatic relations.

16 In both these cases, it appears that the Soviet leadership was more concerned with the development of Chinese influence than American.

17 Ashok Kapur, "The Indian Subcontinent: The Contemporary Structure of Power and the Development of Power Relations," *Asian Survey*, vol. 28, no. 7 (July, 1988): 693–710.

18 M. V. Bratersky and S. I. Lunyov, "India at the End of the Century: Transformation into an Asian Regional Power," *Asian Survey*, vol. 30, no. 10 (October, 1990): 941.

19 *Ibid.*: 927.

Index

Afghanistan
 and mujaheddin 109, 115, 118, 124–26
 and USSR (*see* Soviet Union and
  Afghanistan)
 bi-tarafi (without sides) foreign policy
  101, 104
 Communist Party of (*see* People's
  Democratic Party of Afghanistan)
 Daoud regime and domestic politics
  102–4, 108
 Karmal regime 114, 115, 117–18, 122–24
 Najibullah regime 152, 157–66
 perestroika and reform 162–66
 Saur Revolution 108–14; early reforms
  110–12
 Soviet aid to 50, 51 (table)
 Soviet arms transfers to 46, 47 (table),
  64–65
 Soviet invasion of 114–15
 Soviet trade with 51, 59, 61
 Soviet withdrawal from 156
agricultural development in Third World
 and South Asia 28–29
Amin, Hafizullah 48, 49, 108–9, 122, 213n
 Afghanistan under 67, 110, 112, 117–18,
  138, 152
 and Soviet invasion 114–15, 121, 159
 and Soviet Union 113–14, 126
Andreasian, R. 25
Andropov, Iu. 114, 139, 214n
Angola 6, 8, 15, 182, 214n
Arkhipov, Ivan 127, 130
August 1991 Coup 9
Avadi Resolution 4
Awami League 74, 75, 80, 82
Ayub Khan 74, 75, 195n

Baikov, Vladilen 137, 214n, 218n
Bandaranaike, Sirimavo 96–99, 105, 142,
 183, 191
Bangladesh
 and China 41, 64, 105, 142

 and India 91, 92, 93
 and USSR (*see* Soviet Union and
  Bangladesh)
 domestic politics (1971–78) 92–93;
  (1978–85) 141; (1985–91) 173, 174
 national liberation movement 74–78,
  81, 83, 91, 104
 reaction to Soviet invasion of
  Afghanistan 116, 141
 Soviet aid to 50, 51 (table)
 Soviet arms transfers to 47 (table), 64
 Soviet trade with 52, 60
basic principles agreement 14
Bessmertnykh, Alexander 156
Bhutto, Benazir 162, 172, 173, 223n
Bhutto, Zulfiqur Ali 104, 105
 and 1971 crisis 74–75, 81
 and Indo–Soviet Friendship Treaty 79
 and Soviet Union 73, 84–85, 93–95, 118
 arrest and death 107, 136–37
 at the United Nations, December 1971
  83
Birendra Shah Dev 100, 144, 174, 223n
Bovin, Alexander 33, 89, 181, 224n
Brezhnev, Leonid 195n, 196n, 203n, 213n,
 219n
 and Afghanistan 118, 165
 and Asian Collective Security 100–68
 and Daoud 103
 and Ershad 174
 and Indira Gandhi 80, 117, 129, 134, 176
 and policy in South Asia and Third
  World 8, 11, 31, 183, 193
 and Taraki 112
 foreign economic policy under 51, 106,
  182
 funeral of 139
 meeting with Mujibur Rahman 84
 meeting with Narasimha Rao 128
 views of foreign policy 9, 12, 17, 30, 37,
  55, 190
 visit to India 130

225

Soviet and East European Studies
Series list continued

For EU product safety concerns, contact us at Calle de José Abascal, 56–1°,
28003 Madrid, Spain or eugpsr@cambridge.org.

www.ingramcontent.com/pod-product-compliance
Ingram Content Group UK Ltd.
Pitfield, Milton Keynes, MK11 3LW, UK
UKHW010041140625
459647UK00012BA/1521